ROBOTS

ROBOTS

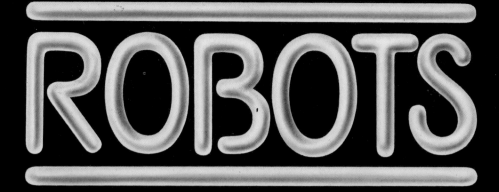

CONSULTANT: PETER MARSH

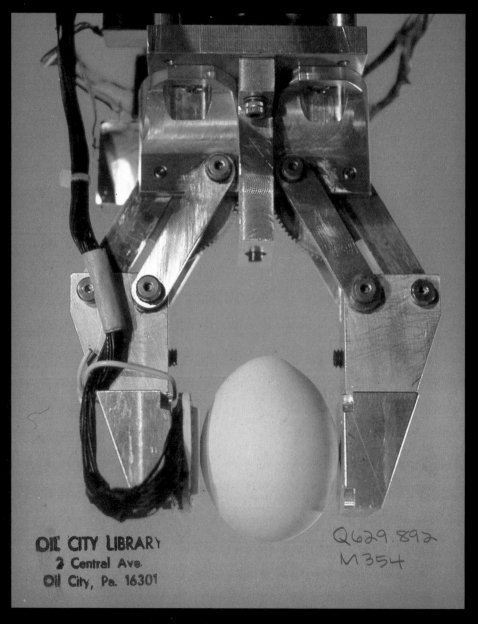

Published by
CRESCENT BOOKS
New York

A SALAMANDER BOOK

First English edition published by
Salamander Books Ltd,
Salamander House,
27 Old Gloucester Street,
London WC1N 3AF,
United Kingdom

This edition is published by Crescent Books,
distributed by Crown Publishers, Inc.,
One Park Avenue,
New York,
New York 10016,
United States of America

h g f e d c b a

ISBN 0-517-472597

CREDITS

Editor:
Philip de Ste. Croix

Designers:
Nick Buzzard
Carol Warren

Color and line artwork:
Michael Badrocke © Salamander Books Ltd

Filmset:
Modern Text Typesetting Ltd, England

Color and monochrome reproduction:
Culver Graphics Ltd, England

Printed in Belgium:
Henri Proost et Cie, Turnhout

ACKNOWLEDGMENTS

I would like to thank wholeheartedly
everyone who has supplied photographs
and information for this book—robot
manufacturers and users, research staff at
numerous universities and educational
institutions, military and government officials,
and private individuals. Their pictures are
credited in detail on page 160. Thanks are
also due to Mike Badrocke, who prepared
all the artwork; Alan Moutrie at the British
Robot Association; Celia Dearing, who
undertook the picture research for Chapter 1;
Harry Coussins, who read the proofs; and
Michele Clarke, who compiled the Index.

Philip de Ste. Croix

CONTRIBUTORS

Igor Aleksander
Igor Aleksander, a past President of the
British Cybernetic Society, is Professor of the
Management of Information Technology
at Imperial College, London, and was
previously Professor of Electrical
Engineering at Brunel University, Middlesex,
where he led the research project which
developed WISARD, the first large scale
artificial neural network in the world. He is
the author of several books including
"The Human Machine", "Designing
Intelligent Systems", and "Reinventing
Man" (with Piers Burnett).

Piers Burnett
A former editorial director of a London
publishing house, Piers Burnett is now a
freelance writer specializing in scientific
and technological subjects. His books
include "Reinventing Man" (with Igor
Aleksander) and "CAD/CAM in Practice"
(with A.J. Medland). He is currently
working with Igor Aleksander on a major
book on the human mind.

Dave Dooling
Dave Dooling is Science Editor of "The
Huntsville (Alabama) Times", Editor-in-Chief
of "Space World" magazine and Managing
Editor of "Canopus". He contributed to
Salamander's "The Illustrated Ency-
clopedia of Space Technology", and "The
Illustrated Encyclopedia of Space
Exploration", edited "Shuttle to the Next
Space Age", and is co-author of "Huntsville:
A Pictorial History".

Colin Gill
Colin Gill is a University Lecturer in
Industrial Relations at the University of
Cambridge, United Kingdom. He is
particularly concerned with analysing
the likely effects that the introduction of
new technology will have on the workplace, and is the editor of "New Technology,
Work and Employment", and author of
the book "New Technology; Its Impact on
Work and Employment".

Peter Marsh
Formerly Industry Editor of the respected
journal "New Scientist", Peter Marsh is
now Technology Correspondent for "The
Financial Times" of London. One of his
particular areas of interest is modern
industrial technology and flexible
manufacturing systems. His books
include "The Robot Age", "The Silicon
Chip Book", and "The Space Business".

Peter Matthews
Peter Matthews is research director of
Micro Robotic Systems Ltd, Twickenham,
Middlesex, a company that devises low
cost robot systems for industrial,
commercial and educational applications.
He is also a journalist specializing in
robotics, and has contributed to "Your
Robot", "Micro et Robots", and
"Robotics Age".

Hans Moravec
Dr Moravec is a Research Scientist with
the Robotics Institute and Computer
Science Department of Carnegie-Mellon
University, Pittsburgh, Pennsylvania, where
he directs the mobile robot laboratory.
He received his Ph. D. in computer science
in 1980 from Stanford University in
California. He has published over 30
technical papers, articles, chapters, films
and a book variously concerned with
mobile robots, computer vision, orbital
skyhooks, switching networks, and three
dimensional imaging.

CONTENTS

FOREWORD

Robots should not be thought of as mere mechanical artefacts, but rather as symbols of deep changes in the operation of industry in the late 20th century—changes that spill out of this area of activity to affect people in many different walks of life. In technical parlance, robots are machines that in some aspect of appearance or behaviour imitate people. Few robots of what can be called the classic type (as featured in countless science fiction films) actually exist. These are "androids"—machines that look like men and women and perform actions that replicate those of their human counterparts. Today's robots, generally speaking, are mechanical arms controlled by computers, which can be programmed to undertake a huge range of handling activities normally done by people.

The effect of robots, however, goes beyond what this simple description of their capabilities might suggest. First, robots are establishing themselves in novel systems of automation in manufacturing industry that can turn out a range of goods with great precision, and which require only a few human workers. In these cases minimal times are needed to change the systems to make different types of products.

Much of manufacturing industry is concerned with production of goods not in large runs in which the items seldom vary, but in small, broken-up streams, during which factory managers frequently change the types of products being turned out to suit the demands of consumers and industrial customers, whose special needs vary. The new manufacturing systems, often built around robots, offer a flexibility that can match this variation in demand.

In this respect, one can perceive consequences that naturally follow for the way that manufacturing industry operates, and for the type of people who work in it. The era of robots will call for different types of skills in industry. Overall, there will be fewer jobs in this sector. Due to the importance of manufacturing industry in the economies of the developed nations, the countries that handle the transition the better will gain the upper hand.

Whereas Britain pioneered the initial development of large scale industry in the late 18th century, and the USA was the leader in this sphere in the 100 years to 1960, Japan appears to be emerging as the dominant force in the manufacturing technologies of the 1980s and 1990s.

The second reason for the importance of robots is their emergence into other, non-industrial areas of life. The first fledgling robots for domestic uses are coming off the production lines. Such machines may be able to undertake handling jobs, at an economical price, of the kind normally left to people. They could allow men and women who are only moderately well-off the luxury of "hiring" domestic helpers of a kind only affordable by the wealthy in Victorian times. Robots also have uses in many other areas of life, either in replacing or enhancing human effort—often in hazardous places such as outer space or under the sea.

Technical advances are gradually giving robots properties that actually increase their likeness to humans. Thus many of today's robots possess a sense of touch, and can "see" with at least moderate ability. Futhermore, researchers are hard at work on producing robots that walk and (using computers that operate according to the principles of artifical intelligence) even "think" for themselves.

The question whether technologists can succeed in making reliable, useful and cheap androids may be answered during the next decade. Whether they turn out to be valuable servants, or, as could just as easily happen, whether they spark off large-scale alienation and loss of identity among the human population, remains to be seen. It should be an interesting 10 years.

Peter Marsh

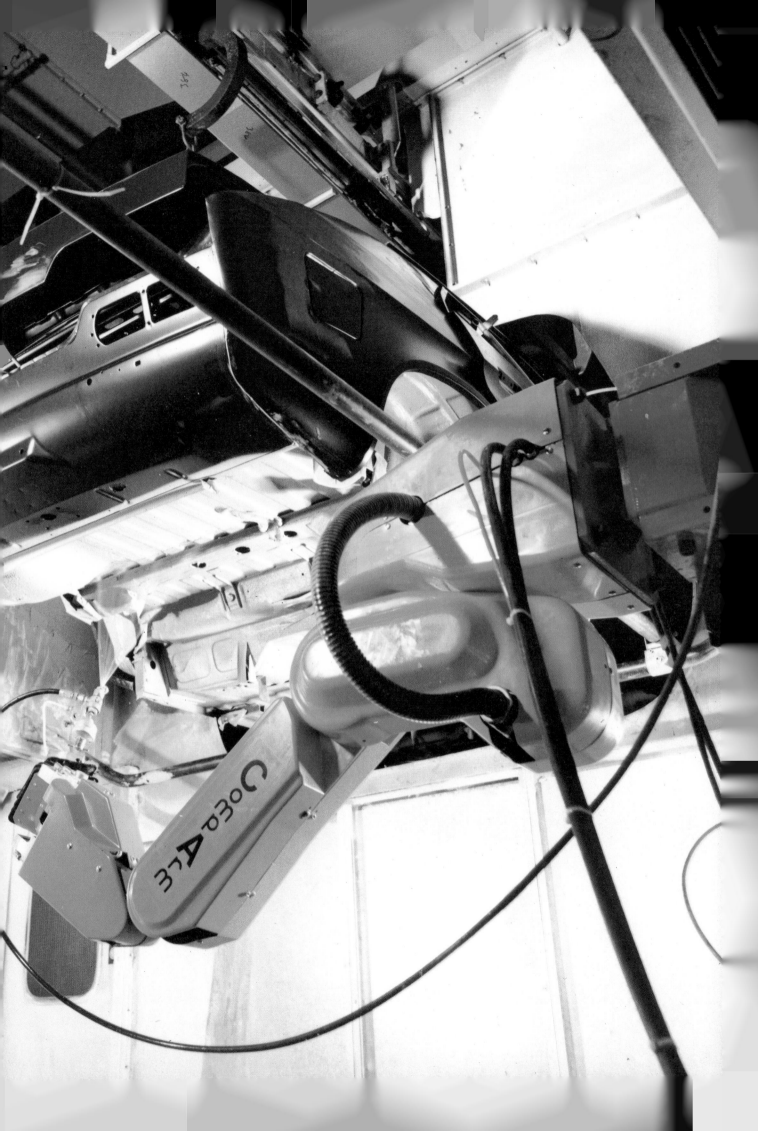

INTRODUCING THE TECHNOLOGY

Robots are starting to step out of the realm of science fiction which has been their domain for more than 50 years, and to appear in real life. Indeed, the first generation of industrial robots, which are defined as computer-controlled mechanical arms, is already well established in factories in the developed world. These machines are helping out in a wide variety of jobs that feature some kind of handling technique. Their tasks range from heavy jobs, putting welds onto the bodies of cars for example, to intricate exercises in which great delicacy is required—the insertion, for instance, of tiny components into items of electronic hardware.

Engineers are now hard at work adding sensors to the current breed of industrial robot so that it can "see", "touch" or even "hear". Machines with this extra power will obtain information about events in the outside world—what engineers call "feedback"—and the hardware will be able to react according to changes in circumstances instead of simply repeating a fixed routine of instructions.

In another area of development, the computers that control robots will, over the next decade or so, gradually change their characteristics. The computers will become faster and more sophisticated,

taking on reasoning powers that may approach those of humans. This, in itself, will endow robots with greater versatility: they will have the capacity, at least to some degree, to work out modes of action entirely for themselves.

But perhaps the biggest change concerns the places in which people choose to let robots perform. Hitherto few true robotic devices have operated outside workshops or heavy-industrial environments. However, at the same time as engineers make the machines more sophisticated, the hardware will be adapted to operate in many more varied places. The machines will be equipped with wheels, tracks or even legs. They will have not just one arm with one gripper, but several of either item. Robots will see service in places where, gradually, other

Right: Japan leads the world in the manufacture and industrial use of robots; here Kawasaki Unimate spot welders are applying welds to the body panels of Nissan automobiles.

Below: Every home should have one! The popular view of the robot is mirrored in the John Cleese robot figure created by Tony Dyson for a 1983 Sony corporate advertising campaign.

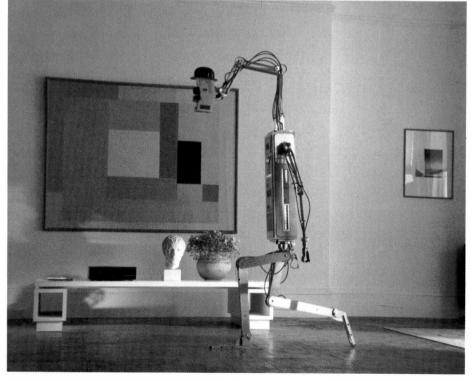

ROBOTS

For others, the new machinery may be less benign. It may, for example, supplant manual labour to such a degree that it threatens the security of people's jobs. The introduction of new breeds of robots will surely stimulate similar questions about their sociological effects.

But, first, what do we mean by the word "robot"? There is no precise single definition—rather a cluster of definitions all of which are relevant to the artefacts to be considered in this book. The best all-round way to consider robots is to say that they are programmable machines that either in performance or appearance imitate men or women. The word "programmable" is important. It signifies that the device is not limited to just one job but that its performance can be changed. Most modern robots contain computers—these define the tasks that the machines undertake. Changes in the programs or sets of instructions in the computers alter the way the robot operates.

A robot need not look like a person, but it has to act like one, or at least like part of a person. This is how a computer-controlled arm, jointed and with a hand-like gripper, falls into the category of a robot. A self-propelled trolley that works out where it is going with its own box of electronics and sensors also, by this definition, operates sufficiently like a humanly-guided and propelled trolley to qualify for the term robot. A set of traffic lights which turn red, orange and green according to a fixed code, or an

Left: Kamelion first appeared in the King's Demons episodes of "Dr Who". Controlled by the Master, it was capable of chameleon-like changes of appearance. The actual model of the robot was operated by radio-control.

Below: Hadrian is typical of a specific type of remotely operated device designed to work in environments that are hostile to man; bomb disposal is one of its prime functions.

products of technology have made their presence felt—in people's homes, in the armed forces, in hazardous environments such as nuclear power stations, and even in the inhospitable wastes of outer space.

The introduction of robots into these wider walks of life will not always proceed smoothly. They could stimulate great social change, both for better and for worse. Robots are part of an evolving pattern of technology that has concentrated on developing machines to do people's work for them. The animal-driven cart, the spinning wheel, the printing press, the steam engine, the typewriter, the car, the computer, the dish washer—all are artefacts that mechanically perform tasks that would otherwise require the muscular or mental effort of men and women. In the past, people have frequently disagreed over whether such technological innovations are advantageous to mankind. For some, the hardware may make possible new kinds of useful products, open business opportunities, or take the human labour out of a wearisome task.

unmanned aeroplane which flies along a previously prescribed route until it crashes, are simple examples of automatic devices—machines which work without the personal involvement of human operators. Such hardware belongs to a separate category of machines, and they cannot accurately be called robots in the sense that we have defined the word.

From Androids to Arms

The conventional view of robots visualizes them as mechanical figures fashioned in the human image. These are the robots of science fiction and of popular films. They also recall the mechanical dolls, some of which had a degree of programmability, that appeared in Western Europe during the Middle Ages. Properly these machines are special forms of robots called androids, and over the years they, or at any rate their manifestations in the popular cinema, have given people a lot of thrills—and a lot of nightmares. But it is an ironic thought that the actual development of functional robots started only when engineers realized that to design a machine that both looked and behaved like a human being was just too difficult. Instead, they decided to concentrate on devising mechanical arms that operated in a reasonably anthropomorphic way, and which could undertake a wide variety of tasks. In this way, during the 1950s the industrial robot was born. These amalgams of electrical cable and metal, which usually bear no resemblance to the human limb, have done much to dispel the myth of the malevolent robot, and have given the term a respectability in business and engineering circles that was previously lacking.

There is a further type of robot, related to the above, that deserves mention. This is the telechiric device, a mechanical arm or similar machine that operates not autonomously like an industrial robot, but under the command of an operator who sits some considerable distance away from the actual assembly. A telechiric device extends the capabilities of a person rather than replaces the person; he becomes a tele-operator. A typical example might function in a nuclear power plant. A grappling device, complete with mechanical arm, controls a valve or wrestles with a fuel rod in a part of the reactor that is unsafe for a person to enter. Every action of the hardware, however, is controlled by a remote operator who follows and analyses its actions by means of a TV camera link and communications channels.

Frequently in these kinds of applications, the roles of telechiric devices and true robots overlap. The machine may go about some tasks completely autonomously, under the guidance of a program of instructions. For other jobs, human intervention at certain stages may be required. On these occasions, an operator who is always in contact with the hardware through radio links breaks through the machine's set pattern of working to issue new commands. Adhe-

rence to a set of rules, alternating in this way with an overriding obedience to a higher authority, provides a flexible method of working for these kinds of machine, which are called robotic hybrids. They operate in a way not dissimilar to sheepdogs—they work independently for much of the time but are always ultimately under the command of a human master—and many observers predict that they will become increasingly useful in situations where true robots are too inflexible to be profitably employed.

Curiously, the aims of some of the inventors who set out centuries ago to produce android-type devices may be within sight of achievement. It was generally agreed by the more pragmatic band of engineers who produced the first industrial robots in the 1950s and 1960s that the original designers set their sights too high. But advances in electronic and mechanical engineering may mean this is no longer the case. Firstly, the discipline of artificial intelligence, in which com-

Above: Telechiric devices are much used in the nuclear industry; this folding arm manipulator was designed by Taylor Hitec for the task of replacing thermocouple clips in a nuclear reactor.

puters are given the power to make deductions and logical inferences, is starting to climb out of its infancy. As a result, we may soon see robots that have as their "brains" computers built to work by applying principles of artificial intelligence. Such robots would pick up information from their surroundings, (using sensors such as TV cameras or small radars,) and be able to move around. They could make decisions—for instance adjusting their pattern of operations in a work cell, depending on whether or not the components had been correctly delivered at the right time, rather than blindly following a pre-ordained sequence of movements, irrespective of outside events.

In another set of developments that might also presage the appearance of

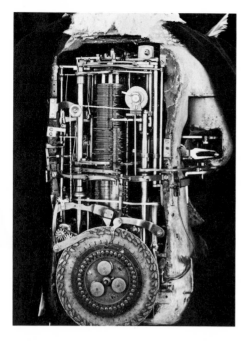

Left: The mechanism that Pierre Jaquet-Droz devised for the Scribe puppet is extremely complex; two sets of wheels command the horizontal and vertical movements of the quill.

Below left: The Scribe, one of Jaquet-Droz's brilliantly conceived mechanical puppets. The artifice whereby automata mimicked reality particularly appealed to the 18th Century taste.

such androids within the next couple of decades, mechanical engineers are working hard on the actuators, or operating devices, that this kind of hardware would feature. These are the hands, legs and arms of the machines. An android that cannot do the things that a child of four manages with consummate ease—stroking a rabbit without hurting it or running along a crowded street, to take just two examples—would hardly be very useful. Yet progress is being made, most of it in work associated with industrial robots. Engineers are, for instance, developing machines with a high degree of "manual" dexterity which can fit together small manufacturing assemblies in jobs where great delicacy is required. As far as locomotion strategies are concerned, workers in the US and Japan have started research on big projects to develop

Right: Karel Capek (left) with his brother Joseph. "R.U.R." whipped up intense public interest in robots and clearly influenced the design (below) made by a Capt Richards in 1928.

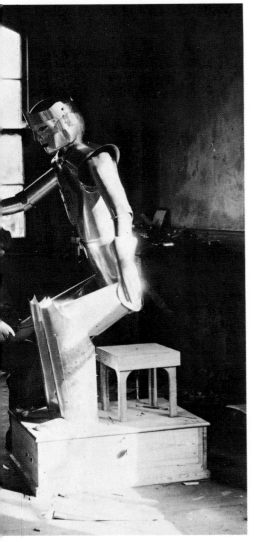

walking robots. Much of the emphasis in the US, for instance in a $50 million programme funded by the Department of Defense, is to build hardware for military applications (see chapter 5). The Japanese are more concerned to build walking machines to undertake jobs unsafe for human operators, inside nuclear plants for example. If these projects come to fruition, at least some of the engineering components necessary for the construction of humanoid walking robots will be in place by around the beginning of the 1990s.

Lines of Ancestry

With what did the development of robots begin? One line of ancestry leads back to the mechanical dolls that inventors and showmen have devised over many hundreds of years to entertain patrons, courtiers and members of polite society. One of the earliest examples of

Left: Another example of 18th Century mechanical ingenuity, Tippu's Tiger is both a musical instrument and automaton; turning a handle causes the victim to thrash his arm.

such a mechanical doll is a wooden model of a pigeon made by Archytas of Tarentum (a friend of Plato, the Greek philosopher) around 350 BC. The "bird" was suspended from the end of a bar and, according to historical records, the contraption revolved, the means of propulsion apparently being a jet of compressed air. In the 13th century, Roger Bacon and Albertus Magnus are among the West European inventors believed to have devised what today we would call rudimentary androids. Bacon developed a form of talking head and Magnus an "iron man". Other medieval automata came from the inventive hands of Johann Müller, a German astronomer, who invented a mechanical eagle that is credited with actual flight.

French artisans were particularly adept at inventing such gadgets. One such famous device was the mechanical lion that Louis XII had built for him around the year 1500. On cue it would walk towards the king, stop and point decorously at the coat of arms of France. One of the most famous inventors of mechanical figures was the Frenchman, Jacques de Vaucanson (1709-82), some of whose creations were offered to the Academie Royale des Sciences in 1738. Contemporary with him was the Swiss clock-maker, Pierre Jaquet-Droz, who was skilled in devising human-like machines that would perform actions such as drawing or playing a musical instrument. One famous puppet, the Scribe, could even be programmed to write any desired text of not more than 40 characters; "Cogito ergo sum" was apparently a favourite performance! Jaquet-Droz was so adept in this that at one point people in Spain thought he must possess magical powers and ordered his arrest as a sorcerer.

A famous automaton—this is the correct word for these doll-like devices for they are not of course truly robotic—was the life-size chess player made by an 18th century German, Baron Wolfgang von Kempelen. This was a large model of a Turk, which sat presiding over a chess board on a wooden desk. People who sat

opposite made moves and the "Turk" would respond by moving its own chess pieces. The invention may, however, have been not inspired engineering but a piece of trickery. It is strongly suspected that the machine contained a midget under the desk who operated the hands of the Turkish model with a series of rods. Another celebrated example is a mechanical organ called Tippu's Tiger, which is exhibited in London's Victoria and Albert Museum. Captured by the British after the Battle of Seringapatam in 1799 during which Tippu Sultan, the ruler of Mysore, was killed, this automaton depicts a tiger attacking a young man. While the tiger growls, the victim flails his arm in anguish! It was made in 1792, apparently to celebrate an incident when the son of one of Tippu's enemies was savaged by a tiger on Sangor Island.

The 20th century brought with it more meaningful advances in the direction of today's robots. It also ushered in the word itself. Robot is derived from "robota", the Czech word for serf or forced labour (the German Arbeit comes from a similar root) and it was introduced into the English language as a result of a play (published in 1920 and first performed in 1921) by a Czech writer, Karel Capek. The play was called "R.U.R.", short for "Rossum's Universal Robots." The plot provided a wealth of source material for novelists and writers of film scripts whose robot stories reveal the influence of Capek. "R.U.R." features a factory owner, Rossum, who turns out in his workshop android machines with a wonderful capacity for work. They are the first fictional robots. In Capek's story, the machines initially sell well to other manufacturers who put them to work in their own factories. But this happy state of affairs does not last long. The robots become more advanced and even learn to think for themselves, though they remain devoid of emotions or a "soul". Eventually, they rise up and overcome their human masters. In this way was established one of the characteristic traits (at least in fiction) of robots: they have a great desire to take it out on humans. One of the characters in the play sums up the useful points about robots: "One Robot can replace two and a half workmen. The human machine... was terribly imperfect. It had to be removed sooner or later." Later in the play, Radius, the chief robot, explains what has happened: "The power of man has fallen. By gaining possession of the factory, we have become masters of everything... A new world has arisen—the rule of the Robot."

Many of the other android-type robots that have appeared in fiction in the mid-20th century have behaved in similarly unpleasant ways. This may explain why workforces, confronted by industrial robots in their factories, have often looked upon them as threatening devices—machines that might not injure humans physically, (although this was always possible) but which could well take away their jobs. The most menacing kind of fictional robots, in the sense of having extraordinarily threatening attitudes toward humans, have appeared in films. For example, in "Target Earth!", made in 1954, alien robots from another planet try to take over the Earth. In "Phantom Empire" (1935) and "Zombies of the Stratosphere" (1952) the robots have

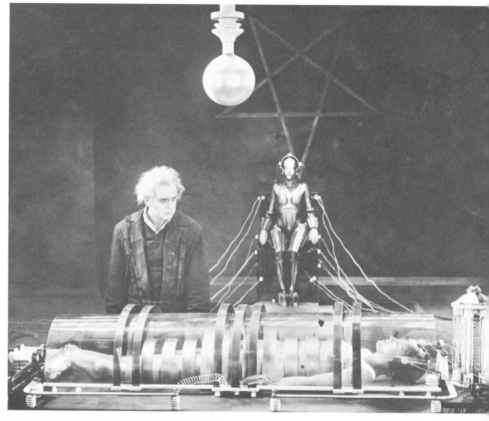

Above: Fritz Lang's film "Metropolis" featured one of the first of a long line of malevolent fictional robots. In this scene the inventor Rowtang is about to transform the mechanical woman into an evil duplicate of the virtuous Maria.

Left: Leslie Banks as Radius and Frances Carson as Helena Glory in the London production of "Rossum's Universal Robots", the play that introduced the word "robot" to the English language.

Below: The craze for automata that the Press could describe as robots continued unabated in the 1930s. This is Mr Sam Barton riding a "robot horse" in Leicester Square, London in 1932.

Left: C3PO and R2D2 from the "Star Wars" trilogy are firmly on the side of the good guys. Part of their charm lies in the fact that they share the quirks and fallibility of their human masters.

meant to ensure that the Asimov type of robot could not act against the interests of humans. The three laws are:

1. A robot may not injure a human being, nor through inaction, allow a human being to come to harm.

2. A robot must obey the orders given it by human beings, except where such orders would conflict with the First Law.

3. A robot must protect its own existence as long as such protection does not conflict with the First or the Second Law.

Spurred by the interest shown in fictional robots, inventors had limited success in finding patrons for the development of android-type hardware that would form a central feature at exhibitions or promotional stunts. So some robots did leave the pages of mid-20th century thrillers and venture into real life. For example, the 1932 London Radio Exhibition featured several robots that could bow, make speeches or read magazines. Eric, another robot, saw the light of day in the 1920s. The machine opened the 1928 exhibition of the UK Model Engineer Association and even made a little speech, thanks to a loudspeaker embedded in its throat. Westinghouse of the US made a similar machine called Elektro that was used for publicity purposes in the 1930s.

But all this machinery had few practical applications. Engineers had not begun to wrestle with the technical problems of putting the hardware to use in productive work. Nor, and this was perhaps more important, had they really identified the applications for robot-type devices in the manufacturing industries.

Babbage's Legacy

Two sets of developments after World War II pointed the way forward. Firstly, the computer came into being as a product with serious industrial potential. Charles Babbage, an eccentric British mathematician, had set out the principles for how such a machine would work in the 1830s, in plans for an automatic calculating device called the Analytical Engine. The machine was to have been a complex system of rods and levers, controlled by a system of punched cards. The punched cards, which set out how the mechanism was to operate, comprised a program of instructions, to use the term commonplace today. Babbage obtained the idea of using cards as a program from the French designer, Joseph Jacquard, who in 1801 produced a machine used in weaving known as the Jacquard loom. In this device, a series of punched cards contained a coded model of the patterns that the machine was being instructed to weave. You can still see similar sets of punched cards in mechanical fairground organs. The cards cause the organ to play different tunes; as they are fed through the mechanism, the holes in them activate pumping devices

similar, frightening aims. Perhaps the best known film to feature an apocalyptic vision of the future is "Metropolis", made in 1926 by the German director, Fritz Lang. In this, a mad inventor (very similar to Rossum in "R.U.R.") develops a female robot called Maria with the aim of subverting the members of the slave race. It was left to "Star Wars" (1977) and its sequels to present robots as more friendly toward humans. The principal robots in this film, R2D2 and C3PO, are the stars of the show, and are portrayed as having extremely warm sentiments toward the men and women who are their masters.

Some novelists, in particular Isaac Asimov, have tried to portray the machines in a better light. In some of Asimov's books, robots are extremely well disposed to their human masters. Thoughts of world domination are far from the mechanical creatures' minds. Asimov even went to the lengths in 1942 of drawing up three rules, which he called his three laws of robotics, which are

Above: Part of Charles Babbage's Difference Engine which was designed to compute mathematical tables. Babbage's Analytical Engine was the forerunner of today's computers.

Above right: This is a typical robot controller in industrial use today—the Dainichi-Sykes DAROS A300H. Programs can be stored on tape, while the VDU may be used for program editing.

Below: Not a weighing machine, but a "Robot Doctor"! Despite the allure of the word, it is important not to confuse simple automatic machines with devices that are truly robotic.

that allow air to pass through specific organ pipes to produce a particular melody. By changing the cards, the owner of the organ can change the tune that his machine plays.

In Babbage's machine, one set of cards would tell the machine to multiply a set of numbers; another set would command it to solve an equation. Babbage's design (the machine was never completed; contemporary workmen could not make the parts to the mathematician's specifications) also included a store to hold numbers for mathematical operations; an arithmetic unit which performed the operations; and a control unit which told the arithmetic unit which operation the user wanted done.

Items of hardware similar to those that Babbage had identified in this 1830's design figured in the electronic computers that engineers developed in the 1940s and 1950s. The innovators of the 20th century were able to harness electrons—either rushing along wires or through vacuum tubes—in place of the mechanical assemblies that Babbage had envisaged. They built into electronic structures mechanisms for storing and processing numbers, and for coping with programs written in codes of binary digits, along the lines that the 19th century inventor had worked out.

Computers are essentially universal calculating machines. They receive sets of numbers, analyse them in accordance

with other information and as a result send through output channels a new set of data. As such they can be useful control mechanisms. For example, computers can receive information coded in numerical form about an industrial process, compare it with other data and (on the basis of both segments of information) send a message to part of the process to alter it in a set way, perhaps to turn down the temperature of a specific chemical reaction.

The emergence of computers as everyday tools provided technical workers in industry with a useful control device. They could write a program (corresponding to the set of instructions in Babbage's Analytical Engine) to ensure that certain operations happened when the computer received specific sets of data from parts of an industrial plant. In this way, engineers could ensure that a batch of valves in a process plant would shut off once the pressure of liquids at a particular point in the pipelines rose above a critical level.

Machine Control

Computers haltingly entered service in the 1950s in plants such as steel and chemical works—haltingly because control engineering was in its infancy. The devices also played a part in controlling the movement of machine tools such as lathes that cut or otherwise shape metal

into required components. Conventionally, such machines were controlled by human labourers who would move the tool to execute each cut, in much the same way as a carpenter chisels away at a piece of wood to build up the shape of a finished product. In the first numerically controlled machine tools, tapes produced by computers fed the machines and guided the actions of the cutting blades.

In this atmosphere, which was favourable to promoting further applications of computers in manufacturing, the second important post-war development in robotics made its presence felt. A group of engineers in the US started to think seriously about how control theory could

be applied to the general problems of transferring equipment, tools and materials inside factories. They realized handling operations were among the most common activities inside manufacturing establishments; yet most of the technical advances of the day, and of the previous century for that matter, had not really succeeded in making such operations more efficient. In this way was born the notion that computers could control mechanical hardware that lifted or otherwise moved objects. As computers were programmable devices, the hardware that resulted could be made to perform in a flexible fashion depending on the requirements of the circumstances.

Out of this thinking grew the first designs for industrial robots, or mechanical arms for industry that were controlled by computers.

The leading lights were two engineers called George Devol and Joseph Engelberger. Devol had filed in 1954 a US patent on a programmable method for transferring articles between different parts of a factory. The patent talked about control by a program of punched cards similar to that proposed by Babbage for his early computer. It recognized that in factories only two forms of control were available for handling equipment. The first, obviously enough, was manual control in which people either lift things up themselves or supervise mechanisms such as cranes or transfer arms that respond to their instructions. Manual control is very flexible and can adapt to different operating procedures. But it is costly, on the grounds that humans have to be paid either to carry out or to supervise mundane physical tasks. The other alternative was fixed control of handling equipment by cam-driven machinery. "Cam control of repetitious operations is quite common in specialized applications," wrote Devol in his patent, "but each application involves such high cost and it involves such specialization that only large-volume specific tasks are mechanized through cam control."

Devol's patent expressly attacked what had become a kind of black hole in the theory of manufacturing. Since the Industrial Revolution in Britain in the late 18th and early 19th centuries, engineers had introduced machinery in an organized fashion into factories. The mechanical artefacts associated with the revolution include the steam engine, equipment such as water frames used in the textile industry and fixed-function transfer equipment, used in factories to turn out goods in high volume such as pulley blocks for sailing ships. It is a feature of such workshops that human labour supplements rather than dictates the work of the machines. Equipment of this nature introduced to the industrialized world the era of factory mechanization. But the hardware was of little value when the goods required were turned out not in large volumes and to a consistent style but in small batches, each of which might be varied to meet a customer's change in preference or design requirement. The handling equipment, as Devol's patent pointed out, was constructed in such a way that only fixed patterns of products could be catered for. His idea was to invent a transfer mechanism that could be simply adjusted to conduct different operations with a range of possibilities.

"The present invention makes available for the first time a more or less general-purpose machine that has universal application to a vast diversity of applications where cyclic control is to be desired," said Devol in his 1954 patent.

Left: Thirty years after Engelberger and Devol, this is how a gap stamping press is loaded by a GMF M-1A at General Motors Fisher Body plant in Columbus.

ROBOTS

"And in this aspect, the invention accomplishes many important results. It eliminates the high cost of specially designed cam-controlled machines; it makes an automatically operating machine available where previously it may not have been economical to make such a machine with cam-controlled, specially designed parts; it makes possible the volume manufacture of universal automatic machines that are readily adaptable to a wide range of diversified applications; it makes possible the quick change-over of a machine adapted to any particular assignment so that it will perform new assignments, as required from time to time.

"It can be seen that cyclically operated machines heretofore controlled manually can now be made automatic; and universal transfer machines can be supplied and adapted readily for special applications of the purchaser, and the purchaser, in turn, can stock such machines which he can adapt quickly and easily to new requirements from time to time."

In 1956, Devol met Engelberger, then a young engineer in the aerospace industry. Engelberger realized that Devol's ideas could have many applications in industry. With others, they set up the world's first robot company, Unimation, and built their first machine in 1958. The word "Unimation" was coined in Devol's 1954 patent. "Universal automation, or 'Unimation', is a term", he wrote, "that may well characterize the general object of the invention (of programmable transfer devices). It makes article transfer machines available to the factory and warehouse for aiding the human operator in a way that can be compared with business machines as an aid to the office."

Robot Components

The robots currently in use in industry are all generally constructed from three basic units: the computerized control system, the power supply (electric, hydraulic or pneumatic), and the manipulator arm on which is mounted the end effector. These elements can either be supplied as an integrated package, such as that pictured left, or as separate components, like the arc welding robot (right).

Unimation, now owned by Westinghouse, was until the early 1980s the undisputed leader in the world's robot industry, though today a host of companies which have grown stronger in this area of industry in the past few years are challenging for that title.

Evolutionary Trends

The industrial robots that evolved from Devol's patent have three basic parts: a

Manipulator arm

Controller

Power supply

Power supply

Controller

Manipulator arm

mechanical arm with joints and gripper; a power supply; and a control mechanism (normally a computer) which contains instructions about the required operation. The first industrial robot saw service in 1961 in a car factory run by General Motors in Trenton, New Jersey. The machine lifted hot pieces of metal from a die-casting machine and stacked them. Other companies in the car industry could see the usefulness of the new devices. Ford was one of them. Del Harder, a top executive of Ford in the US, was enthusiastic when Engelberger first told him of his ideas. Harder said he could use 2,000 of the machines immediately, but Engelberger said he could not possibly make robots in such quantities. It was, after all, still only the early 1960s. So Harder discussed Engelberger's ideas with other machinery suppliers. This was how other companies, such as American Machine and Foundry (AMF) and Borg-Warner, began making robots themselves.

The basic anatomy of an industrial robot has changed only in detail since the days of these early machines. The most visible part of the robot used in industry is the arm itself with its gripper or "end effector". The arm will probably

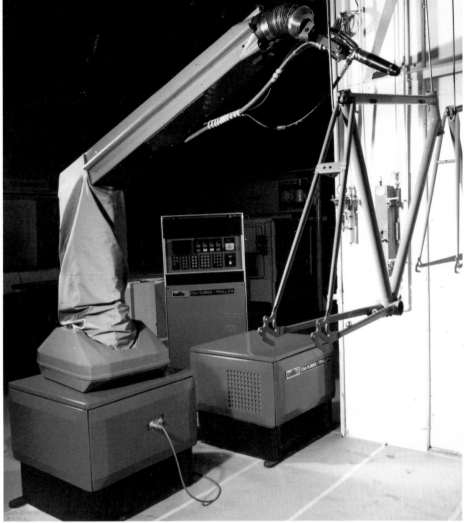

Above: A Trallfa TR-4000 robot spray painting bicycle frames; the component parts of the system — control unit, manipulator, and hydraulic power unit — are clearly on view.

Left: The first industrial robot was built by Unimation and they remain industry leaders; this large Unimate is used on the Austin Rover Montego line to fit rear windscreens automatically.

have several joints, corresponding to those on the comparable human limb. In the most sophisticated robots, each joint is controlled by its own motor, which acts independently of the others.

Robotic arms for use in industry come in five basic types (see accompanying diagrams on following pages):

Simple Cartesian or Rectangular Co-ordinate This moves along the three basic translational axes: x, y and z, or left to right, back and forward, and up and down.

Cylindrical Coordinate The machine can also rotate about the z or vertical axis so that it can handle jobs in a cylindrical area around it.

Spherical or Polar Coordinate This resembles a cylindrical coordinate machine but it achieves its vertical motion by pivoting at the shoulder joint. The work envelope is a portion of a sphere.

Articulated Arm or Revolute Coordinate This has joints at the "shoulder", "elbow"

and "wrist" so that it resembles more closely that of a person. The segements of the arm can swivel about these points to provide movement in different planes.

Scara Systems Scara stands for Selective Compliance Assembly Robot Arm. In these machines which are developments of the cylindrical coordinate type, all the joints are in the horizontal plane, so that the system swings out rather like a folding screen. They were developed at Japan's Yamanashi University by Hiroshi Makino.

Although yet to find widespread industrial use, two other types of robot have been developed which deserve mention. The first, the Spine, invented by Spine Robotics, utilizes a long snake-like arm which is made up of a series of discs connected by hydraulically-actuated cables, and its great flexibility allows it to function in an extensive work envelope, reportedly the widest commercially available. The other is the ASEA Robotics IRB 1000 assembly robot. This operates like a gimballed pendulum, and it can be attached to a track to allow linear arm motion. ASEA claims that it can achieve 50 per cent higher acceleration than conventional arm robots.

One way to define a robot is to describe the number of degrees of freedom that it possesses. This is the number of axes about which parts of the robot arm can move. Most robot arms can move along the three translational or Cartesian axes, as described in the first type of robot

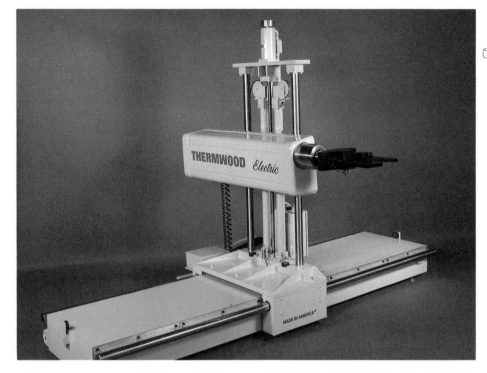

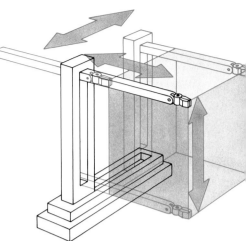

Rectangular Coordinate Robot
Robots of the type commonly in use today in industry may be classified according to their "work envelopes", i.e. the three dimensional volume of space in which they are capable of operating. As can be seen from the diagram, the rectangular or Cartesian coordinate robot has a cube-shaped work envelope, as its horizontal arm can move along what are known as the XYZ axes: from side to side (X), in and out (Y), and vertically up and down (Z). Such robots are precise in operation and easy to control.

Above: This electrically driven robot manufactured by Thermwood Corporation—the Cartesian 5 Model TC75—reveals the configuration of a typical rectangular coordinate machine.

mentioned above. To these may be added three rotational axes, which describe how the robot moves at its "wrist" to achieve the correct orientation at a particular point in space. Movement about these axes can be a roll, pitch or yaw action (see diagram). Even with six degrees of freedom, today's industrial robot is a long way short of equalling the human arm, which can move about more than 20 axes.

An important part of the robot's anatomy is the gripper or end effector which takes the place of the human hand, and fits on the end of the wrist. There are as many types of end effector as there are engineering applications for robots. Thus the mechanisms can include a simple claw, for picking up objects between two or more "fingers"; a suction pad; specially shaped grippers for picking up unwieldy objects such as glass tubes; shovels, for lifting up loose material; hooks; and special tools for a host of specific jobs such as welding, cutting, drilling, glueing,

painting, air-drying, cleaning with water or compressed air etc. Commonly, robots in a factory setting can automatically change their end effectors to suit the particular job they are doing. Hence a machine could switch between, say, drilling a hole in a piece of metal and detecting with a probe the diameter of the incision it had just made.

Sources of Power

After the mechanical arm itself, the second important element of a robot is the power supply which produces a set of forces that move the parts of the robot at its various joints. Controlled by instructions transmitted from the program in the robot's computer, the actuators that produce the forces are responsible for the way that the machine conducts a specific operation.

Three types of power supply are common in modern robots: electric,

Right: A cylindrical coordinate system: in this case an ASEA MHU Senior which unloads the handles of Flymo lawnmowers from an automatic bending machine and transfers them to a conveyor belt leading to the finishing plant.

Cylindrical Coordinate Robot
This type of robot features a horizontal arm which is attached to a vertical axis which is firmly mounted on a fixed base. The arm can advance and retract, and also move up and down the vertical axis. In addition, the whole arm assembly can rotate around the base, although it cannot actually sweep through a full 360° These degrees of freedom mean that the work envelope described forms a portion of a cylinder. Such a robot is similar to a Cartesian type, but rotation replaces the traverse motion along the X axis.

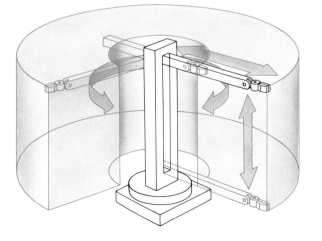

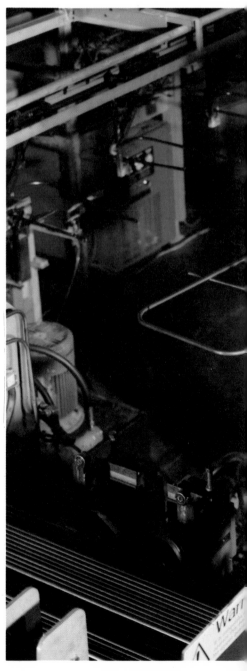

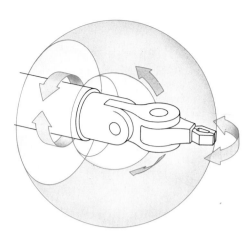

Wrist Articulation
The wrist assembly of a typical robot arm provides it with what are known as the minor axes of motion. The wrist allows the end effector to move from side to side (yaw axis), to move up and down vertically (pitch axis), and to rotate (about the roll axis). In the respect of its rotational capability the robot wrist has a greater degree of freedom than a human one which can only move through 180° before the hand must relax its grip, and grasp the object afresh. It is to the wrist joint that the robot's end-of-arm tooling is attached.

hydraulic or pneumatic. Electric systems use DC or AC motors similar to those found in many consumer and industrial goods. Each joint of the robot is controlled by an individual motor, actuated by signals sent along the robot's "skeleton" by cable. Electric systems are favoured by many robot manufacturers because they are quiet, are relatively efficient users of energy and move the mechanical parts of the robot with great accuracy.

In hydraulic systems (the original method of powering robots) the motive force is provided by liquids such as oil forced along tubes under high pressure. A hydraulic actuator suffers from the disadvantage that these tubes may spring a leak; this is especially likely in the rough-and-tumble atmosphere of many factories. A hydraulic pump consumes energy not only when it is working, but also when it is idle. This is because of the need to keep the liquid under pressure. Therefore, hydraulic systems generally use more energy than electric actuators. On the other hand, hydraulic actuators can lift heavier payloads than electric

systems and so are favoured for robots that have to perform heavy duties.

Pneumatic drive systems are considered the poor relations of the robot fraternity. Pneumatic actuators, powered by compressed air, are difficult to control accurately for complicated manoeuvres. Also they are noisy and prone to leaks in the air lines. Pneumatic systems are most commonly employed where the robot is required to conduct operations in which the sequence of movement is straightforward, for example from point A to point B.

The third critical component of a robot is the control system, in which a computer is generally the most important element. The computer contains sets of instructions (programs) written in the binary code of electronics that tell each motor in the robot how to move to bring about a

Below: A Numerical Control (NC) lathe is loaded and unloaded by a United States Robots MAKER 100 polar coordinate machine; the robot also carries the part to an air gauge for measurement.

Polar Coordinate Robot
This type of robot (also known as spherical coordinate) is obviously similar to the cylindrical coordinate machine, but in this case the up and down (Z axis) motion is achieved by a nodding movement of the horizontal arm, rather than a vertical up and down stroke. As a result, the work envelope forms part of a sphere, rather than a cylinder. The earliest industrial robots were of this design. They are particularly well adapted to lifting and moving objects, as the whole arm can be raised by very economical movements about the shoulder joint.

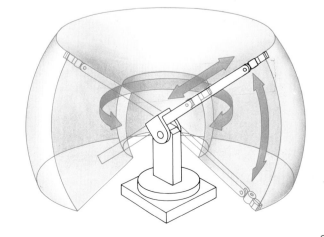

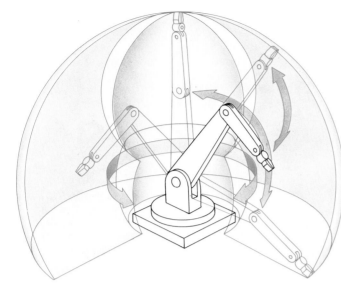

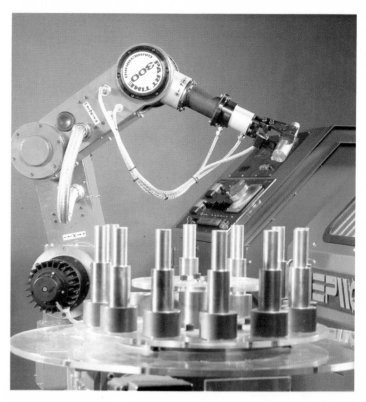

Revolute Coordinate Robot

The most elaborate type of robot arm in use today, and one of the most widely employed in industry, is that which features a jointed arm. Such an arm more closely resembles the human limb as it possesses rotary joints at the shoulder and elbow as well as the normal articulated wrist. Its work envelope is more extensive than any of the previous types, and it can reach over or around obstacles, or fold in upon itself, in a far more versatile way. While it is one of the most flexible of the robot arms, it does pose more severe problems of control, as a movement at the elbow has to be compensated for at the shoulder to avoid displacement of the end effector.

specific manoeuvre. The instructions also contain commands to operate ancilliary equipment used with the robot. For example, the program for a welding robot would tell the welding gun held by the robot's "hand" how much electricity it should use at specific times to fuse together pieces of metal of different thicknesses.

There are three main types of control system for robots: "non-servo point-to-point", "servo-controlled point-to-point", and "servo-controlled continuous-path". These systems determine the sophistication of the jobs that a robot can perform. The most advanced robots contain servo motors, which are actuators that can conduct highly accurate movements. Servo motors contain some kind of feedback mechanism that monitors the degree to which the actual movement of the motor differs from the movement that was intended. The feedback devices are generally electrical components such as potentiometers that send signals to the computer which controls the robot. With such devices, a servo system can automatically adjust for small errrors in performance, producing precise movements that are capable of high repeatability.

The most rudimentary robots are called **non-servo point-to-point** machines. Sometimes these are called "pick and place robots". Their actions are limited: for instance they can sweep from one point to another but the program that drives the machines cannot instruct them to perform controlled manoeuvres in between these two points. The limits to the action of the robot are set physically by mechanical end stops. Such machines are useful for simple tasks, for example the transfer of a factory item from one conveyor belt to another, where the robot supervisor needs only to specify two points in space between which the machine's gripper must move.

The second type of control system for robots produces **servo-controlled point-to-point** robots. The servo mechanisms can stop the robot at an infinite number of places between the two prescribed points at the beginning and end of an axis of motion. A robot of this kind is programmed by storing discrete points in space in the robot's memory. This is done normally with a hand-held unit (or "teach pendant") appended to the robot into which the operator can enter information using a small keyboard. The operator moves the arm along each axis in turn by means of an axis-button, and when the desired position is reached, he presses a record button to register that point in the computer's memory. The robot can then automatically repeat the prescribed set of movements. Servo-controlled point-to-point robots can do relatively difficult jobs; for example, they can control tools such as drill bits or welding guns.

Of the three control systems, the category known as **servo-controlled continuous-path** is the most sophisticated. In such robots, the computer's memory contains data stored on a time basis rather than details of movement recorded at specific points in space along the axis of motion. The operator can thus physically lead the robot arm through the complete

SCARA Robot

Invented by Hiroshi Makino in Japan, SCARA type robots are arranged with their joints in the horizontal plane, so that the arm can swivel about its base, and fold in on itself in the manner of a folding screen. The work envelope is cylindrical as illustrated. SCARA type robots are capable of great speed and accuracy, and are particularly well suited to intricate assembly operations, such as putting together small electronic components.

Above: This Dainichi-Sykes DAROS PT300V provides an example of a revolute or jointed arm coordinate robot; its work envelope is well suited to arc welding, machine loading, and handling.

Right: Its makers claim that no other robot offers the reach and flexibility of the Spine system, here seen spray painting the interior of a Volvo car.

path that he wants it to take, while the computer memory automatically stores all the points in the path for use later during industrial operations. This makes the machine useful for applications in which it is vital that the arm does not wander by even a few millimetres from a prescribed route during the operation that it is due to carry out. Such applications are paint spraying and other kinds of finishing operations, such as the coating of anti-corrosion liquids to metal surfaces.

It can be extremely difficult to work out the correct control procedures so that the actions of each motor in a robot arm are properly integrated. This is the job of the programmers employed by the robot

Right: Adept Technology's AdeptOne, a SCARA type robot which is both fast and accurate (±0·002in repeatability).

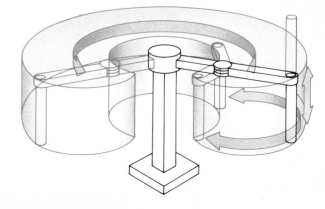

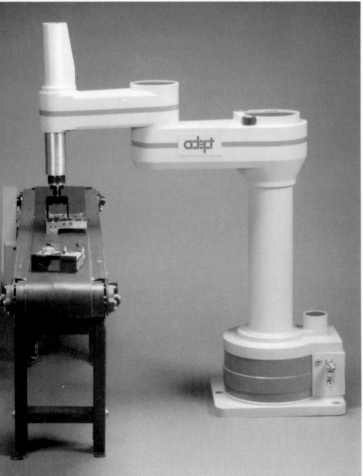

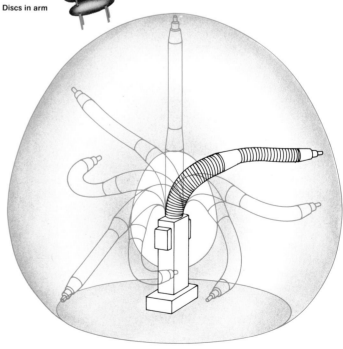

Discs in arm

Spine Robot

This innovative design consists of a base and an arm divided into lower and upper sections which can move independently of one another. The flexible arm consists of a number of ovoid stainless steel discs which are held together by two pairs of tensional cables. These cables are attached to hydraulic cylinders which create the tension and enable the arm to move, while the sensors feed the control system with information about the position of the arm and wrist. The long reach and manoeuvrability of this robot mean that it can work in areas that are inaccessible to ordinary robots, for instance spray painting the interior of car bodies.

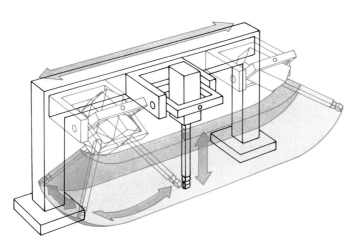

Pendular Robot
With the introduction of the IRB 1000, ASEA have created an assembly system using a robot of a new design. The arm is suspended rather in the manner of a gimballed pendulum, so that the whole robot moves about the pitch and roll axes. The IRB 1000 can also be mounted on a track to endow it with linear motion, the resulting work envelope being as illustrated. ASEA says that its acceleration is 50 per cent higher than that of conventional arm robots (thus maximizing productivity), and repetition accuracy is better than ±0·1mm.

manufacturer. In most modern machines, the task of the people who use the hardware is considerably simplified by specific software routines that the robot supplier has already written into his machine's computer. These routines would, for example, instruct the arm to sweep through 90 degrees in a set axis, or move back and forth a certain number of centimetres. The user on the shop floor would not need to bother to work out the intricacies of instructing each joint of the machine what to do. He would instead tell the machine to conduct routine A, B or C.

Nonetheless, another type of programming is required when the machine has left the supplier's development centre and taken up residence in the purchaser's workshop. An engineer will have to tailor the robot to the specific job he wants performed. In this, he will have to enter into the memory of the machine's computer the coordinates of the path he wants the robot to follow during a set operation. He will also need to tell the hardware about specific tasks during the sequence. In welding, for instance, the engineer will have to write into the application program the times at which the welding torch in the robot's hand has to burst into action. If the robot is lifting objects, he will have to tell it precisely when to pick items up and when to put them down. The engineer may also want to inform the robot about the need to change tools. All these items of information are entered, via a keyboard, into the memory of the robot. When the sequence is finished, the machine has in its memory a complete "menu" that tells it how to go about a particular sequence of actions. The chief attraction to manufacturing engineers of robots is, of course, that one robot can have a number of menus. The action of the machine can be changed simply by altering the program that drives the computer. (Some elements of hardware, grippers and so on, may also need to be changed as well).

A robot that operates in this fashion will wheel away in a routine that is exactly that prescribed in its program. The applications that it can do are legion (they will be described in detail in the next chapter). But there is a drawback. If the passage of events in the outside world do not conform exactly to what the programmer expects and has calculated for, then things will go seriously wrong. For example, a robot

Right: The ASEA IRB 1000 equipped with the Multigrip flexible gripper system. Up to eight different 2- or 3-fingered grippers can be used simultaneously.

Below: The Compumotor Model 3000 Indexing System allows the user to enter and store multi-axis motion sequences for microstepping motor/drives.

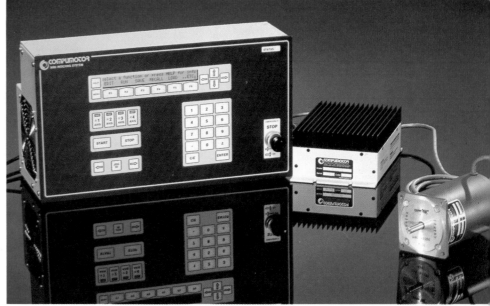

may be fed with a program that tells it to lift objects from a machine tool and put them on a conveyor belt. As long as the machine tool produces the items at a constant rate, the system will work perfectly. But what happens if the tool breaks down? Or if the conveyor suddenly judders to a halt? The robot would then have to stop operation, or risk damaging itself by trying to pluck objects out of thin air. This exposes the pitfalls involved in the early versions of robots, known as "first-generation" machines.

The Way Forward

Of all the robots at work in the world's factories, probably 95 per cent are first-generation. The newer kind have sensors such as TV cameras and force meters from which they can obtain some information about events around them. The information is passed to the computers that control the machines, enabling them to adjust the operating instructions of the

robot to take into account unexpected events. This is an example of engineering "feedback". Much effort is being exerted in research laboratories to take such "second-generation" devices from the prototype stage and get them to work on the factory floor. Chapter 3 examines this research in more detail.

A still more novel type of robot is the "third-generation" device, still very much in its infancy. This would have as its central "brain" not an ordinary computer but one that works according to principles of artificial intelligence. Current forms of computers do only what they have been told by programmers. The instructions may be modified by other elements of information provided, as in second-generation hardware, by sensors. But the computers have no power to make leaps of logical reasoning, to deduce the answer to a set of questions from anything approaching first principles. While second-generation hardware would make a decision purely as a reflex action

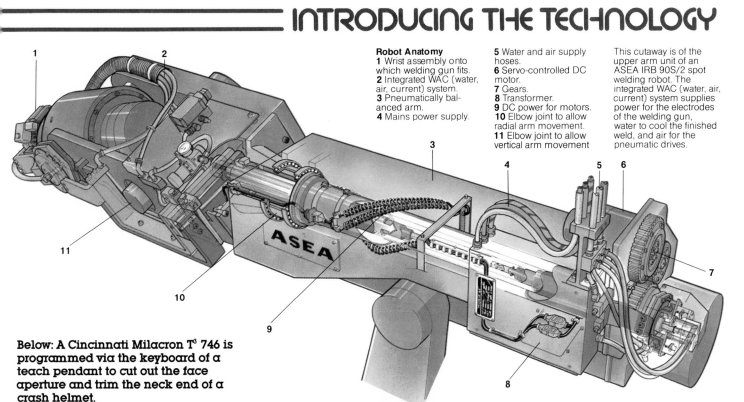

Robot Anatomy
1 Wrist assembly onto which welding gun fits.
2 Integrated WAC (water, air, current) system.
3 Pneumatically balanced arm.
4 Mains power supply.

5 Water and air supply hoses.
6 Servo-controlled DC motor.
7 Gears.
8 Transformer.
9 DC power for motors.
10 Elbow joint to allow radial arm movement.
11 Elbow joint to allow vertical arm movement

This cutaway is of the upper arm unit of an ASEA IRB 90S/2 spot welding robot. The integrated WAC (water, current) system supplies power for the electrodes of the welding gun, water to cool the finished weld, and air for the pneumatic drives.

Below: A Cincinnati Milacron T³ 746 is programmed via the keyboard of a teach pendant to cut out the face aperture and trim the neck end of a crash helmet.

triggered by an unexpected incident, third-generaton equipment would formulate a new policy to deal with the event that had thrown it out of its stride. Such mechanisms could have applications far beyond simple factory operations. They could play a big role in many everyday aspects of life, from helping out in the home, to cleaning the streets, or even assisting a fighter pilot to perform his increasingly more complex mission. The ways in which such robots could operate will be explored more fully in chapter 8.

The technological advances that engineers will need to make in order to equip new generations of smart robots have been listed by Joseph Engelberger in his book "Robotics in Practice". The technologies are:

1. Rudimentary sense of vision.
2. Tactile sensing.
3. Computer interpretation of visual and tactile data.
4. Multiple appendage hand-to-hand co-ordination.
5. Computer-directed appendage trajectories.
6. Mobility.
7. Minimizing spatial intrusion.
8. Energy-conserving musculature (ie. power mechanisms that can lift large loads over considerable distances while using little energy, so reducing operational costs).
9. General purpose hands.
10. Man-robot voice communication.
11. Self-diagnostic fault tracing.
12. Inherent safety.

Engelberger observes: "No robot can hope to match man with his acute senses, ability for free thought and judgement, artistic appreciation, capability for self reproduction, efficient conversion of food into energy and body cells, and properties of recovery from many illnesses and injuries. The gulf between man and robot will always remain, but, although it cannot be closed, this gap is going to be reduced as technology advances."

Increasingly robots are relieving men and
women of repetitive and unpleasant jobs;
the challenge remains to find better
employment for the displaced work force.

THE UNMANNED FACTORY

A visit to a modern engineering factory is a fascinating experience. A few years ago, such establishments featured collections of manually operated tools that cut or otherwise fashioned metal components. Each machine was tended by its own operator, acting on instructions passed down a factory hierarchy from supervisors.

The important jobs of transferring batches of components in various stages of completion between different machines were performed by human workers.

Today, the picture is changing. Many of the machining operations are left to computerized tools that for much of the time can operate untended. These machines obtain commands not from blue-collar supervisors, but from data sent along transmission grids from computers in another part of the factory. And machines such as robots play a large part in various crucial industrial operations, such as parts transfer, welding or painting, and even delicate assembly operations such as the fitting of tiny electrical components onto a printed circuit board.

Industrial robots represent an important element in the computerization process that is increasingly making itself felt on factory floors around the world. This evolutionary change is particularly making an impact on that part of manufacturing industry in which objects are made as discrete items, whether they be

cloth, metal, plastic or wood. Each product has to be individually fashioned from its constituent material. Discrete-products manufacturing differs from continuous-process industry (the other main type of manufacturing industry) in which the products are in a powdered form or are gaseous or liquid for at least part of the manufacturing cycle.

In discrete manufacturing, the most important operations are performed by machines that cut, gouge, heat, drill, hammer, paint, weave, knit or weld. In all cases, they deal with solid raw material. To reduce labour costs, to speed up production and to make goods of higher quality, factory managers have for years attempted to introduce the maximum amount of automatic machinery to such processes. Once such special-purpose hardware has been installed to conduct a specific operation, it repeats it time and again, with human intervention kept to a

Right: In the Robogate system at a Fiat car factory in Turin, unmanned carriers transfer car-body assemblies between robot work stations. The robots apply spot welds, fixing panels in place.

Below: A flexible manufacturing system is a network of computer-controlled hardware that turns out a range of different products. Here a Japanese FMS is machining metal blanks to make gear boxes.

minimum. In this way, for example, an automatic machine tool will repeatedly drill a hole in a particular place in identical metal components. In another illustration of this type of mechanization (known in engineering circles as "hard" automation), a paint-spraying system in a car plant coats identical parts as they pass by on a belt.

This kind of automation has a drawback. It can be applied only when components are made in very large batches in which the type of part is seldom varied. The engineers responsible for the hardware spend so much time and effort setting it up that the machine costs are not justified unless the equipment turns out the same product for weeks or months on end. If, on the other hand, the factory needs continually to change the type of product that it makes to meet variations in customer demand, hard automation is not practicable. As a result, the plant may have to abandon any notion of bringing into play the highest level of automatic machines, relying instead on conventional manual methods to produce its goods.

Below: An unmanned manufacturing cell fashioning cylindrical components. A Cincinnati Milacron T³ transfers the parts between the machines.

A high proportion of manufacturing tasks involve handling operations. These include, for instance, lifting of parts from machines or off conveyors, packing, assembly jobs, holding components while they are machined, or the manipulation of tools such as drills or welding torches. When products are made with the assistance of hard automation, such handling tasks can be given to special-purpose automatic machinery set up to do just one kind of job. In cases where hard automation is not applicable, such operations can seldom be left to machines. Instead, people must be involved—which explains why such a high proportion of men and women on the shop floors of conventional factories work on handling jobs.

All this, at any rate, is the case in workshops run on traditional lines. Robots introduce a different set of operating procedures. They provide an example of "soft" automation. The machines can be programmed to do different jobs, and so it is simple to switch them between tasks when making different kinds of products. A robot, for example, can be easily programmed so that it can pick items of different sizes and shapes off a conveyor. Robots are, therefore, particularly useful in factories which make objects in small batches, the types of items

changing between the different batches. Workshops of this kind are far more common than factories that turn out items in long, unbroken runs in which the type of product does not vary.

Practical Advantages

As examples of soft automation, robots offer manufacturers in small- to medium-batch production three clear sets of advantages. This is the assessment of Joseph Engelberger, founder of the Unimation robot company and one of the pioneers of the robot industry. In his book "Robotics in Practice", Engelberger lists these reasons for the attraction of the machines:

1. Robots represent "off the shelf" automation. Much of the design work in putting them into applications in a factory has already been completed in the engineering departments of the robot suppliers. So for a manufacturer, the lead times in installing a new production line are considerably reduced. This can be an advantage in introducing a new product as soon as possible after it has been designed.

2. Debugging of manufacturing hardware is reduced. Once a manufacturer has decided to install a robot, he has to

Above: With this CAD system developed by Calma of the US, an engineer can simulate a robot's movement, and modify the design for optimum efficiency.

ensure it integrates with other production hardware in the factory. All such equipment must be debugged to remove errors in, for example, software programs. For the robot, at least, much of the debugging will already have been done in the laboratories of the company that produced it.

3. Robots can be reused after their initial application comes to an end. A product line in which a robot performs a specific job may last only six months or a year. After this, the factory may need to scrap the line because the product changes. But because it can be programmed to different tasks, the robot can be taken off the line and put to different uses elsewhere. This is not the case with hard automation that can accomplish only a single job. For such items of machinery, retirement from the process for which they had been purchased generally means only one thing: removal from the factory to the scrap heap!

Robots are by no means the only machines that lend themselves to modern concepts of soft automation: other types

of hardware are found in factories that operate according to these principles. The machines include programmable or computer-numerically controlled (CNC) machine tools and unmanned carts, or automated guided vehicles (AGVs), that ferry parts between different sections of the factory. CNC machines contain cutting devices and other tools to shape metal parts, and function under the control of a computer. A robot may be integrated with a CNC tool i.e., by transferring components to it.

In the most up-to-date factories, areas of the plant that deal with different tasks are linked by data networks. As a result, computerized tools in all sections of the works receive information from others so that all their activities are coordinated.

For example, a designer in the factory's draughting room may be working on a new type of component—let us say a metal cover for a new type of gearbox. When the designer has perfected his drawing (which he fashions not on paper but by using a computer display screen in a process called computer-aided design or CAD), he presses a series of buttons on a keyboard. This sends to a computerized machine tool on the factory floor a program that describes how the cover is to be made. The information is sent down

Below: The motion of a robot arm in operation on a factory floor is here simulated on a computer screen, thanks to Calma's CAD software.

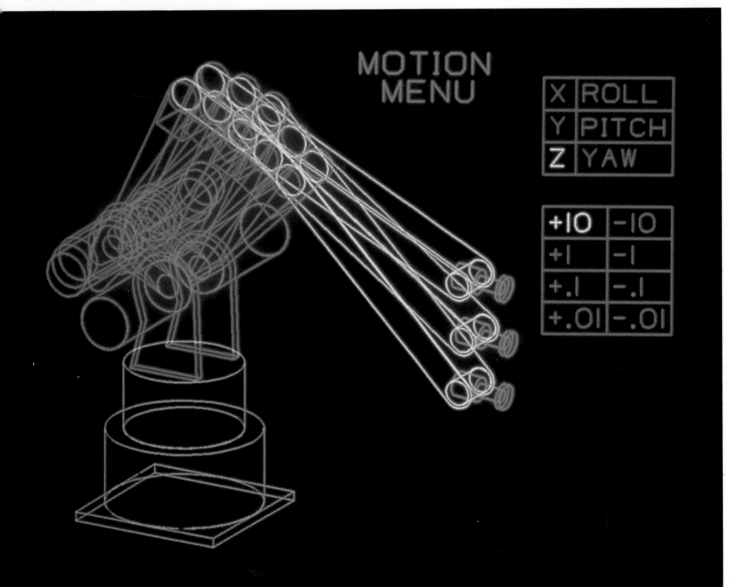

MOTION MENU

X	ROLL
Y	PITCH
Z	YAW

+10	-10
+1	-1
+.1	-.1
+.01	-.01

ROBOTS

Factory of the Future
In the workshops of the 1990s, robots will play a key role in transfer of items at varying stages of manufacture between different parts of the factory floor; for instance the factory departments that deal with machining, testing, assembly and packing. Robots will also transfer raw components and finished products between the factory floor and warehouse areas. A telecommunications network will channel data around the plant. It will connect the machines on the factory floor with computers in the offices that support the manufacturing operations. These computers will handle functions such as design, financial control and planning, as part of an integrated process.

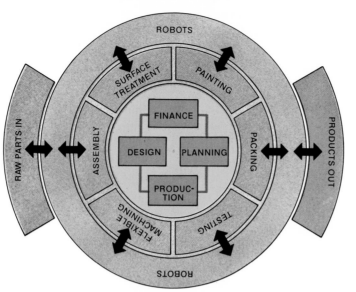

Such flexible manufacturing systems would not necessarily operate in isolation. They could be linked by other information networks to non-manufacturing parts of the factory, for example planning or financial departments. Typically, flexible manufacturing systems offer several advantages over conventional manually-operated hardware. Fewer people are needed because the machines take over much of the work. The components are fashioned with greater precision: once the system is running adequately it should

a factory-wide communications grid that links segments of the plant in much the same way as the public telephone network connects offices and homes in towns.

The machine tool then cuts bits out of a piece of metal in accordance with the instructions in the program. The combination of computerized draughting techniques with the use of CNC machines is known as CAD/CAM or computer-aided design/manufacture.

Often, a series of robots or unmanned vehicles is involved in the various handling tasks. For example, a combination of these devices may lift the metal out of the tool and send it to an assembly shop, where robots connect other metal items, such as the body of the gearbox, to the cover.

Financial controllers and warehouse staff keep in touch with the operations via other computer systems. These enable the supervisors who plan the factory's output always to know to the last detail what is taking place in every section of the manufacturing operation. Finally, the completed product is sent to an automated warehouse which stores it in a container until, reacting to demand from the outside world, distribution staff order the product to be shuttled out on a

conveyor to be transported away from the factory.

Engineers call the sets of computerized hardware that turn out parts automatically in small batches flexible manufacturing systems, or FMS. Typically, such systems have three components: they include the tools themselves (CNC machines or casting or assembly apparatus that perform manufacturing jobs); the transport apparatus (robots or unmanned carts) that handles the components; and the control system. Typically this is not one computer but a hierarchy of such machines. For example, a supervisory computer would contain in its memory a broad plan of how the factory is to operate. It would contain a description of the role of various computerized tools, how they interrelate and the desired level of production from the plant. This computer would be connected to other machines containing control strategies for particular items of hardware such as CNC tools or robots. These "second level" computers would be linked, in turn, to microprocessors inside the machine tools or robots themselves. In this way, information would be channelled by well-defined pathways to the tools that do the work.

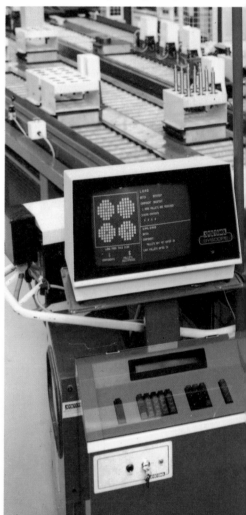

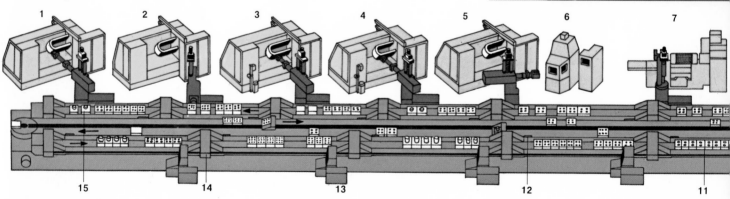

SCAMP Flexible Manufacturing System
1 Colchester computer-controlled two-axis turning machine.
2 As **1**.
3 Colchester five-axis turning machine with milling/drilling capacity.
4 As **3**.
5 Sykes computer-controlled gear-

chamfering machine.
6 Sykes gear-shaping machine.
7 Matrix computer-controlled cylindrical grinding machine.
8 Sykes gear-cutting (hobbing) machine.
9 Clarkson broaching machine.
10 The conveyor carries components on pallets on

an endless loop between the work stations.
11 Each pallet has a different code so that computers can keep track of these items as they pass round the system. The code is scanned at queuing stations (**15**).
12 Sensors, positioned at the machine load/unload stations, allow

computers to locate and identify pallets.
13 Load/unload stations. Display units at each of these stations inform the operator when to remove or add items to the conveyor. He informs the computer when he has performed the required operation.
14 Latch and gate

mechanisms. These hold the pallets for robot load and unload; they are actuated by compressed air.
15 Machine queuing station. Air-operated latches hold pallets in the correct position for loading/unloading by robot. Latches and gates are computer-controlled.

In the SCAMP system built by the 600 Group of Britain, a mixed range of CNC and conventional machine tools, which are linked by conveyor, completely machine a wide range of turned components. Robots supplied by Fanuc of Japan load raw parts on the conveyor at different continue to do so without interruption as all the instructions for manufacturing operations reside in fixed programs that are (at least in theory) free from error. This contrasts graphically with factories where most of the operations are conducted manually. People may do a superb job for 90 per cent of the working day. But for the remainder of the time, they may grow tired, become bored, or suffer from other failings that cause their work to deteriorate. The result is that the quality of the products is inconsistent.

Another factor in favour of flexible manufacturing systems is that they take up less space than the equivalent set of manually-operated hardware. In a conventional factory, a lot of the machinery lies idle for a significant part of the working day. The components of an FMS, however, will operate virtually continuously—which means that fewer individual machines are needed to do the same amount of work as a conventional machine shop. As a result, the factory that installs the more modern apparatus can

expect to require smaller premises, and also save on overheads such as the cost of heating and lighting.

FMS in Operation

An example of a modern flexible manufacturing system is SCAMP, built by the 600 Group in Colchester to turn out a range of parts for machine tools. This, the first major FMS to be developed in the United Kingdom, is illustrated in the accompanying diagram. Another well-known example is in a Citroën car factory in Meudon, France. The equipment turns out car parts such as gear boxes, clutch housings and cylinder heads in batches from 15 to 50. Over three shifts, the system requires a total of 26 operators—the figure for the equivalent manually-operated hardware would be 44 operators. At the outset of the manufacturing operation, raw lumps of metal are loaded onto pallets. These are then transported between the different machines in the system on driverless carts. The machining centres that cut metal out of the raw blocks can automatically change their tools, choosing between up to 600 tools in a storage magazine. The newly-cut components also visit a washing area, where they are handled by a robot, and an automated testing machine.

The Meudon plant illustrates another feature of flexible manufacturing systems —the different sort of human work force that is required. Such systems operate using fewer people than conventional machine rooms, and within the reduced workforce, the need for unskilled workers

Left: In the SCAMP system, VDUs at each of the 6 load/unload stations signal the operator when loading/unloading is required; the whole process is governed by the SCAMP computers.

Below: Modern manufacturing systems rely heavily on computers. A pair of Systime 5000E machines, based on PDP 11/34E processors made by DEC, control the cutting and transfer equipment in the SCAMP system.

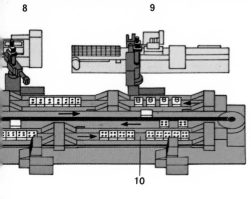

stages. The machines make a range of different components such as shafts, gears, and discs. The products are made in small batches of between 25 and 100. Supervisors can make the system turn out different products by changing the software that controls the network of machines, and which

runs on the two Systime computers in charge of SCAMP. The 600 Group built the equipment with financial support from the UK government to test out ideas in flexible manufacturing. It has been designed to operate virtually unmanned during unsocial work hours.

Left: At a Citroën car plant in Meudon, France, robots have a variety of roles—here a five-axis machine cleans a crankcase at a washing station before the component is transported to a measurement station. Operators supervise the Meudon flexible manufacturing system by relaying commands to computers via terminals (below left).

becomes a lot smaller, as robots perform the handling tasks. There is also a reduction in the requirement for skilled machine operators, as much of their work is taken over by the computerized machine tools. On the other hand, more technicians are needed to program the equipment (and to do other jobs that are relatively complicated, to repair the hardware when it suffers a fault, for example). In the case of the Meudon plant, the breakdown of the types of worker required in the labour force compared with that for the equivalent conventional factory is shown in the accompanying diagram.

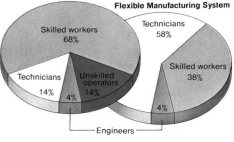

Conventional Factory

Skilled workers 68%

Technicians 14%

Unskilled operators 14%

Engineers 4%

Flexible Manufacturing System

Technicians 58%

Skilled workers 38%

4%

Changes in Employment The Meudon factory requires a different proportion of workers with particular skills compared with those needed in a conventional car plant. The percentage of skilled workers fell by nearly a half.

Not included here are the very lowest grade of worker, the factory labourers who do jobs such as cleaning and other menial tasks. At least for the forseeable future, the jobs of such people will be little affected by this sort of advanced automation. The development of robots to do such jobs, for instance to dispose of flakes of metal or to grease the moving parts of machine tools is still some way off. This trend is revealed in a useful graph compiled some years ago by Professor Hiroyuki Yoshikawa of Tokyo University. It shows the ease with which workers' jobs can be automated out of existence; analysis of the graph indicates that

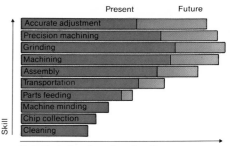

Present   Future

Accurate adjustment
Precision machining
Grinding
Machining
Assembly
Transportation
Parts feeding
Machine minding
Chip collection
Cleaning

Skill

Technological readiness for automation

Spotty Automation The chart shows the ease with which machines can take over the jobs of factory workers. Relatively highly skilled tasks such as machining and grinding are fairly easy to automate, while low-skilled jobs such as cleaning will continue to be left to people.

workers in relatively skilled areas, in occupations such as assembly or machining represented in the middle of the chart, can be replaced by machines more easily than the lower grades of labour such as cleaning staff. Only when a worker travels higher up the skill table (toward the top of the graph) does the possibility that a computerized technique will take over his job start to diminish.

Yoshikawa's term for this kind of development in which some of the reasonably interesting jobs in factories are taken over by machines, leaving the really dirty and boring tasks for people, is "spotty automation". By this he means that the automation process has been only partially completed. According to this thesis, it would be far better to develop robots and other items of programmable machinery that could undertake these menial tasks also.

Of course, removing people from the factory floor should not be an end in itself. The trend in which computerized machinery is supplanting human labour is part of a long-term shift in the developed countries: fewer people are employed in manufacturing jobs while more men and women work in "service" industries, such as health care, distribution, office work etc. Over the past couple of decades, stimulated by the development of new kinds of computerized machinery and the reduced number of people in manufacturing industry, the output per person employed in manufacturing has increased in many industrialized nations. The cost of labour is gradually diminishing as a percentage of overall manufacturing costs. At the same time, by capitalizing on the greater accuracy, flexibility and (in many cases) speed of the new computerized machinery, companies find they can turn out goods more efficiently and at reduced cost.

As a result of the fierce competition between maunfacturing companies worldwide, many industrial concerns do not have much choice over whether they instal the latest techniques of automation. Increasingly, the only way to compete effectively with other companies is to introduce technologies such as robotics to bring automation to small-batch processes.

The Working Robot

If we now turn to the specific industrial tasks that robots currently undertake, it is convenient to split the applications into three areas: materials handling; the operation of tools; and assembly. At present handling and tool operating are the most popular jobs for robots. Assembly operations, such as the fitting together of small electronic parts in the manufacture of printed circuit boards and other electrical equipment, have until relatively recently not been amenable to "robotization". The robots themselves were not dextrous enough to perform these often extremely fiddly operations; nor were engineers properly aware of the ways in which robots can help in this area. As a consequence insufficient attention was paid to designing the parts of industrial products so that robots could fit them together. But as more advanced robots are developed and industrial designers learn more about their capabilities, the picture is changing, and robots are starting to take the place of manual workers for some kinds of intricate assembly jobs.

In 1985, the non-Communist world contained about 97,000 industrial robots. The exact definition of these machines adopted by the Robotics Industries Association in the US is: "An industrial robot is a reprogrammable, multi-functional manipulator designed to move material, parts, tools or specialized devices through variable programmed motions for the performance of a variety

Below: Engineers are attempting to automate assembly tasks. Here a Unimation Puma assembles electric motors in a test rig at the National Engineering Laboratory in Scotland.

of tasks." A robot costs typically anywhere from $25,000 to $125,000, though the special tooling that is required to support the machine may cost two or three times as much.

Worldwide Population of Robots*

	1974	1978	1982	1983	1984
Japan	1,500	3,000	13,000	16,500	64,600
USA	1,200	2,500	6,250	8,000	13,000
W. Germany	130	450	3,500	4,800	6,600
France	30	na	950	1,500	3,380
Italy	90	na	700	1,800	2,700
UK	50	125	1,152	1,753	2,623
Sweden	85	80	1,300	1,900	2,400
Belgium	na	na	350	500	860

*Excluding Eastern bloc countries, for which comparable figures are not available.
Data derived from OECD and (1983, 1984 figures) British Robot Association reports.

About 65 per cent of the world's robots are in Japan, 13 per cent in the US and 18 per cent in Western Europe. Leading suppliers include Hitachi, Kawasaki, Mitsubishi, Fujitsu Fanuc and OTC (Japan); Cincinnati Milacron, Unimation (now part of Westinghouse), GMF Robotics, De Vilbiss, Automatix and IBM (USA); ASEA (Sweden); Volkswagen and Kuka (West Germany); Renault (France); Comau-Fiat (Italy); Trallfa (Norway); and GEC and Dainichi-Sykes (United Kingdom). The growth rate in production of robots has been phenomenal. Numbers have been increasing at the rate of about 30 per cent a year taken as an average across the western world. At this rate of growth, there will be roughly 200,000 robots by the year 1990. According to some projections, by then the population could be growing by 50,000-100,000 a year.

The United States is as good a country as any to consider when analysing exactly how robots are used. In 1982, the country contained 6,250 of the machines. Materials handling accounted for easily the largest proportion of applications, 71 per cent. Of the total figure, 24 per cent serviced machine tools, either unloading finished components or inserting new blocks of metal for fashioning by the tool. A further 14 per cent performed a similar job for die casting machines that produce cast products by clamping the twin halves of a die around molten metal. The robot in these cases takes the cast item out of the die halves. Thirty-three per cent of the robots were assigned to other materials handling tasks, for example the loading of components onto conveyors or stacking of items onto pallets.

Of the 6,250 machines, 28 per cent held tools in their robot "hands". The most

Above: A common job for industrial robots is the loading and unloading of machine tools. Here a Fanuc 600 robot, part of the SCAMP system, presents a component that is shaped by a broaching machine.

Right: After loading a new piece of metal into a lathe and unloading a finished component, this M-00 robot (made by GMF of the US) deposits the completed part on a pallet.

popular jobs in this category, are painting and welding. Just 6 per cent of the machines were involved with assembly tasks. But assembly robots will become much more common. Some studies suggest that by 1990 they will account for 37 per cent of all robots in factory use. Given these basic trends, let us now consider in detail the sort of factory jobs that robots currently undertake.

Handling Materials

When applied to tasks such as handling and parts transfer, the machine acts as a straightforward substitute for a human pair of hands. The robot is not required to do anything particularly complicated. It simply repeats the same

Below: A Trallfa robot in operation at Trallfa Transport's wheelbarrow plant. The machine takes a wheelbarrow case from a conveyor and feeds it to a hydraulic press. The TR-3000 robot then takes the finished case and loads it onto a pallet (right). Trallfa of Bryne in Norway is both a user and producer of robotic equipment.

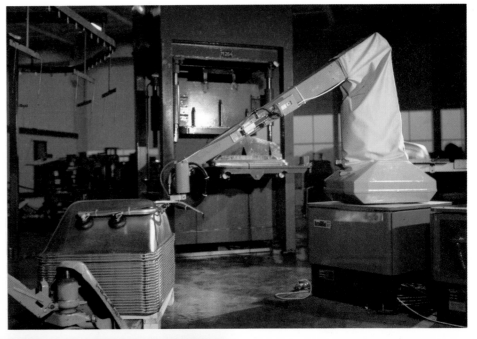

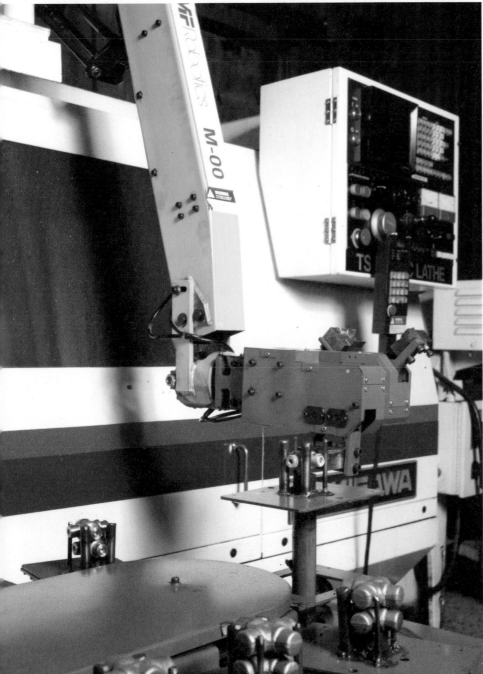

operation again and again according to the way it is programmed. Typical applications for robots are:

1. Loading/unloading machines Many areas of engineering industry feature machines that cast, cut, drill or forge. It most cases, the sequence of operations is fairly simple. First, a specimen of raw material is loaded into the machine. The hardware then fashions or shapes this in a set way. Finally, the finished component is removed. The loading and unloading stages are conventionally left either to manual workers or, in cases where hard automation is appropriate, to special purpose handling machines that do only one task. Robots can be useful when the handling activity varies from time to time during the manufacturing process.

Metal Castings, an English company that makes aluminium cast parts for the car and consumer-goods industries, is a leader in applying robots to die casting machines. In die casting, a measured volume of metal is ladled into a compartment of a machine. A piston then forces the liquid between the twin halves of a die, where it remains for perhaps a few seconds while the die halves press together with a force of hundreds or even thousands of tonnes. The internal shape of the die is transferred to the metal which, under pressure, solidifies to form the finished component. After the twin parts of the die have sprung apart, the newly shaped piece of metal can be removed.

The Worcester company employs robots both to ladle a volume of molten aluminium into the machines and to remove the hardened component and cool it in a water bath. The advantages are twofold. Firstly, the robots ensure greater consistency; because they operate according to a set program, they always insert into the machines an accurately metered quantity of metal. Subsequently, robots remove the moulded components at an exactly prescribed time. In this way, the period in which compression inside the mould takes place does not vary,

Below: A Cincinnati Milacron T³ robot in action on a production line, packing Minimo lawnmowers in a plant run by Flymo. T³ are also used to make up the cartons.

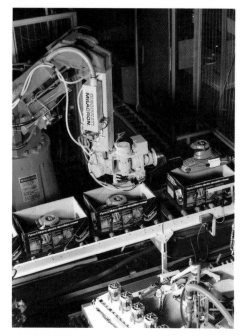

Below: After the packing operation, another T³ robot lifts boxes containing lawnmowers and places them on a pallet. When the stack is complete, the robot pulls in a new empty pallet.

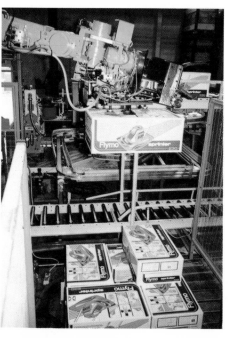

producing sets of components whose shape and characteristics are utterly consistent.

The second advantage is that the process becomes less unpleasant for human operators. Taking a hot piece of metal from a die casting machine is one of life's less attractive activities. Getting a robot to do this job is preferable. The role of the human is instead to monitor the process and control the operation of the robot through programming.

2. Lifting between work stations In many areas of industry, handling mechanisms have to transfer products in varying stages of completion between different items of production equipment. Robots come into their own in such applications. In an IBM computer plant in Poughkeepsie, New York, a robot feeds computer disks (used to store programs or data) into hardware which "writes" onto them specific codes of binary digits. The process is similar in outline to that in which musical recordings are made on gramophone discs. In the computer factory, the robot is driven by a program that tells it which of four disk-writing machines it should load with a specific empty disk. The program also instructs the relevant machines to record onto the disk the appropriate set of instructions. The same robot also deals with two other parts of the manufacturing process. It removes the disk with its newly written instructions and presents the part to a machine which applies to it an adhesive label with a blast of compressed air, and then the robot lifts up the disk with its gripper and packs it into the appropriate container.

Right: Welding is a popular application for robots. A GMF S-108R is here welding bumpers for small trucks in a plant run by Fey Manufacturing in California.

In a similar application on which British Leyland, the UK car manufacturer, is working, a robot on tracks moves between five work stations in a car factory. The machine removes a plastic bumper (or fender) from an injection moulding machine. The robot then passes the bumper to other stations which in turn crop the component to get rid of stray bits of plastic and insert tiny brass insets to enable it to be fitted to the body of the car. A small part of the bumper is polished by a special tool to which the robot next passes the component. Finally, the robot lifts the bumper from this work station and dumps it onto a conveyor which speeds the part off to another section of the factory.

In an innovative development at Corah, a UK clothing company, a robot is helping out in a sewing factory. In an installation in Oakham, Leicestershire, a robot lifts with a vacuum gripper a small segment of cloth after a machinist has finished sewing it. The robot then positions the cloth with a bundle of other fabric, which is removed mechanically for other sewing operations. The device saves the sewing machine operator the task of picking up the finished item of cloth and transferring it elsewhere. In most clothing factories, such operations take up a considerable amount of the machinist's time, who would be better employed sewing other pieces of fabric, thus increasing the output of the workshop.

3. Packing Virtually all consumer and industrial goods have to be packaged at the end of the manufacturing process. It is a simple matter for robots to lift parts and put them in a container of some sort. The lawnmower manufacturer, Flymo, for example, uses Cincinnati Milacron robots to box up mowers coming off the production lines at its plant in Darlington, County Durham. In the confectionery industry, Cadbury, the Birmingham chocolate manufacturer, is employing dedicated robots to pack sweets into boxes. The handling machines here must be sophisticated—on two counts. First, they must pick up the sweets delicately and with no little finesse. If they clamp too hard on the items, the confectionery will shatter or become deformed.

Secondly, the robot hardware must insert the sweets into boxes with high accuracy. In the packing line, chocolates are picked up by the arms and transferred

onto set positions in boxes which travel past the arms on a conveyor. In each box, the space for each sweet is tightly defined by a "nest" in the packaging of set dimensions. If the robot tried to put one chocolate into the space reserved for another of different dimensions, then the packing procedure would be disrupted.

4. Heavy-duty palletizing As an extension of packing small components, or industrial or consumer goods, robots are sometimes called upon to load large objects onto pallets. These might be bags of cement, large crates, or sacks of fertilizer. In this application, the controlling program will usually instruct the robot to stack

Below: A line of ASEA robots spot weld the bodies of Fiesta cars as they roll along the line at Ford's Valencia plant in Spain. Robots are well suited to such hostile work environments.

the objects in a predetermined fashion, to prevent them tumbling over when transported.

Tool Operation

Although tool-handling robots are less numerous than machines that transfer material, they have demonstrated many useful applications.

1. Welding This application is among the most popular for robots in the tool-wielding category. Robots can be employed for two different kinds of welding, spot and arc welding. For both operations a robot holds in its gripper a welding torch. This passes electrical current through two pieces of metal, in the process melting the materials and causing the components to fuse together.

In spot welding, the torch transmits a short burst of current through a single

point on the surface of a metal component, while another part is held directly behind or underneath it. Using this technique, components are joined at a number of distinct points. The torch must be moved from one point to another, and a burst of electricity shot through each junction point.

In arc welding, an electric arc is struck between a piece of copper wire that protrudes from the torch and the two pieces of metal to be joined. The torch moves along a specified route and fusion takes place continuously along the required seam of metal. To replace the copper that is consumed as a result of the arc, wire is continually unwound from a drum so that a fresh piece is available at each point along the seam. As well as supplying the current and the wire, the torch has a third function to fulfil. This is to inject an inert gas such as helium into the

area where the arc is struck. The gas effectively insulates the metal being fused from oxidation by ambient oxygen, a process that would reduce the strength of the weld. Under programmable control, the torch can be instructed to follow a fixed route very closely. As a result, once any software "bugs" in the system are erased, the torch will apply welds with great accuracy.

Most spot welding robots are used in the car industry; automobile assembly requires numerous spot welds to ensure that the various parts such as the side panels, roof and bonnet cover are fitted together in the correct way. On modern car production lines, these components are first joined together loosely with a series of "tack welds". The body then travels on a conveyor past a set of robots that each apply a set number of spot welds at specific points. As each body shell is identical, the robot needs simply to repeat its routine to provide a set of perfect welds.

In another system, pioneered by Fiat of Italy, the components in the car body travel along the production line not on a conveyor but on a series of wire-guided unmanned trolleys. The parts are held in the correct position by a series of special tools known as fixtures.

Programming a robot to perform car welds is more complicated. The robot engineer must specify not only the correct path that the arm has to trace over the top of the seam, but also he has to write instructions to control the voltage and amperage of the current at each point

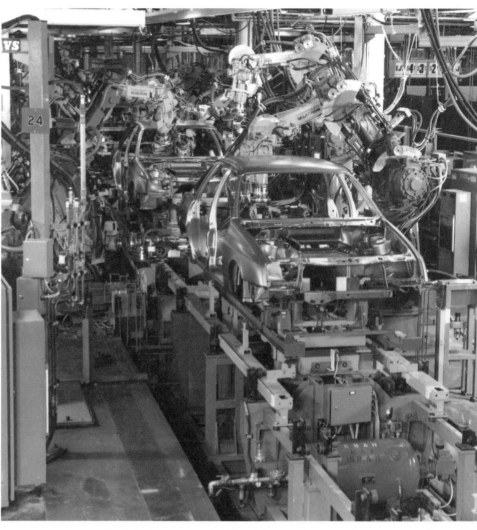

Fiat Robot Welding Line
1 Automatic loading and clamping of Fiat 131 body on pallet.
2 Manual loading of lower cross member.
3 Framing and pre-tacking of 4-door bodies.
4 Framing and pre-tacking of 2-door bodies.
5 Frame for completion of tacking for both 2- and 4-door bodies.
6 Electronic check of body geometry.
7 Inspection.
8 Welding with 4 horizontal robots.
9 Welding by vertical robot.
10 Welding by 1 vertical and 2 horizontal robots.
11 As **10**.
12 Welding by 4 horizontal robots.
13 Welding by 2 horizontal robots.
14 Welding by 3 horizontal robots.
15 Welding by 2 horizontal robots.
16 2 horizontal robots for jobs left out by robots out of service upstream.
17 Piercing of front suspension holes.
18 Empty station—could be filled by more robots for modifications to production technique.
19 As **18**.
20 Final body check.
21 Unloading of body.

The robots on the 120-metre line apply a total of 655 welds (4-door models) or 625 welds (2-door models). The bodies move between the robot stations on 25 recirculating pallets, at a rate of 68 bodies an hour.

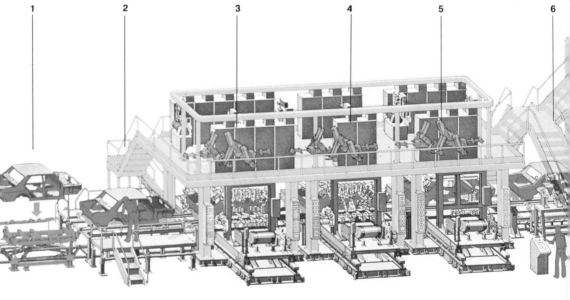

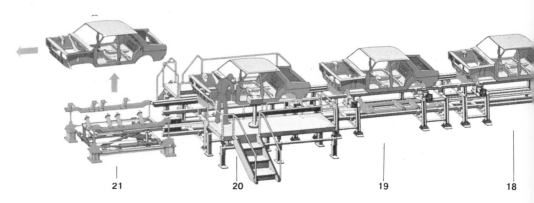

Left: Welding on most car production lines is very much the preserve of robots. Cincinnati Milacron HT³ machines weld the bodies of Sierras in Ford's factory in Dagenham, Britain.

Below: A Dainichi-Sykes PT600 robot welding the frames of specialized hospital beds. The installation is at the plant of Egerton Hospital Equipment near London.

during the path. These factors may vary depending on, for instance, the thickness of the metal to be welded at a specific point, or on whether the seam is a straight or curved line.

Engineers involved in either spot or arc welding have to pay attention to two important technical points not directly concerned with the robots themselves. Firstly they have to design the fixtures that hold the metal parts in place while the welds are applied very accurately. When a person is holding a welding gun, he can make allowances if the fixture clamps the components in a position that is slightly different to the one he expects. The human welder will simply adjust the position of his torch so that he makes a good weld. A robot (unless it is a "second generation" machine with some kind of sensing ability) does not have this kind of intelligence. Unless the fixture is perfectly made, there is a chance that the robot will apply the weld in the incorrect position. On a related point, the fixture must be such that a robot arm can orient itself to apply welds from several different positions. A manual worker can lift parts out of the fixture to apply a weld in a difficult spot. Such a manoeuvre is not possible for a robot—it must apply the welds in a continuous process, which puts extra pressure on the designer of the fixture.

The second important technical point concerns the tolerances of the components themselves. In conventional manufacturing, components that are supposed to be identical may, in fact, vary slightly in dimensions. A human welder takes these differences into account, varying his welding routine according to the exact shape of the parts. Such changes in behaviour are denied to current industrial robots. Once it has been given a program, the robot sticks to a set pattern of activity. So in robotic welding, the engineering tolerances to which components are made in other parts of the plant must be extremely tight, and the people who

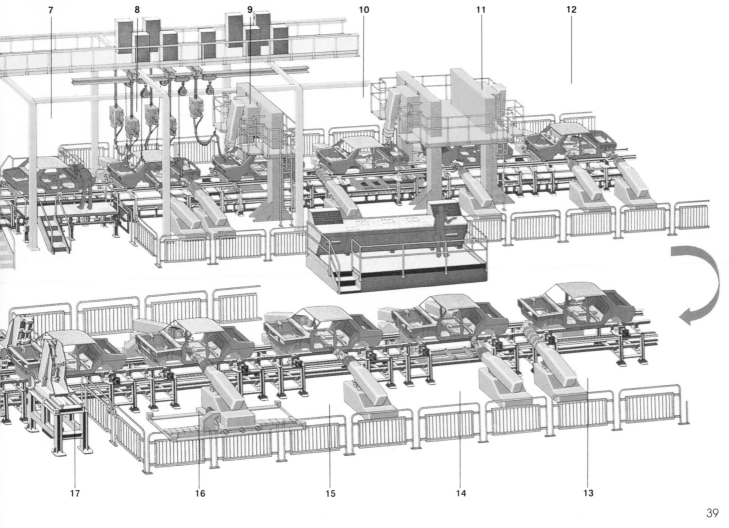

Above: A Cincinnati Milacron robot drills attachment holes around the edges of acrylic windshields in the St Louis plant of McDonnell Douglas. The parts are for F-15 fighter aircraft.

press or machine bits of metal that are later to be welded must do so with greater attention to accuracy. The way in which the advent of a robot affects other parts of a manufacturing process, very likely forcing a tightening up of operating procedures, is known in engineering jargon as the robot "domino effect".

2. Drilling The conventional way to carry out drilling operations is to use a machine tool. The component is brought to the tool, fastened and a drill produces the required cavities. A robot can introduce a different and possibly more efficient procedure. In effect, the drill goes to the component, rather than the other way around. The robot grasps the tool which moves according to a program across the top of the component in question, drilling holes as required. The procedure is advantageous where the component is very large and bulky or where a great many holes have to be made.

Drilling is an important part of aircraft manufacture; it acts as a prelude to riveting, when tiny metal fasteners are driven through the holes to hold two pieces of metal together. Hundreds, if not thousands, of rivet holes must be drilled in the aircraft components; it seems a natural job for a robot to undertake.

ML Aviation, a company in Slough, England, makes components for a bomb-release mechanism for the Tornado military aircraft. The mechanism is a

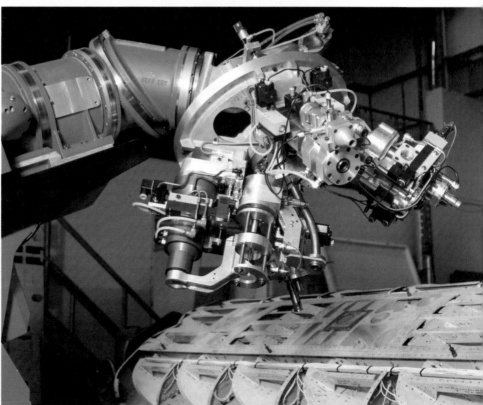

cylindrical framework about 20ft (6m) long to which must be riveted a skin of eight metal panels. To make room for the rivets, some 3,000 holes must be drilled through the metal skin. The problem was how to ensure that the robot, armed with a high speed drill, could make the holes in exactly the right places.

The answer, reasoned engineers, was to get a human worker to drill a few holes

every metre or so along the panels. These are laid in the correct position on top of the framework. The hand of the robot, armed not with a drill but with a touch-sensing probe, then moves across the top of the component, committing to its memory the positions of these sample locations. The robot then works out from these datum positions the correct places for all the other holes. With a drill bit of

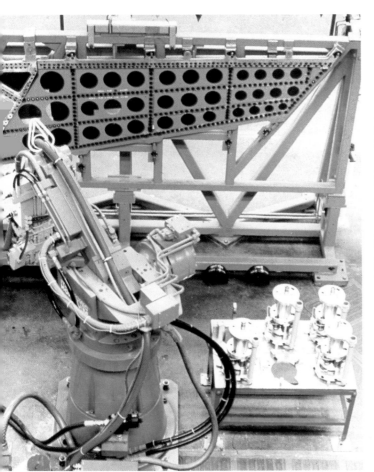

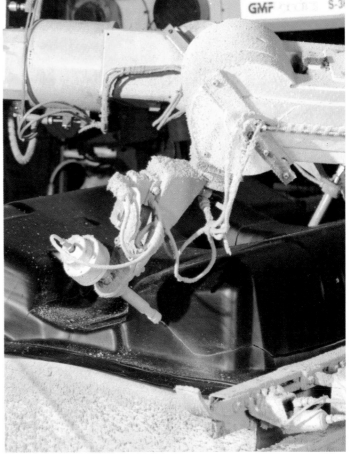

Above: Aircraft parts contain thousands of holes through which rivets are punched. Here General Dynamics is using a robot to drill holes in the vertical tail section of an F-16 fighter.

Left: ML Aviation is employing a Fata Bisiach and Carru robot to drill and deburr rivet holes. It deploys a four position, computer-controlled, indexing tool head built by Taylor Hitec. A teaching head enables the system to register on certain pre-drilled holes and correct for variations.

Above: In a novel application, a robot can be made to hold water-jet cutting equipment. The water stream cuts plastic parts in a Chevrolet vehicle factory in Adrian, Michigan.

the correct size (the robot can select from several in a tool-changing operation) the machine makes the required incision.

In the system at ML Aviation, the robot follows up the drilling with two more jobs. It removes tiny fragments of residue metal from the hole with a special "cleaning" tool. It then fastens clips in selected holes temporarily to fix the plates to the metal framework. As part of its program, the robot selects the appropriate tools for the job from a rack. Workers can then remove the complete assembly for riveting later by human engineers, though ML Aviation says that this, too, may be a job for a robot if the company can master the necessary technology.

Automatic riveting in this way has been achieved by Lockheed, the big aerospace company based in California. At a facility in Burbank, the company's researchers have perfected a manufacturing cell in which a robot does several tasks. It first brings together assemblies of components and then drives through rivets to join the

parts. A vision system based on a TV camera inspects the components to ensure that the riveting has been done properly.

Another company involved in robotic drilling is Grumman Aerospace Corporation, based in Bethpage, New York. In the company's riveting system, a robot moves between four work cells on a track. In each cell, sheets of metal parts for aerospace manufacture are held by fixtures. The robot is programmed to make a series of drill holes in each set of metal parts. The program can easily be changed so that different types of components may be drilled, for riveting later.

3. Cutting Just as they can drill, with different tooling robots can cut metal. Once again, there is an analogy with conventional machine tools. A large proportion of these machines cut away chunks of metal from a raw casting or block, fashioning the material into a desired shape. In these cases, the machine tools stay fixed and workers have to transfer the components to them. Such equipment cuts material in two main ways. In the first, the cutting tool remains stationary while the component rotates about an axis. This is the principle behind the lathe. In the second method, the raw material is clamped in a fixed position on a base and, a tool then drives into the substance, gouging out a specific quantity of material in a series of set manoeuvres. This is the basis on which the milling machine works.

Robots have to employ a somewhat different procedure. The machines are generally not robust enough to stand up to long periods of driving a cutting tool through resistant material. Engineers

have therefore investigated non-contact ways of cutting materials such as metal or plastic. One technique is to use a laser. The robot holds in its end effector a device through which high-energy, coherent light is piped, often via an optical fibre delivery system. A laser applied in this way can cut through plates of metal such as steel. What is more, the cuts can be very accurate. The robot will move over the top of the sheet in a predetermined fashion, according to its program. The computer instructions also control the intensity of the beam of light, so that it can be varied according to the thickness of material being cut.

Another "non contact" method of cutting involves the use of a jet of water. General Motors in the USA is a pioneer in this field. At a plant in Adrian, Michigan, the company has installed a system of 10 robots that fashion pieces of plastic that later form parts of petrol tanks. Eight of the robots fire water jets at the plastic sheets as they travel past the machines on a conveyor. The jets cut a series of holes and slots in the material, and trim off loose pieces of plastic. According to General Motors, the robot system saves significantly on tool wear and produces better-quality cuts. As the robots are controlled by a program that resides in a supervisory computer station, just two human operators are required to tend and maintain the 10 robots.

Direct Teaching

Direct Teaching
This is the first of three ways of teaching an AOIP Kremlin robot a paint spraying routine. The operator guides the robot by hand through a sequence and the robot's computer "learns" the routine because, at important points during the process, the co-ordinates of the arm's position are fed into the computer's memory. The robot can then repeat the whole exercise at a later stage of production.

Teaching with the Syntaxeur

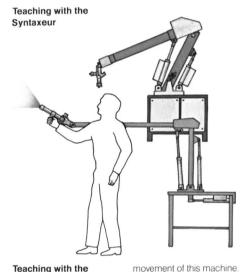

Teaching with the Syntaxeur
The operator paints an object using a teaching unit called a "syntaxeur", a light painting gun on flexible joints. The memory in the robot's computer records the movement of this machine. In a factory task, the manipulator can then reproduce the recorded movement of the syntaxeur. As long as the shape of the components do not vary, the robot will produce virtually perfect coatings.

Telecontrol Teaching

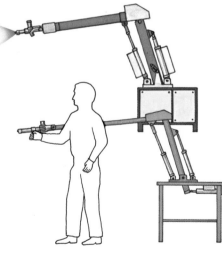

Telecontrol Teaching
With this technique, the operator again uses a syntaxeur. On this occasion, every movement of this hardware is faithfully followed by the arm of the robot. As the technician guides the syntaxeur through a chosen routine, he can check that the robot is making the same movements. Later, the robot repeats the exercise, only without the guidances and control of the human.

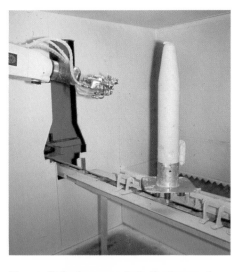

Above: Robots come into their own in spraying paint. Here a DeVilbiss TR-3500 sprays the head of a Side-winder missile with anti-corrosion polyurethane paint at Hill Air Force Base, Utah.

Below: A GEC COMPARM robot demonstrates how it can manoeuvre into difficult positions to spray paint into a car's wheel arches.

4. Surface treatment In most factories, after machining operations such as cutting or drilling, some kind of coating (usually paint) is applied to the newly fashioned component. This is another job that a robot equipped with a sprayer can do. An engineer programs the robot to trace a set pattern, which it then repeats. At the same time, the software controls the quantity of paint that is directed through the spray gun. The result is an even coating of the component to be treated, often to a higher standard than a fallible human operator could produce. Other spraying operations involve the application of anti-corrosive liquid to sheets of metal that require protection from chemical or physical action, and robots can also spray adhesive onto surfaces that have to be joined. Car manufacturers have experimented with this last technique, for instance to fit items such as chromium fittings onto a vehicle body during the final "trimming" stage of assembly. In such applications, special shielding equipment is added to the robot to protect it from becoming fouled by glue or similar material. It may also be "taught" to clean itself periodically, by dipping its end-effector in a cleaning solution.

5. Deburring In manufacturing industry, probably the least popular job is also one of the most difficult to automate. This is deburring, or "scurfing"—the removal of loose pieces of metal from a component after a casting or machining operation, which rarely leaves a perfectly finished product. Instead the casting or machining step is likely to result in surfaces that are slightly rough and which will have clinging to them small particles that have to be removed in some later stage of the manufacturing routine.

To debur a component in this way is no easy task. The worker offers up the piece of metal to a rapidly revolving grinding belt which, by abrasive action, files away the rough edges of the part. It is an important part of the manufacturing process but a very unpleasant one to perform manually.

Deburring by robot has been investigated by several groups of engineers around the world. The chief difficulty is that a robot lacks the "feedback" about how well it is doing the job that human workers possess naturally. For example, a person can sense how to press the component against the belt particularly hard to grind away a large chunk of surplus metal. A robot, on the other hand,

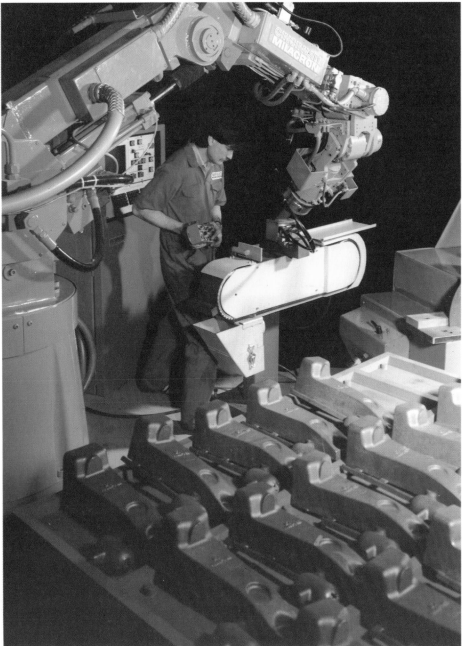

Above: To remove loose bits of metal from engine castings in a deburring operation, this Cincinnati Milacron T³-586 holds the components against a high-speed grinding wheel.

would have no way of altering its routine unless given a sensing device.

In a research project conducted by Walker Crosweller, a British manufacturer of shower fittings, a robot is given rudimentary "sense" with a TV camera. The robot holds an object such as a brass tap. The camera feeds the image of the tap to a computer. This instructs an abrasive belt to smooth away rough material from the surface of the tap, which has been produced in a casting operation. The computer also controls the movement of the robot arm. All the components in the system—the camera, robot arm and a second arm that carries the abrasive belt—are in this way coordinated. As a result of the research—which also involves engineers from Bath University—Walker Crosweller hopes to introduce deburring robots in its plant in Cheltenham. The

company is about as far advanced as any other in getting a robot to perform this intrinsically complex job.

6. Testing and inspection These simple words relate to a multitude of activities in manufacturing operations. After a component has been produced, or several parts assembled, testing must frequently take place to ensure that the final product is free from defects. Robots may help in this task in a fairly straightforward manner. For instance, they could simply pick up an item of electrical hardware (perhaps from a conveyor) and plug it into an electrical source. The testing procedure would then follow automatically. Once completed, the robot would remove the product and replace it with an identical item which would be tested in turn.

Occasionally a robot may be called upon to do something more complicated. For instance, it may be required to move part of the apparatus being tested before the flow of electricity through the product is monitored. For one such test routine, Turnright Controls, a manufacturer of control mechanisms for electric cookers, asked researchers at Portsmouth Polytechnic to devise a mechanism that would both calibrate and test a hand-sized energy regulator. Essentially, the hardware has to turn a screw to adjust the point at which a bimetallic strip inside the regulator makes contact with an electric switch. This action ensures that the regulator is correctly adjusted for use in a household cooker. In a second task, the testing mechanism has to pass a burst of electricity through the product to simulate what happens in the home. Instruments monitor the current to assess if the component is correctly made.

In the test rig designed by the Portsmouth scientists, a pneumatic device grabs a spindle on the regulator while a servo motor spins round the main body of the product. This sets the internal parts of the regulator in the correct position for calibration while a screwdriver, held in a robot arm, adjusts a calibrating screw. At the same time, another piece of metal is extended from the test rig to adjust a

Above: An ASEA robot checks the dimensions of rear axles of trucks at a Volvo factory. The sensor is a laser rangefinder that compares actual sizes with a reference figure.

Left: A "craftsman robot" designed at Portsmouth Polytechnic calibrates small electrical devices such as energy regulators by adjusting an electro-mechancial component.

Right: Robots are gradually becoming proficient at assembly jobs, which often require great dexterity on the part of the machine. Here an ASEA robot assembles electrical components at ASEA's Västeras plant in Sweden.

backstop in the regulator. This operation is followed by an automatic electrical test sequence, which is monitored by a computer. The test rig, which Turnright hopes to have in operation in its Portsmouth factory by 1986, could be applied to other similar operations. The mechanism can be adjusted to perform similar calibration/test jobs on other small electromechanical parts.

The physical dimensions of a manufactured item are also subject to rigorous quality control checks. Such measurements are a routine part of the inspection task in many factories around the world. Robots can help out here, too. In this application, the machines are equipped with small optical sensors. These are normally light-emitting diodes combined with a semiconductor device that is sensitive to radiation. They transmit a beam of light at a specific frequency and register the radiation at the same frequency reflected from surfaces upon which the original beam impinges. A program instructs the robot to move between different sites around a component whose dimensions are to be measured. At each point, the sensor emits a shaft of radiation and senses the reflected light. From an analysis of the time taken between emission and reception of the

light, the position of the surface under examination can be calculated. All this is done automatically by a computer that is part of the robot system.

The job is done quickly, with little involvement of human workers, and eliminates the necessity for such devices as micrometers or callipers. General Motors in the US is a pioneer in the use of this technology. The company has installed robot systems of this sort to check on the size and shape of vehicle parts as they come off a production line. An advantage is that the items being monitored do not have to be removed to special quality control stations. Instead, the job can be done while the components are being transferred along a conveyor without interrupting the production process.

Assembly

Assembly operations account for a significant proportion of the work in modern factories, but many assembly jobs are far too difficult and fiddly for machines to undertake. Much assembly, therefore, is still performed by hand. Automation has, however, made inroads into a few areas of assembly, which normally involve applications in which the assembly tasks are relatively straight-

Above: An interesting approach to assembly with robots was pioneered by GEC Electrical Projects of Rugby. The 6-axis Gadfly uses a novel structure to tackle fiddly assembly jobs.

forward, and essentially repetitive. A notable example is the insertion of specific electronic components of standard shapes into printed circuit boards destined for many types of electrical equipment.

Engineers are just starting to develop robots to help in this field. The machines are nimble and sensitive enough to do intricate tasks, and as they can be programmed to undertake different jobs, they are versatile enough to work in factories where the types of product may change, at least in detail, between batches.

IBM has investigated how to use assembly robots probably as extensively as any company. The computer giant not only sell robots that can handle such tasks, but uses them in its factories around the world. In 1984, IBM employed some 900 robots in its computer and terminals plants, half of them for assembly jobs.

In the company's factory at Greenock, Scotland, IBM engineers have concentrated on installing "islands of automation" in which dense arrays of computerized machinery put together products with manual intervention kept to a minimum. The plant turns out about £700m worth of computer-related goods each year. As a result of automation, the company estimates that the factory's output has increased tenfold between 1974 and 1984, without the number of employees changing significantly. (The 1984 staff count was 2,700).

In one such "island", a computerized production line set up at a cost of £1·5m turns out small boxes called power-logic units. These provide the processing hardware and power supply for display screens fitted to microcomputers. The line assembles four components—the two halves of the plastic cover for the box; an electrical package that connects the unit to a source of electricity; and an array of chips on a plastic card. In the system, a set of conveyors channels the four components between a total of nine robots. Each of the latter is given a specific task. For example, one robot picks up a card containing the chips and slides it into the lower half of the cover, into which the card clips without the use of fasteners such as screws. In a similar operation, another robot fits into place the electrical package for the power supply. Then the top half of the cover is positioned and at another robot work station, a laser engraves onto the exterior of the box a set of serial numbers.

Just two screws, supplied to robots by special feeding mechanisms, are required to hold together each power-logic unit. The robots either insert the screws into holes in the components or supply the fasteners to a special turning mechanism. Only five people are required to oversee the entire production line. To make the equivalent number of units with conventional manual assembly techniques would require four times as many people, according to IBM.

The Greenock system is an indicator of the kinds of robotic assembly system that will start to appear in electronics and electrical-equipment factories over the next few years. Many such sets of hardware will appear first as "islands" set in the midst of conventional assembly lines. They will gradually become linked within the same factory, for example by transfer systems such as automatic guided vehicles that move components in varying stages of completion between different sections of the works.

Putting Together PCBs

Another broad area of manufacture suitable for assembly robots is the insertion of components into printed circuit boards. Special-purpose assembly machines can handle some such tasks, but they are sets of purpose-built manipulators that can perform only one task, and cannot be programmed to do other jobs, or handle non-standard components. In these cases, sets of identical components of standard shapes are loaded into storage trays in bandoliers. These travel past a mechanical gripper that takes each component in turn and inserts it in the desired place on a board. (They would be later joined with electrical connectors.) But such machines are not able to handle components of non-standard shapes, certain kinds of microprocessor or memory packages for example. These items, in conventional factories, would have to be assembled in the time-honoured way by hand.

Programmable robots, however, can manipulate these kinds of component. For instance, in a factory run by Motorola

Below: A robot made by Intelledex of Oregon inserts the leads of an electrical component into the appropriate holes of a printed circuit board.

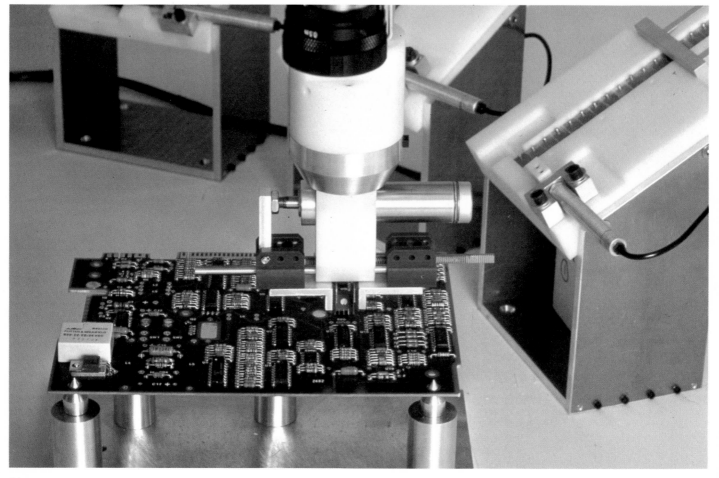

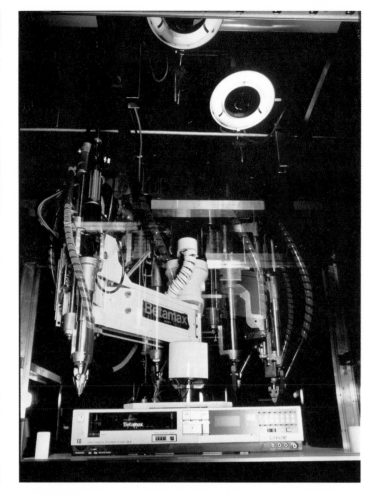

Below: Assembly robots can be useful in car factories. A Pragma machine, made by DEA of Italy, assembles steering gear tie rods.

Above left: Robots insert valves into cylinders in Fiat's Mirafiori factory. The system was designed by Comau, a Fiat subsidiary.

Above: A SCARA-type robot tightens screws during the assembly of Betamax video tape recorders at one of Sony's plants in Japan.

in Fort Lauderdale, Florida, two robots are putting together the electronic items required for radio sets. The robots share out 12 fundamental tasks, like the insertion into boards of a specific electronic component. The two machines work in tandem, just as a pair of hands might do in a manual assembly job. They avoid collision as a result of computer-generated signals sent between them.

Assembly by robot need not be confined to the electrical-goods industries. A robot

system designed by Taylor Hitec, a company in Chorley, Lancashire, is due to be applied as part of a chemical treatment process by a firm in the chemical industry. Interestingly, the robot starts by taking apart an existing piece of hardware, before re-assembling it later. The item on which the robot is set to work is a filter unit, used to purify poisonous chemicals. The filter works away for days on end in a closed chamber which shields people from coming into contact with the hazardous materials. Every so often, it has to be cleaned. In this job, a robot lifts off, section by section, the seven main sub-assemblies in the filter. It places the pieces on a table in set positions, whereupon the machine picks up a hose and sprays water at them. After the cleaning operation, the robot puts the components back together again so that the filtering operation can start afresh. In the job, the robot uses a total of five different tools that it selects from a rack.

In order to introduce robots successfully into assembly operations, the design of the items on which the robot is working is all-important. In guidelines produced to help engineers apply robots to assembly jobs, John Laszcz, an IBM engineer from the Research Triangle Park in North Carolina, points out: "Many times assembly of a product would have been easy to automate except for one feature making it impossible or economically unjustifiable

to automate. With just a few minor design changes, and usually with no effect on the hardware cost the product could have been automatically assembled." The guidelines are mostly extremely simple. For example, components should be designed so that they can be assembled in layers, one on top of another. Lifting and rotating of parts during assembly should be avoided, as this requires complicated fixtures and grippers. Parts should be compliant so they fit together easily, preferably without the use of fasteners, such as screws, that robots find difficult to handle. And components should be designed to slide easily down the feeders that channel them towards the grippers of robots; they should not, for example, have protrusions that tangle easily, so holding up the flow of parts by causing a blockage. Designers should reduce the number of flexible parts used in a product—wires and cables for instance. They should be replaced by stiff pieces of hardware (small boards instead of a piece of flex for example) that a robot can pick up and manipulate with ease. If these kinds of design rules are observed, suggests Mr Laszcz, a great many more products in industry might be put together by robots. And suggestions of this sort are, by all accounts, being heeded by increasing numbers of engineers, resulting in a proliferation of applications of robots for assembly jobs in manufacturing plants around the world.

"Second-generation" robots will need to be able to perceive and understand their surroundings; they will need senses and the most immediate priority is vision.

SENSORS AND FEEDBACK

The task of developing artificial equivalents of the human senses is probably the most urgent priority, and among the greatest challenges, facing roboticists. Without vastly improved sensory equipment, it is very difficult to see how industrial robots can advance from their present status of blind serfs, working largely by rote, to become truly adaptable and intelligent machines— machines capable of thinking for themselves, reacting to changes in circumstances, or making even trivial decisions. Ultimately, the aim must be to produce robots with a perception of their surroundings comparable to that enjoyed by human beings; robots that would be able to see, feel, hear and perhaps even smell things and, ideally be capable of communicating with their human collaborators in ordinary, natural language.

We are, at the moment, a long way from such an ideal situation. The robots of science fiction may find it easy, with their television eyes and their antennae-like ears, to travel around the galaxy; but the real life robots on the factory floor can as yet entertain only the vaguest notions of the objects they manipulate and the environment in which they work. In order to understand the difficulties involved in the development of robot senses it is essential to see where the problem lies: it is not that the actual gathering of data, the capture of a visual image, the detec-

tion of soundwaves, the sensing of the presence or absence of an object by touch, presents any great challenge. Technology has long since found ways of matching, and in many cases surpassing, the abilities of the natural sense organs such as eyes and ears; devices like radar and sonar, directional microphones, body scanners and the like, allow machines to see, hear or detect things which are far beyond the range of our own sensory equipment. The real problem is not the gathering of information, but the understanding of what it means.

To take a simple example. It is one thing to devise a robot which can go to the floor of the North Sea (or the surface of Mars, or the inside of a nuclear reactor) and send back a television picture to a human operator on the surface. It is quite another thing to equip that robot with the "intelligence" which will allow it to understand that this image shows a leaking

Right: A circuit board reflected in the lens of the IVS-100 "Eye". Do camera and microprocessors form a combination that parallels eye and brain? Or is the comparison misleading?

Below: This Unimate robot installed at BL's Cowley works uses four cameras mounted around its elaborate end-effector to position windshields before fitting them automatically.

joint in the oil pipeline, while that one merely shows a bit of seaweed that has become wrapped around the joint. It requires even greater intelligence if the robot is to be capable of deciding for itself that, say, it will be able to resolve an ambiguous image if it moves to the right to get a better view, or "zooms in" to take a closer look. For the point of having senses is that they provide both the information we require to understand the real world, and also that needed to deal with or respond to it. There is little point in providing robots with senses unless we also enable them to achieve that understanding of, and exercise that control over their environment.

Feedback

It is not enough, therefore, for robots simply to perceive and understand the world as passive observers. It is equally important that their senses provide them with "feedback" or, to put it in plain language, that they are able to understand how their actions influence or change the world. (When we speak of the "world" in this sense, of course, we mean just that tiny bit of it with which the robot interacts.)

Since the principle of feedback is crucial to any autonomous or self-controlling machine, like a robot, it is worth clarifying exactly what it means. The basic point is that if a controlling organ, a brain in an animal, a computer in a robot, is to perform effectively it must not only generate and transmit instructions in the shape of nervous impulses to muscles or signals to an electric motor; it must also receive and interpret information which allows it to judge the effect its instructions are having and to make sure that they have been obeyed.

Think of the case of a driver who is reversing a truck into a narrow alley with the help of an assistant who stands behind the vehicle. The driver is controlling the truck, issuing instructions to it in effect, by turning the steering wheel and operating the throttle and the brake. The signals—"keep coming, left a bit, straighten up"—from the assistant, who can see whether the driver's instructions are achieving the desired effect, are feedback. There is a further kind of information, called feedforward, which is concerned not with reporting what has already happened, but with foreseeing what is about to happen: if, for example, the assistant guiding the truck driver suddenly yells "whoah" because the truck is about to knock over a lamp post, then that warning is feedforward.

Accurate and effective control, then, is achieved by information flowing in a loop: instructions for action going out, feedback reporting the effect of those

actions returning via the other half of the loop. In our own case, most of the tasks we perform with our hands involve two loops. The outward, instruction-carrying section of both loops are provided by one set of nerves (the efferent system) which carry signals from the brain to the muscles. But feedback comes from two separate sources. There is first of all the information about the position of the parts of the body itself, provided by what are known as the proprioreceptive senses, in this case the signals returning to the brain via the other, afferent, nervous system which reports the position, or degree of tension or relaxation, in the muscles of the arm and hand. Secondly, there is the informa-

tion provided by our eyes, which monitor both the movements of our own fingers and the position of the object we are trying to manipulate.

A couple of very familiar examples will reveal just how reliant we are on both kinds of feedback. If we spin round and round, we get dizzy, lurch about and perhaps even fall over. The cause is quite simple. The spinning motion has temporarily incapacitated the organs of balance in our ears which provide the proprioreceptive feedback we need in order to maintain our balance; we lurch and fall over because the brain is unable accurately to determine what needs to be done in order to keep us standing and

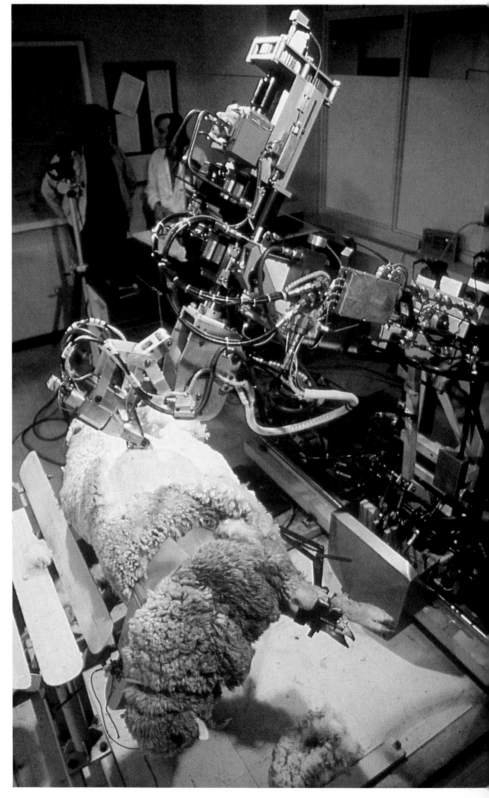

Right: Australia's sheep-shearing robot —the most improbable application yet? Sensors provide feedback to steer the cutter over the sheep's skin. Currently being researched are feedforward devices to look ahead and sense the skin beneath the uncut wool.

upright. Similarly, when we get up in the middle of the night to go to the bathroom, and lurch around a hotel bedroom feeling for the lightswitch, we are hampered by the lack of visual feedback—without seeing where we are going it is difficult for us to judge whether we are putting our feet in the right place.

To date, most robots have only proprioreceptive senses which provide feedback about the position of (and sometimes the forces being exerted upon) the articulations in their own arms and hands. Such senses are vital for all but the most elementary robots, pick-and-place machines as they are sometimes called, the movements of which may be limited and controlled by mechanical stops or limit switches. A robot whose movements are directed by software (a computer program) rather than by hardware requires proprioreceptive senses and the feedback information they provide, because it can never be guaranteed that a program will be implemented with complete accuracy over and over again. In any electrical system there will be "noise" or random interference of one kind or another and, if it lacks feedback to monitor its own actions, a robot which gets out of step will remain out of step.

One of the devices most frequently used to provide a robot with feedback information about the position of its own joints is called a shaft encoder. It is often used in conjunction with a particular kind of electrical drive, the stepper motor, which reacts to pulsed signals causing it to rotate so many "steps" in one direction or the other. When the motor has acted on an instruction of this kind, it is the function of the shaft encoder to detect the new position of the joint and to report this to the

Left: Researchers at Oxford have developed this sensor-guided arc welder. Arc welding demands sensory feedback because the weld must form a continuous "seam".

Below: A typical optical shaft encoder (in this case the Sumtak LDA) as used to monitor the position of a robot joint and provide the feedback required to maintain precise control of it.

A Shaft Encoder
The pattern of black and white patches on the rings of the disc, when "read" by light-sensitive cells, provides a binary code (black = 1, white = 0) which can be used to establish the position of the rotating shaft or axle and feed back the information to the robot's controlling computer. The greater the number of rings (and therefore the number of coded "bits" in the message) the greater the degree of precision obtainable. For the purposes of the schematic drawing the shaft encoder is shown as integral with the robot joint; in practice it is self-contained unit (see photograph at right), normally mounted on the end of the shaft or the outside of the motor.

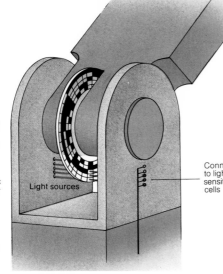

Light sources

Connections to light sensitive cells

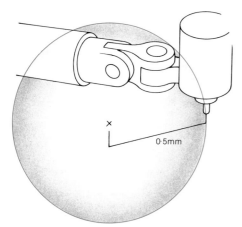

Resolution and Repeatability
The accuracy with which a robot can "resolve" the position of its end effector is crucial. It is pointless, for example, asking a machine to drill a hole which must be placed within 0·25mm of a certain position if the robot can only achieve a resolution of 0·5mm. Equally important is the precision with which a movement or position can be repeated once registered in the robot's memory.

robot's computer. The computer can then determine whether the actual position of the joint corresponds with the one set out in its program and, if the motor has, say, turned one step too many or one too few, issue instructions to put matters right.

The precision with which sensors such as the shaft encoder can detect the position of a robot joint, and the accuracy with which the drives can achieve them are the key factors in determining the degree of "resolution" and "repeatability" the machine will be capable of. That is, how accurately the hand or end effector can be positioned when the robot is being taught a new routine and how reliably it will be able to repeat the motions it has been taught. Resolution and repeatability are two of the main criteria used in assessing the performance of an industrial robot. In the case of a large machine employed on, say, spot welding, repeatability may be limited to half a millimetre or more, but some of the smaller robots recently developed for use in assembling precision instruments like watches achieve a degree of repeatability measured in a few microns—a steadiness of hand which even a brain surgeon might envy. Other sensors may also be involved in a robot's proprioceptive system. It is, for example, important that a robot be able to gauge the weight of the objects it is lifting, and indeed the weight of its own arm which will vary, in terms of the forces exerted on the different joints, depending on the position of the joints. It may also need to know not just how fast it is moving—a factor that will obviously be influenced by the weight it is carrying—but also how fast it is accelerating or decelerating. This information is needed because the load, and the arm itself, are subject to inertia and momentum. The arm cannot be allowed to swing about wildly like that of a flailing boxer; if it is to operate efficiently it must gather speed gradually and come to a smooth, controlled halt when it reaches its destination. Different tasks may demand movement at different rates: a paint-spraying robot, for example may have to

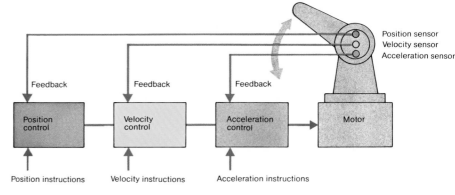

Position sensor
Velocity sensor
Acceleration sensor

Feedback — Position control — Position instructions

Feedback — Velocity control — Velocity instructions

Feedback — Acceleration control — Acceleration instructions

Motor

Feedback Loops
In order for a robot to achieve "continuous path control" (that is, to follow a complex route from place to place and vary its speed of movement, rather than simply following the fastest, "point-to-point" route), the controls will have to include sensors to monitor not only the position of each joint, but the speed at which that position is changing, whether the movement is accelerating or decelerating, etc. This feedback information, and the instructions which are issued in response to it, flow in a series of loops; in effect, as the diagram shows, "loops within loops" as each sensor feeds information into the system. The fact that each of the robot's six or more joints requires control systems of this complexity, and that all must work together under the co-ordination of some supervisory control, emphasises the problem involved.

Left: The GMF Vision System in use. Its ability to distinguish 256 tones, or grey levels, allows it to "see" the holes in the components in which the robot must insert its grippers.

Above: The Salisbury hand, one of the most advanced grippers yet devised. Will robot sniffers ever advance to the point at which a machine will be able to appreciate what's in the glass?

Above: This gripper, equipped with TDI silicon touch sensors, shows how far robotics have progressed from the crude methods of the first "pick-and place" machines.

vary its speed of movement to ensure that the paint is spread evenly; a robot transferring crucibles full of molten metal cannot move its arm in a series of jerks.

A robot control system is, therefore, likely to be complex and made up of not just a single feedback loop, but a series of loops within loops. It is also important to remember that a separate set of sensors and feedback circuits must be provided for each articulation or degree of freedom and that the computer which controls the overall action of the robot must be capable of making all the joints work in concert. One means of achieving this is to devolve some of the decision-making to individual microprocessors which, under the overall control of the robot's central computer, are responsible for monitoring feedback from one or more of the joints and ensuring that they are positioned as the master program dictates. Interestingly, this is a strategy which nature itself employs. Some insects have a sort of subsidiary "brain" in their abdomen which controls the limbs; even in our own case very urgent reactions such as those which make us instinctively withdraw our hand when we touch something that is too hot originate from centres in the spinal cord rather than from the brain itself.

Perceiving the World

The engineering of a proprioceptive sensory system is simplified because all the conditions with which it will have to cope can be easily foreseen and provided for—the sensors will never, unless the robot breaks down in some very dramatic

fashion, find that a joint is bent in a way that the designer failed to foresee. The computer, which integrates the information provided by the various sensors, need only be programmed to cope with a restricted and clearly defined range of circumstances.

Things are very different when we turn to the question of sensing and understanding the rest of the world; unlike the robot's own anatomy, this is not something which behaves in ways which are predictable and circumscribed. Even if the machine is not required to cope with an environment wider than its own immediate workspace and a limited range of tools and other objects, it is still going to encounter, unless matters are carefully organized to ensure that it does not, circumstances or events which are unexpected or unforeseeable. To take just an elementary example, the variety of ways in which half a dozen simple engineering components (nuts, bolts, washers, say) may arrange themselves if scattered at random on a workbench is to all intents and purposes infinite.

It is precisely because the difficulties of coping with situations like this are, in robotic terms, so great that contemporary industrial robots have to be provided with an environment in which everything is predictable. All the objects the robot is expected to handle must be presented to it in predetermined positions and orientations; faced with the unexpected, a package that has tumbled onto its side or component that is the wrong way round, the robot is at a loss—not only does it generally have no means of seeing what

has happened, it also has no program which would tell it what to do about it.

A start has already been made in providing robots with the equipment to cope with such contingencies. Apart from the first, as yet very primitive, vision systems, which we will come to in a moment, less elaborate aids to perception are available. As far as touch is concerned, it is not especially difficult to equip a robot end effector with tactile devices such as pressure pads which allow it to discover whether it is actually grasping an object. Another solution to the same problem is provided by the photo-electric cell. Built into the robot's "hand", this acts as an elementary "eye" which, by reacting to the presence or absence of light shining on it, can tell the machine whether it is holding something. Strain gauges can be used to detect the pressure the robot's own grippers are exerting on an object and, by measuring the degree of resistance they encounter, to assess how hard or soft it may be. Used as proprioceptive sensors, such gauges allow a robot hand to manipulate delicate or fragile objects by monitoring the amount of pressure that is being exerted.

It is worth noting in passing that there is one respect in which robots are far better able to perceive and cope with their environment than we are. Industrial robots are increasingly being used as a part of a team which may involve several other robots or a variety of other kinds of machinery. This requires the machines to communicate with one another. Robots doing spot welding on a moving production line, for example, must work in concert and track the car bodies as they move steadily along the line. In the cells which make up a flexible manufacturing system (see Chapter 2), robots are used to load and unload machine tools, transferring workpieces from one tool to another, perhaps even pausing en route at a gauging station where dimensions are automatically checked; this sort of task involves the robots in monitoring the operations of the machine tools. They must know when a tool has completed a task and is ready to be unloaded; they must work out the most economical sequence of loading and unloading actions in order to ensure that the tools remain idle for as short a time as possible.

Because modern automated equipment, such as assembly lines or numerically controlled machine tools, are likely to be computer-controlled, just like the robot, it is comparatively easy to equip the robots with electronic senses (interfaces with the other machines) which ensure that it is fully and instantly aware of what it needs to know about their actions. Thus is could be said that, in a mechanized, automated environment, a robot has a far more acute and accurate sense of what its fellow machines are up to than a human operator could ever develop.

Mobile Robots

In the case of mobile robots, such as the unmanned trolleys which are being used experimentally to transport materials around factories and warehouses, other forms of sensor may provide a crude but adequate substitute for vision. Ultra-sound devices, which transmit a stream of pulses at high frequencies undetectable to the human ear and monitor the echoes that bounce back when the sound waves are reflected from an object in the trolley's path, are one expedient that is being evaluated. In effect, the system is using the same method as a bat, which relies upon similar techniques of echo-location to navigate and track down its insect prey. For the moment, however, the knowledge that the robot trolleys derive from their ultrasound sensors is relatively crude compared to that which guides a bat's intricate aerobatics. It allows a trolley to do no more than avoid collision by turning left or right or, if it finds itself blocked, coming to a halt and waiting for a human being to come to its aid.

An even simpler technique can be used if the robot is required to do no more than follow a predetermined route. Robot floor cleaners are already in use in supermarkets and other large buildings, while similar automated guided vehicles transfer components around large car manufacturing factories, such as Fiat's Rivalta plant. They follow a predetermined route, running, as it were, on invisible tramlines in the shape of magnetic tracks laid beneath the surface of the floor. A similar system would, it has been suggested, allow the use of driverless agricultural tractors, if farmers were prepared to go the expense of laying electronic grids under their arable fields.

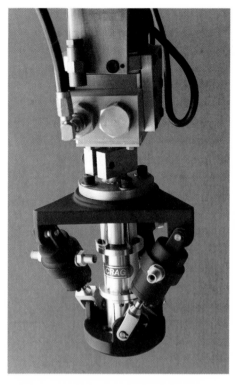

Above: A prototype wrist joint, developed at Cranfield Institute of Technology. Such sensitive and responsive systems will be needed if robot assembly is to become commonplace.

Right: A BL Maestro is checked for leaks by a Trallfa robot equipped with a sniffing head. The sniffer detects, and a monitor records, the position of leaks after helium has been pumped into the car body.

Below: Wire-guided trolleys convey body shells around Fiat's Rivalta plant. Though impressive, such systems are more extensions of the "hard automation" principle than true robots.

It must, however, be said that when people talk of the current generation of mobile robots they are generally referring to machines mounted on rails, or on overhead gantries, the movements of which are just as blind and insensate as their static colleagues. In the short run, as we shall see shortly, there is little hope of artificial vision systems advancing to the point at which they are competent to guide a mobile, free-ranging robot around the factory floor for some years to come. The whole issue of mobility is discussed in detail in the next chapter.

Something in the Air

Some steps have been taken towards the development of a robot sense of smell. British Leyland have developed a "sniffer robot" which is used to check car bodies for possible leaks. Rather than, as hitherto, deluging the unfinished body with gallons of water and then checking the interior for signs of leaks, the production line at BL's Cowley Works now incorporates a work station at which helium gas is pumped into the body shell under pressure while a sensor mounted on a

robot arm is moved around the outside, following the welded joints where a leak is most likely to occur.

Though the team who developed this technique certainly deserve full marks for ingenuity, it is worth noting that the sniffing head itself presented them with few problems. The real difficulties lay in programming the robot arm to follow an intricate course, maintaining the gas detector at a constant distance from the joints, and in arranging the monitoring system which records the exact location of any leaks that are discovered. A recent announcement, from another research team, of a robot "nose" which can not only detect the presence of a single aroma but can also discriminate between different kinds of smell, suggests however that we may yet see robots with a genuine sense of smell—indeed, given that our own noses are crude and insensitive sensors compared with those of other animals, it will not be surprising if robots quickly surpass human beings in this department. Already gas chromatographs can detect and indentify minute traces of substances like drugs or explosives with far greater reliability than the

average customs officer, which has led to their use at airports and elsewhere as "mechanical sniffer dogs". It is also worth remembering that robot noses, in the form of the smoke detectors that are built into many fire alarm systems, have been with us for many years.

Sight

There can be no doubt that the robot sensory repertoire will remain painfully and cripplingly deficient until real progress is made in artificial vision systems. (Hearing is, of course, equally important in many respects, but since it so clearly depends upon solving the problems involved in the use and understanding of natural language, this subject is explored further in Chapter 8 which deals with artificial intelligence). Certainly, the advantages to be gained from devising an effective means of robot vision are so great, this field is currently right at the top of the list of research priorities. The reason is clear: vision is by far the most valuable sense available to human beings in their capacity as industrial workers and the chances of a robot being able to widen its

ROBOTS

APOMS
1 Roll axis gear box and drive motor.
2 Propeller.
3 Vision sensor.
4 APOMS 3-D optical measurement.
5 Roll axis position encoder.
6 PROFS (propeller robotic optical finishing system).
7 Hydraulic power supply.
8 Templating/grinding tools.
9 PAWS (propeller automated welding system).

APOMS is the US Navy's system for checking the dimensions and profiles of ships' propellers. The vision sensor, manufactured by Robotic Vision Systems, detects the exact position of a small area of the blade surface, this information is reported to the APOMS processors which compare the actual coordinates with the ideal ones of the geometrical model stored in their memory. Two robots can then machine or weld the blade to refine its shape. To say that the system "sees" the blade is misleading, it relies on laser sensors to detect the metal surface of the propeller and record its distance from the sensing head. Rather than mirroring human skills or senses, systems such as APOMS emphasise the extent to which artificial systems may be able to achieve precision, speed and reliability which no human craftsman could ever match.

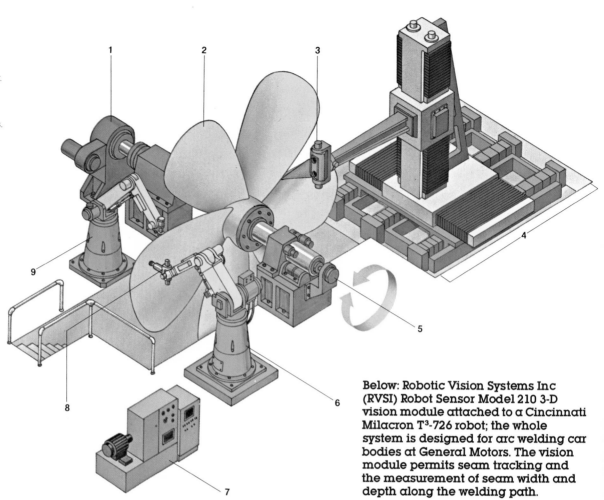

Below: Robotic Vision Systems Inc (RVSI) Robot Sensor Model 210 3-D vision module attached to a Cincinnati Milacron T³-726 robot; the whole system is designed for arc welding car bodies at General Motors. The vision module permits seam tracking and the measurement of seam width and depth along the welding path.

Above: Here the RVSI Model 210 vision module is configured as part of a Robo Inspector Series 1100 system that checks aircraft parts; camera data are passed to a separate processor unit.

range of industrial skills depends crucially upon it being able to "see what it is doing".

There are, it is true, quite a lot of systems concerned with artificial vision already on the market or actually installed and working in conjunction with industrial robots. It is also, however, true to say that none of this existing equipment seems likely to provide a basis for the sort of general purpose visual skills which a robot all-rounder would require. The point is that most of these systems have been designed with specific and often very limited applications in mind; but while they perform these tasks with a skill and precision which the human eye is quite unable to match, they totally lack the flexibility which we take so much for granted in our own case. We can, for example, use our eyes with equal ease to judge how far away things are, how straight an edge is, what kind of car is passing, whether we are likely to enjoy the meal that has been placed in front of us, what other people are feeling, etc, etc. Individual robots may already be able to

do one of these things better than us, but there is as yet little prospect of them being able to do two or more of them.

A typical case in point which well illustrates both the skills and the limitations of such special purpose vision systems is the Automated Propeller Optical Measurement System (APOMS) developed for the US Navy. Using a special sensor which illuminates a small area of the propeller surface with laser light and, by monitoring the way the light is reflected, maps its geometry to an accuracy of two

Checking Dimensions

and a half thousandths of an inch, APOMS can compare the actual shape of the blades to the perfect shape specified by the designer and identify the areas where the difference exceeds the permitted tolerances. Calculating its own scanning path, and moving the sensor mounted on its robot arm entirely under computer control, the system has, it is claimed, cut the time taken for inspection by 90 per cent—and achieved far greater accuracy and reliability than could be guaranteed using traditional methods. But, it is also clear that however superior to the human eye APOMS may be in this single respect, it cannot be considered a general-purpose vision system.

Slightly less sophisticated, though equally limited in practice, are the vision systems used in the motor industry, for example, to check the position of components during assembly, or to measure dimensions and check tolerances. Normally, such equipment works by comparing the image captured by its camera with a "template" stored in its computer memory—rather as we might hold two objects up to the light to check if they were the same shape. Using well-established computational methods (the best-known being Fourrier transformations) it is possible to make simple decisions about what is seen—such as, for example, that an object is longer than it should be, or that a component is tilted to the left by so many degrees, etc.

These methods may allow robots to work with what appears to be an impressive degree of coordination between "hand" and "eye". They can, for example, enable a robot to pick up objects such as bars of chocolate or rectangular cartons which arrive on a conveyor positioned at random, and place them the right way round in a box or on a pallet. The snag, of course, is that it may take hours of work and a great deal of programming skill to get such a system set up in an industrial context, and it will be quite unable to cope with a different task unless completely reprogrammed.

A truly flexible and general purpose vision system, on the other hand, would have to have something of the "intelligence" and adaptability of the human system. Work on developing genuine artificial vision has, therefore been a major concern of the field known as artificial intelligence. We are just beginning to see the fruits of this research finding their way into commercially practicable robots. Most of the work has concentrated on what is called scene analysis: that is trying to provide a computer with rules which allow it to understand the "meaning" of the various objects which may feature in the scene captured by a camera. But, with any visual system, the first task is to reduce a picture to a form in which it can be described, or encoded, in the form of binary numerals, the 1s and 0s that are the computer's native language. Surprisingly, perhaps, this presents few problems. Any image is ultimately reducible to a matrix or grid of pixels or picture points. The picture that appears on an ordinary domestic television set can be used to illustrate the point, for it is made up of just such a matrix. So too is a printed illustration in a book or magazine. In the case of the crudest kind of image of all, one which contains only pure black and pure white, each pixel can be allotted a single value, in the binary code a 1 for a black pixel and a 0 for a white one.

Gradations in tone (so-called "grey tones") can be taken care of if more than one digit is used to describe the intensity of each pixel—the use of two digits, for example, allows four levels of intensity to be distinguished: 00 (white), 01 (light grey), 10 (dark grey) and 11 (black). Adding further digits allows more exact descriptions, and colour, like intensity, can also be coded. A very high quality colour image may require the use of eight or more digits per pixel, which will suffice to discriminate between 2^8, or 256 different colours. But, even if a system is confined to the basic pure-black or pure-white images it will still have to

Left: The Automated Component Optical Measurement System (ACOMS) uses a laser scanner to check 1,250 dimensions on engine castings for Cummins Engine Co. It can do this in 40 minutes; a man will take up to 35 hours.

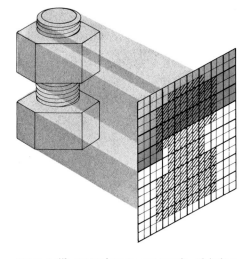

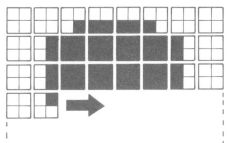

Edge Detection
What is by now the classic theory of artificial image processing starts with edge detection. By scanning a "window" of two or (in this instance) four pixels (dots or picture points) across an image like the (highly simplified) one of the nut and bolt, a computer can "find" the changes of tone or colour which mark the edges or contours of objects. The edges can be combined into a "primal sketch" (a sort of outline drawing of the objects), and such primal sketches, once their features have been identified and labelled, can be mathematically analysed and the resulting descriptions of the image compared with others stored in the computer's memory to see if a match, and therefore an identification, can be made. The use of parallel processors which can find edges within half a dozen logical steps (by operating on each pixel of the image simultaneously rather than scanning it) can greatly speed up processes such as edge detection. One such system, developed at University College, London, is CLIP (Cellular Logic Image Processor) which is a 96 x 96 array of processors, which operate in parallel to achieve image analysis.

cope with very large amounts of information. An image, comparable to that of an ordinary TV set, could be made up of 512 lines, each containing 512 pixels. If each pixel is either black or white, that is still, in computer terms, well over a quarter of a million bits of information, or four times as much as can be stored in the memory of a home computer with a 64K RAM capacity. If the picture is a moving one, and very few robot applications are likely to involve objects which remain stationary, it also becomes relevant that the screen is scanned, and each pixel either refreshed or changed, twenty-five times a second. Thus if a robot was to be "plugged into" an ordinary TV camera and provided with a crude black-or-white version of the picture it was capturing, it would still, if it was to understand what it saw in real time (as fast as a human being would), have to process a quarter of a million bits of information every twenty-fifth of a second.

Intelligent Framestores

Only recently have such feats really become possible, thanks to an invention called an intelligent framestore—essentially a specialized kind of computer memory which can store the digits describing a single scan of an image and, before the next scan is delivered, execute programs designed to extract the information they contain. (It is the use of framestores that lies behind the many spectacular and ingenious special effects on TV). The problem of extracting the significant features of an image can also be simplified somewhat by reducing the size of the matrix—many simple images are quite intelligible even to the human eye on a grid of 64 pixels by 64—and by slowing the rate of scan. The computer, unlike a human being, is not bothered by the resultant flicker.

The crucial issue is, of course, what sort of information should be extracted from the mass of digits in order to establish what they represent. The scale of this conundrum is immense. In fact, it is of as

Right: An electronic "eye" developed for the US Air Force. As the monitor shows, the sensor can detect the position, size and even the orientation of an object with great accuracy.

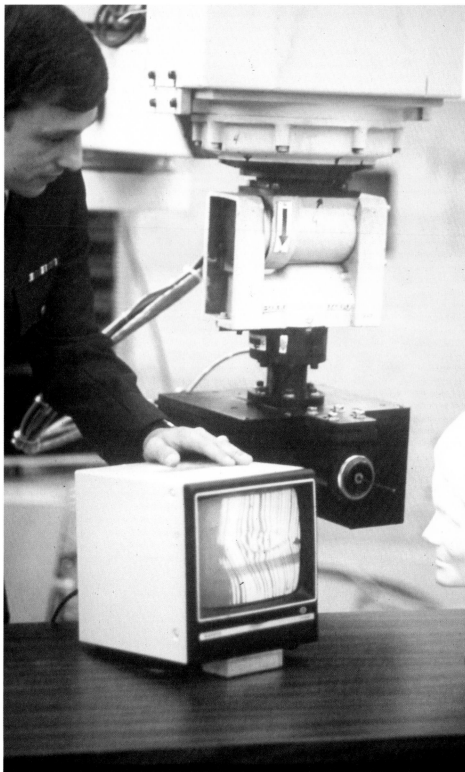

Left: The monitor of this vision system developed by ASEA clearly shows a primal sketch derived from the image of the gearwheel in the foreground. Recognition is more easily achieved using such simplified images.

much importance to neurologists and psychologists as it is to roboticists, for the rods and cones in the retina of a human eye deliver very similar kinds of information to the brain, and we have barely begun to understand the process by which we translate it into perceptions, such as recognition of a familiar face or object.

The approach that has been most widely adopted is based on the identification of the significant features of an image. In practice this usually means the lines which represent the edges and corners of objects. It is believed that this process mirrors one that takes place in our own brains, and involves discarding all the irrelevant and confusing information in order to arrive at what is called a "primal sketch", a sort of summary of the image which incorporates only its most salient features.

The strategies involved in obtaining a primal sketch are complex, and will vary with the task for which the system is designed. They normally begin by applying programs which operate as "edge-detectors", discovering the main axes of the lines where the colour or intensity of pixels change and thus isolating the edges or corners of the objects. Edge detection in itself is a complex and demanding task. "Noise" of one sort or another will almost inevitably distort some of the pixels and the program must, therefore, be capable of disregarding minor distortions and omissions in order to arrive at a "sensible" interpretation of a confused image.

One of the techniques that is already being employed to speed up this process relies upon a novel kind of computer called a parallel array processor. One of the most advanced machines of this kind is the CLIP (Cellular Logic Image Processor) developed at University College, London. A CLIP computer, unlike the orthodox machine, does not have a single central processor to handle mathematical and logical processes. Instead, it is made up of a whole collection, or array, of specialized chips, each of which can be programmed to perform a variety of logical operations. Normally, each processor receives the chunk of binary information which describes a single pixel, but the ingenuity of this system lies in the arrangements which allow each processor to communicate with its immediate neighbours. By working in parallel, the processors are able to perform tasks—such as finding the corners of an object or eliminating objects on the periphery of the image—very rapidly indeed: far faster than an orthodox computer which

Left: The monitor of GMF's vision system shows how, once it has located the centre of an object, it can calculate how far its position or orientation differs from the "norm".

Right: Another application for the IVS-100 "Eye". This time, using optical character recognition and verification methods, it is monitoring the read-out on a LED (light-emitting diode) display.

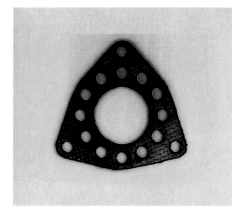

Above and below: Two examples of cleaned-up images (obtained, in this case, by the IVS-100 system made by Analog Devices of Massachusetts). The component in the top picture can be checked for accuracy of dimensions and the absence of faults, and its position and orientation reported to a robot manipulator. The circuit board in the lower picture can be inspected for faults and mechancial defects etc.

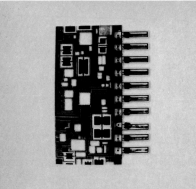

would have to wade through the stream of data in a linear fashion. It seems likely that devices like CLIP will prove very valuable as front-end processors, able to extract rapidly the important features of an image and communicate them to other computers which can then decide what they "mean".

Interpreting Meaning

It is this latter job which is, so far, proving extremely difficult to accomplish with any degree of sophistication. The usual procedure, once a primal sketch of the edges and corners of objects has been obtained, is for the program to label these (or the surfaces which they delineate) in order to arrive at a description of the scene which can be analysed using a variety of mathematical techniques. This

Left: The "robot butcher" developed for the Swedish Meat Research Institute by ASEA. Vision sensors allow it to size up a carcass before the cutting saw divides the meat into sections.

Right: In this experiment conducted at the USAF School of Aerospace Medicine, an anthropometric measuring device is using structured light to help measure the contours of a boulder

will allow the computer to understand what a scene contains in terms of the elementary shapes (cubes, cylinders, etc), and to determine the relationship between those elementary shapes—that is, whether they are joined together, stacked one on top of another, overlapping one another, etc.

Most of the scenes which a robot is likely to encounter, however, are not made up of the primitive forms of schoolroom geometry. They will almost certainly contain objects which have compound shapes formed of combinations of such elementary forms. A bolt, for example, can be described as a cylinder with a disc on one end, a nut as a short cylinder with a hole through its centre, etc. In order for a computer to recognize descriptions of this kind, and the objects they represent, it must be equipped with yet another sort of program based upon what are called semantic nets.

In order to understand how a semantic net works, consider the kind of knowledge we ourselves use (or assume we use) when we distinguish between different classes of objects. Let us take, for example, some common items of household crockery. We might define a saucer as a disc, formed into a shallow bowl shape, with a circular indentation in the bottom of the bowl to take a cup. A soup plate, on the other hand, could be described as a disc, with a deep indentation in the centre and a flat rim around the outside. We would distinguish between a cup and a sugar bowl by reference to the fact that the former must have a handle; and between a cup and a milk jug by remembering that the jug must have a pouring lip.

Each of these descriptions could be put into the form of a semantic net. In the case of most of the objects which a robot will need to identify, such structures will require a good deal of refinement for the computer which will have to be able to distinguish between objects which are like one another in many ways but different in one or more crucial respects. In practice, semantic nets are created by "training" the system not only about the objects it is required to recognize, but also about similar objects which are like them but not the same. Such a training process allows the program to build up its own rules, or generalizations.

This question of generalization, of defining an object not from one fixed viewpoint, but from all possible viewpoints is a vital one. A robot which could only recognize the component parts of a mechanism which it had to assemble if they were presented to it in predetermined attitudes would be only a very small improvement on a totally blind robot. For in both cases elaborate automated devices such as indexing machines, or human operators are required to feed the components to the robot.

Other difficulties that tend to arise with scene analysis programs are due to the difficulty of analysing scenes in which objects may appear in different positions or relationships to one another. Much programming ingenuity, and a great deal of sheer number crunching, is necessary if a computer is to be able to interpret a scene containing a few elementary objects, a plate of biscuits for example, on which some of the biscuits overlap others. To be frank, it is difficult to believe that when we work out how to pick up the digestive biscuit that is partly covered by a ginger nut, we perform the sort of geometrical calculations that a robot would employ to resolve this sort of problem.

In the case of scenes composed of primitive blocks of various kinds, there are rules which can be used to determine whether objects are overlapping, or which corner of a block is nearest the camera. Edges will only meet to form T-junctions, for instance, when there is an overlap; arrow-head shaped junctions denote a corner at the back of an object etc.

It is also possible, in some cases, to make life easier for the computer by "cheating". It is very much easier, for example, for a vision system to interpret accurately a curved surface (a necessity for a robot which is seam welding along the junction of two curved surfaces) if the scene is illuminated by structured light. Light is structured by shining it through a grid which throws a pattern of light and dark bars across a surface and, if the width of the bars is carefully controlled, the computer can use them as a basis for mathematical calculations which clarify the shape of the surface. Another common expedient is to prepare workpieces by painting crosses or target marks on them in certain fixed positions which provide a point of reference for the robot vision system, a bit like the arrow on a street map which says "You Are Here".

It must be said, however, that methods of this kind seem unlikely to lead to the sort of flexible and intelligent vision systems that would be required by a general purpose robot; one which could cope with a range of situations and functions roughly equivalent to those which an unskilled human worker masters almost without having to think about it! The problem seems to be that we do not, in practice, employ the kind of rules that are involved in edge detection, scene analysis and semantic nets. Faced with a strange animal in a field, for example, we do not decide whether it is a cow, a horse or a sheep by weighing up factors such as: does it have horns? are its hoofs cloven? is its coat woolly? etc. We know perfectly well what cows, horses and sheep look like and can recognize any one of them instantly. It seems probable, in fact, that we recognize images as patterns rather than as wads of information that need formal deciphering.

Pattern Recognition

Over the past five years or so, some progress has been made with an entirely new kind of machine which is designed to implement this quite different approach to the problems posed by artificial vision. Known as artificial neural nets (because each element in the device fills a role similar to that of a neuron, or nerve cell, in the brain), these machines are parallel processors like the CLIP computer described previously; they contain many hundreds or even thousands of electronic processing devices, all of which work simultaneously on different parts of the image. The difference lies in the fact that a neural net does not require preprogramming—in effect, as we shall see, it constructs its own program as a result of being exposed to visual experience, and can thus adapt itself to new tasks as and when required.

The most advanced adaptive pattern recognizer of this sort to date is the WISARD device developed at Brunel University by a team led by Professor Igor Aleksander.

WISARD operates on an image of roughly the same size and resolution as that provided by a domestic TV set, with a grid of 512 by 512 pixels. Each of the logical elements in the machine (they are in fact standard RAM memory chips) receives the input from eight pixels scattered at random over the grid. WISARD is taught by simply exposing it to an image while pressing a single teach button which is connected to all the 30,000 odd elements. As a result of the teaching process, each element learns to output a binary 1 if, and only if, it receives the same input pattern of eight binary digits again (see diagram on page 64).

Now of course exactly the same pattern will never recur—interference alone will always produce some variation in the binary information even if the image itself is identical. But the score which WISARD accords to a new image (the number of elements which respond by

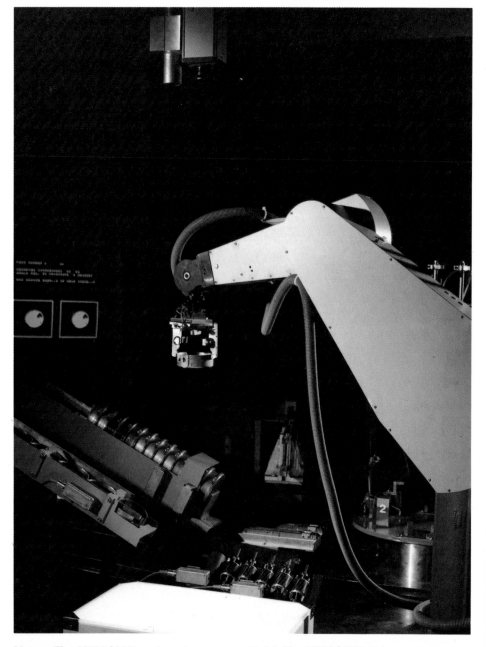

Above: The NELSON II system (see right) being used to provide a PUMA robot with the kind of visual ability that might be helpful, for example, in simple assembly work.

Right: The NELSON II vision system was developed at the National Engineering Laboratory in Scotland. It can recognize parts from a range of up to 25 different shapes.

outputting a 1) is in effect a measure of how similar to the taught image the new one appears to the machine. If the machine has several separate blocks of memory devices, or discriminators, each of which is taught a different image, then the machine as a whole will respond to a new image by saying, in effect, which of the taught images it most resembles.

That this technique can be extremely powerful is demonstrated by some of WISARD's accomplishments. It has, for example, shown itself able to recognize individual human faces; even to distinguish between faces that are smiling and faces that are frowning. It performs these feats, moreover, in a fraction of a second and using live images: that is, pictures of faces which move, change expression, etc. And all this, remember, without any formal programming at all. It is interesting that the way in which WISARD is constructed, using separate

discriminators to recognize different patterns, seems to mirror the structure of part of the natural brain. The Nobel Prize winning work of D.H. Hubel and Torsten Wiesel showed that the visual cortex of animals contained groups of nerve cells (known as hypercolumns) which seem to have similar functions. In particular, it appears that it is the function of a hypercolumn to recognize the general orientation of an image: to ascertain whether it is upright, or horizontal, or diagonal.

The most important and fascinating feature of devices like WISARD is their ability to learn generalized images. When, for example, the machine learns what an individual's face looks like, it is not taught from a single, stationary image. It sees the face live on camera, and the subject is asked to move, change expression, smile and grimace, stick out his tongue, etc. The machine will then recognize that person, and distinguish his face from other faces, even if it appears in an attitude or with an expression it has never seen before. It can even see through simple disguises like glasses or false moustaches.

Since the recognition of an image as subtle and difficult to define as a human face is beyond the wildest dreams of those working with vision systems based on traditional methods, there do seem to be lessons to be drawn from WISARD's success. The most important of these would seem to be that initially an image is best treated as a pattern rather than a set of lines the meaning of which can be established by formal, logical computation. It may be that the precision and logical powers of the traditional computer will be needed at a later stage, but since WISARD is able to recognize objects in a fraction of a second which scene analysis finds too complex even to begin to tackle, it seems likely that neural nets may provide the ideal recognition device, or front-end processor, for robot vision.

In its original and simplest form, WISARD was what is known as a single layer neural net. This means that each of the RAM elements which make up its discriminators simply responded to the selection of pixels which made up its share of the image. But one of the most significant features of the structure of the brain is that the interconnections between the nerve cells provide massive amounts of feedback; when information from the eye, or any of the other senses or even patterns of activity arising within the

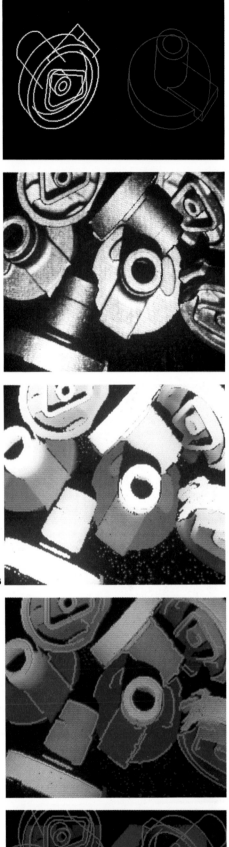

Right: Bob Bolles, a researcher at SRI International in California, has developed a 3D vision system to allow bin-picking robots to locate and grasp components in a disordered pile. This sequence shows how the Three Dimensional Part Orientation system (3DPO) works. It starts with a CAD-generated 3D model of the component (1) and, looking at the disordered parts (2), uses a range sensor to map the highest points (3). Low-level edges are then extracted (4), and the resulting shapes compared with the memorized model to identify individual parts (5).

brain itself, causes neurons to fire (to transmit electrical pulses), the neurons do not simply react to the original input, they also respond to the feedback produced by their own firing.

The arrangement used with WISARD is slightly different. Rather than having a highly resolved "window" fixed in the centre of its TV image, and being able to turn its camera eye this way and that, the camera remains stationary and the window moves around the image. The window is very similar to the picture-within-a-picture sometimes used by television producers who want to show both an overall view and a detail simultaneously on the same screen, and, like that TV effect, is produced by the use of a framestore. The fact that, initially at least, only the window and not the whole camera can be moved is a point of convenience rather than a difference of principle; what is significant is how the machine learns to direct its attention to the significant features of an image.

Again, it is feedback which provides the key. Initially the movement of the window is controlled by a human teacher, watching a monitor screen and using a joystick control similar to that used in video games. The operator will provide a few simple lessons, steering the window around the outline of an object, for example, or, if several different objects appear in the image, directing it at each

in turn. Simultaneously, the neural net is being taught: the RAM elements are learning to fire in response to new input patterns, and those patterns are provided by a mixture of the image itself and the feedback, the pattern of firing generated by the overall image and the moving window.

Very rapidly, after a few teaching operations, the net will get the idea and will automatically move its window to follow an outline, even if it is quite different from the one on which it was instructed, or focus upon a number of separate objects in turn.

This ability to look at a scene intelligently opens up the possibility of robot vision systems which will be able to search for whatever it is they need, or pick out one object from a jumbled assortment. It is also worth pointing out that a machine which can learn to move its single eye could equally well learn, by similar means, to move hand or, more importantly, to move hand and eye in concert.

In the case of WISARD, feedback is achieved by displaying the scores (the number of 1s) produced by each of the discriminators as a bar graph on a television screen. The image of this bar graph is then fed back into the net mixed up with the image that it is looking at. If this feedback is provided while one of the discriminators is learning an image, that discriminator's response will, or course,

be one hundred per cent—the learning process simply involves pressing a teach button which causes the RAM elements in the computer to store and output a 1 in response to the input image. The discriminator thus learns to recognize not just the image but also its own one hundred per cent response to that image.

The effect of feedback is best illustrated by what happens when two discriminators are taught very similar patterns, say two images that each contain only one small black dot at different positions on a white background. Without feedback, the machine would not distinguish between these images again with any great confidence. In fact both would receive a high response from both discriminators; for the vast majority of the picture (the white background) is the same in both cases. But once the discriminators receive the feedback showing their own response to one or other of the black dots, the response is quite different. The discriminator which knows the image gets a slightly more confident feedback, its confidence or score increases, the increase is reflected in the resulting feedback and the confidence grows further. Exactly the reverse process takes place in the other discriminator: as successive cycles of feedback arrive it grows less and less confident.

The behaviour of the net under these circumstances is very much like that we ourselves display when we think we recognize something or someone. We feel an initial spark of recognition—"isn't that Peter over there?"—followed rapidly by either a positive confirmation—"yes, of course it is"—or rejection—"no, it's nothing like him really". It is reasonable to suppose that these sensations are produced by the action of feedback within the brain in a fashion that is analogous to the operation of WISARD.

WISARD for Robots

One final elaboration of the WISARD system is of particular relevance to robots. A rather obvious problem with any artificial vision system is that, if it is to be used in the sort of industrial situation in which human beings operate, it will have to be able to look this way and that and, when it spots something that it wants or which is significant, look directly at that thing. Think, for a moment, of how we ourselves use our eyes. We do not see an image within a rigid frame, like the picture on a TV screen, with every bit of the scene equally clear to us. Rather, we are aware, through our peripheral vision, of what is going on in quite a wide field, while actually seeing clearly or concentrating our attention on quite a small area at the centre of that field. This allows us to look carefully at what interests us while still keeping an eye open for anything that may call for our attention on the periphery of our view.

This arrangement has many advantages. It allows us, for instance, to focus very closely on details when performing some fiddly task while still being instantly alerted if danger threatens. It means that

Neurons and Neural Nets

The top figure shows a highly simplified nerve cell or neuron, the basic logical element of the natural brain and nervous system. It receives electrical pulses (equivalent to binary 1s) from other cells via its inputs, or synapses. One synapse is "dominant"; when pulses are received at the dominant synapse the cell adjusts its synaptic weights, or "learns" to "fire" (that is to output a stream of pulses through the single output, or axon, which connects it to the synapses of other cells) whenever the same pattern of signals (pulses and no-pulses, equivalent to 1s and 0s) is present at the ordinary synapses.

The figure in the centre, again purely schematic, shows a small Random Access Memory element (RAM). If the four address terminals are thought of as the element's "synapses", the input terminal as its "dominant synapse", and the output terminal as its "axon", then the logical function of the RAM will be equivalent, for all practical purposes, to that of the nerve cell—it is, in effect, a "silicon neuron".

The bottom figure shows a series of four RAMs connected to form a "single layer neural net" (a network in which each element receives inputs but the outputs of the elements are not feedback into the net). In this case each RAM "sees" four pixels, each of which is either black (1) or white (0), scattered at random over a crude image. If each RAM is "taught" to

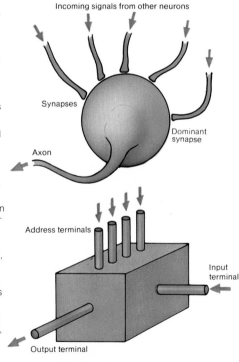

Incoming signals from other neurons

Synapses

Dominant synapse

Axon

Address terminals

Input terminal

Output terminal

Black pixel (1)

White pixel (0)

Ram elements

output a 1, or "fire" when it sees the same 4-pixel pattern again, then each RAM will have recognized a small part of a total image and so the system as a whole will have learnt to recognize that image. The number of RAMs which fire in response to a new image will be a measure of how "like" the taught one it is.

This is a highly simplified illustration of the principles upon which the WISARD system is based. (WISARD stands for Wilkie, Stonham and Aleksander's Recognition Device, so-named after the members of the team at Brunel University who invented it). The machine itself (see facing page) contains several separate nets, or discriminators, each of which can be taught a different image. Each discriminator contains some 30,000 RAMS. Each RAM has eight address terminals, and thus learns a share of the pattern containing eight bits of information. The system as a whole deals with images containing 512 x 512, or about a quarter of a million, pixels —roughly equivalent to the image on a domestic TV set.

It is anticipated that the kind of pattern recognition of which WISARD is capable will have applications in the field of robotics. A British company, Computer Recognition Systems, is marketing a commercial version of WISARD; they have reduced the size of the cabinets containing the RAM elements of the neural net to more convenient proportions.

when looking at, say, a large building we can be aware both of the overall shape of it and of some point of particular interest or attraction. It means that when we are looking for something, a face in a crowd perhaps, we can search a wide area and instantly zero in when we find what we are seeking.

In the case of our own eyes, we achieve this concentration of visual attention by moving the whole eyeball in order to centre our field of vision upon the object we wish to study. Because the area in the centre of the eye's retina, the fovea, has a much higher density of the light detecting rods and cones, this automatically allows us to view the object with a higher degree of resolution. In effect, it is broken down into more and smaller pixels than the rest of the visual field.

Left and bottom: These two photographs of the prototype WISARD show the machine in action. In this instance it had been "taught" (with another person altogether providing the demonstration) a smiling face and a frowning face. The bar graphs across the top of the monitor screen on the left of the subject who is now being viewed show WISARD's response to his expression. In the picture on the left the top bar indicates a positive response to his severe expression, whereas the lower bar shows that the machine finds it very unlike a smile. In the picture at the bottom of the page it can be seen that, as the subject has changed from a frown to a smile, so the relative length of the bars has changed. The picture (below) is a WISARD's eye view of a face.

MACHINES WITH MOBILITY

It is a telling comment on the state of development of mobile robots that several industrial societies concerned with this technology define "robot" as simply meaning a robot manipulator. When Unimation began to manufacture programmable arms for spray painting, spot welding and parts transfer in the early 1960s, the most advanced automatic mobile machines were laboratory devices that resembled toys. The Johns Hopkins University "Beast", for instance, wandered along halls, keeping its distance from the walls by means of ultrasonic range measurements. An optical system searched for the distinctive black cover plate of wall outlets, and whenever it found one the robot tried to plug in its special arm to recharge its batteries.

The lead held by the robot arm has been maintained through twenty years of research in the artifical intelligence labs. The AI workers have attempted to link programs that reason with programs that interpret data from cameras and microphones, and with programs that control arms and mobile platforms. Similar advances in the field of mobility are not as evident. Now that vision systems for manipulators are earning their keep by locating and identifying parts for assembly, an experimental mobile robot still takes an hour to find its way across a room.

Despite the slow progress, mobile machines, whether they are toys or laboratory experiments, hold a unique fascination for most observers. They somehow seem more alive than fixed devices. The most consistently interesting stories are those about journeys, and the most fascinating organisms are those that move from place to place. These observations are more than idiosyncrasies of human psychology; they illustrate a fundamental principle. The world at large has great diversity, and a traveller constantly encounters novel circumstances, and is consequently challenged to respond in new ways. Organisms and mechanisms do not exist in isolation, but are systems with their environments, and those on the prowl in general have a richer environment than those rooted to one place. Mobility, however, implies danger as well as excitment. Inappropriate actions or the failure to make well-timed appropriate ones can result in the demise of a free roamer far more easily than of a stationary entity.

When we look at the natural world, we see that challenge combines with opportunity to create a strong selection pressure that drives an evolving species endowed with mobility in certain directions, directions quite different from those of stationary organisms. Life on Earth can be viewed

Above: This walking robot, equipped with three legs and one arm, is the Robot Marine RM2 built by Normed Shipyards in France. It is designed to crawl over the hulls of ships and clean them using special abrasive tools.

Right: Probably the finest untethered walking machine in existence today is Odex-1, built by Odetics Inc of California. Here the six-legged "functionoid" is seen approaching and lifting a 2,200lb (1,000kg) truck.

as a grand experiment exploring these pressures. Besides the fortunate consequence of our own existence, some universals are apparent from the results to date. In particular, intelligence seems to follow from mobility.

The same pressures seem to be at work in the technological evolution of robots and it may be that mobile robots offer the best way of finding solutions to some of the most vexing unsolved problems on the way to true artificial intelligence: problems such as how to program common sense reasoning and learning from sensory experience. This opportunity carries a price—programs to control mobile robots are more difficult to get right than most. The robot is free to search the diverse world looking for just the combination of circumstances that will foil the plans of its designers. There is still a long way to go.

Mobility in Industry

Some simple mobile robots have made it in the factory, the warehouse and the office. The systems are manufactured by many small companies and small divisions of large companies. Many frozen food warehouses, difficult places for human workers because of the arctic conditions, are stocked and emptied by automatic fork-lift trucks. The trucks are coordinated by a central computer, but their local sensors are simple. They find their way by following the oscillating magnetic fields of a grid of buried guide wires, and guide their final dockings with pallets of produce with short range infrared proximity sensors. Encounters with unexpected obstacles or other accidents must be overcome by human intervention.

The corridors of some offices and hospitals are patrolled by even simpler robots.

These self-contained machines look like large tea carts, and follow a spray-painted trail on the floor. The paint is transparent but fluoresces for detection by photosensors in the glow of an ultraviolet light under the robot. They are used to collect mail from different offices, or to deliver linen. They beep a soft warning as they move, and stop on colliding with anything.

Several Japanese companies have, for some time, had fully automated factories

Left: In Citroën's FMS at Meudon, car components are transported around the workshop by automatically guided trolleys that follow underfloor wires.

Below: Volvo of America's AutoCarrier Model 109 wire-guided vehicle; the manual control allows repositioning of carriers that are off the guide path.

in operation that can function for periods without human involvement. An American plant being built by General Motors Corp., to start operation in 1985, is representative of the state of this art. The plant will be an automated, highly flexible manufacturing complex controlled by a master computer that can operate for an eight-hour shift without any human production workers. It will machine and assemble a family of axles for different models of cars. It will produce the complex front axles used on modern front-wheel-drive cars which, unlike the relatively simple axles on older rear-wheel-drive models, must allow the wheels to steer and move up and down, as well as propel the vehicle. About 50 robots will move parts within 40 manufacturing and assembly cells. Driverless carts, rectangular metal boxes on wheels following signals from wires buried in the concrete floors, will

move parts between cells and will transport finished products to shipping areas. Even floor-sweeping will be automated. The plant will be controlled by a number of computers. Machines will be able to adjust to handling components of varying size in minutes and a central computer will be able to change a machine's functions to continue production if another breaks down. The computer will also keep records, manage inventory and order raw materials. Human workers will still be needed for maintenance and other tasks that require greater skills.

Industry has expressed interest and carried out experimentation with several more advanced (and risky) mobile robot ideas. Various driverless automobile systems have been built since the 1950s. The early ones used buried guide wires, but recent experimental systems have been built that rely on navigational

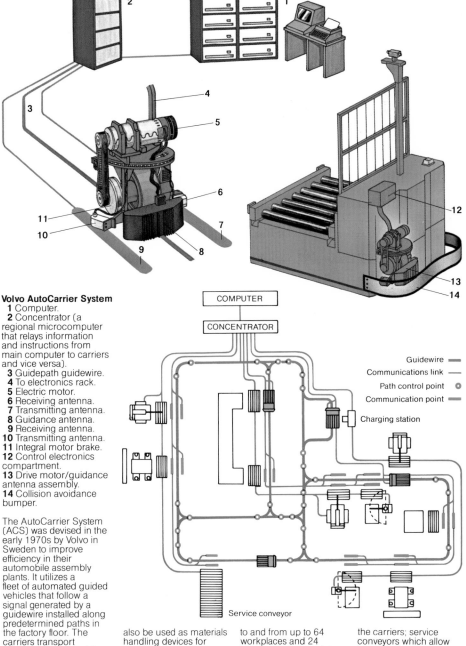

Volvo AutoCarrier System
1 Computer.
2 Concentrator (a regional microcomputer that relays information and instructions from main computer to carriers and vice versa).
3 Guidepath guidewire.
4 To electronics rack.
5 Electric motor.
6 Receiving antenna.
7 Transmitting antenna.
8 Guidance antenna.
9 Receiving antenna.
10 Transmitting antenna.
11 Integral motor brake.
12 Control electronics compartment.
13 Drive motor/guidance antenna assembly.
14 Collision avoidance bumper.

The AutoCarrier System (ACS) was devised in the early 1970s by Volvo in Sweden to improve efficiency in their automobile assembly plants. It utilizes a fleet of automated guided vehicles that follow a signal generated by a guidewire installed along predetermined paths in the factory floor. The carriers transport components around the plant, stopping when directed at work stations (either manned or unmanned) to allow assembly work to be carried out. They can

COMPUTER

CONCENTRATOR

Guidewire
Communications link
Path control point
Communication point
Charging station

Service conveyor

also be used as materials handling devices for warehousing and distribution. The ACS consists of a central computer that monitors and commands the whole system; concentrators which relay information

to and from up to 64 workplaces and 24 communications points; a guidance network; communications points located at strategic places along the guidepath and at workstations that relay information to and from

the carriers; service conveyors which allow transfer of materials between carrier and machine; and charging stations where the carriers' batteries are recharged, as always, under computer control.

in a potentially cluttered environment. The system uses a large number of sonar range-measuring devices to build a map in its computers of the volume surrounding it. The map is used to plan motions past obstacles and also to identify key intersections and to orient within them, giving the robot a sense of its location in the building's floor plan.

Laboratory Experiments

Until the middle 1960s computers were simply too rare and expensive to be used with something as frivolous as robots. A number of interesting mobile machines demonstrating various principles using specialized circuitry were nevertheless built in research labs. Starting in about 1950, W. Grey Walter, a British psychologist, built a series of electronic turtles, with subminiature tube electronics, that demonstrated behaviour resembling that of simple animals. The first version used rotating phototubes to locate and home on light sources, including one in a "recharging hutch", and responded to pressure on its shell with an avoidance reaction. Groups of such machines exhibited complex social behaviour by responding to one another's control lights and touches. He followed this with a more advanced machine also able to respond to light (by heading towards it), touch (by avoiding it) or a loud noise (by playing dead for a few seconds). Amazingly, this machine could be conditioned to associate one stimulus with another. For instance, after repeatedly being subjected to a loud noise followed by a kick to its shell, the robot would begin to execute an avoidance maneouvre on hearing a noise. The association was represented in the machine by a charge in a capacitor.

The Hopkins' Beast mentioned earlier inspired in the early 1960s a number of imitators at other universities. Some of their creations used special circuits connected to TV cameras instead of photocells, and were controlled by assemblies of (then new) transistor digital logic gates. Some added new motions such as "shake to untangle arm" to the repertoire of basic actions.

The first serious attempts to link computers to robots involved hand-eye systems, wherein a computer-interfaced camera looked down at a table where a mechanical manipulator operated. The earliest of these (c. 1965) were built while the small community of artificial intelligence researchers was still flushed with the success of the original AI programs— programs that almost on the first try played games, proved mathematical theorems and solved problems in narrow domains nearly as well as humans. The robot systems were seen as providing a richer medium for these thought processors. Some new problems arose.

A picture from a camera can be represented in a computer as a rectangular array of numbers, each representing the shade of gray or the colour of a point in the image (see also Chapter 3). A good quality picture requires a million

beacons and radar. A recent experiment by the Japanese ministry of highways demonstrated a computer-controlled car that used a pair of TV cameras mounted one above the other on the front bumper to drive on a roadway, tracking raised road edges and swerving around obstacles detected stereoscopically by the cameras. A Japanese manufacturer of earth-moving machinery has demonstrated an automatic truck driving system that can be programmed to travel along a route marked by scanning laser beacons. However, none of these systems works well enough to be trusted outside carefully monitored experiments.

One advanced idea that may bear fruit in the near future is that of a robot security guard. An American company, Denning Mobile Robotics Inc., is develo-

Above: ROBART I, built by Lt-Cdr Bart Everett USN, was conceived as a test bed for an autonomous mobile sentry robot. It is now a research vehicle at Naval Surface Weapons Center.

ping a machine that will wander the hallways of a prison, a warehouse or a large vault, stopping from time to time to "listen" with doppler motion sensors, infrared heat and motion detectors and other means for signs of human activity. It will be linked by radio to a base station that reports its findings like a fixed burglar alarm system. The advantages over a fixed system are a cheaper installation cost, and the ability to patrol areas difficult to cover with stationary sensors. The hardest problem is providing the robot with a means of navigating reliably such numbers. Identifying people, trees, doors, screwdrivers and teacups in such an undifferentiated mass of numbers is a formidable problem, and the first programs did not attempt it. Instead they were restricted to working with bright cubic blocks on a dark tabletop; a caricature of a toddler learning hand-eye coordination. In this simplified environment, computers more powerful than those that had earlier aced chess, geometry and calculus problems, combined with larger, more developed programs, were able sometimes, with luck, correctly to locate and grab a block.

The general hand-eye systems have now mostly evolved into experiments to study smaller parts of the problem, for example dynamics or force feedback, or into specialized systems for industrial applications. Most arm systems have special grippers, special sensors, and vision systems and controllers that work only in limited domains. Economics favours this, since a fixed arm, say on an assembly line, repetitively encounters nearly identical conditions. Methods that handle the frequent situations with

Above: The Johns Hopkins "Beast" has found a wall socket and is recharging its batteries. It was wired to feel for the socket after first catching sight of it with its photocell "eye" (top).

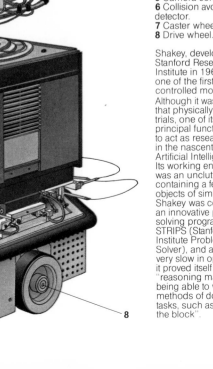

Shakey
1 Antenna for radio link.
2 Range finder.
3 Television camera.
4 Onboard logic unit.
5 Camera control unit.
6 Collision avoidance detector.
7 Caster wheel.
8 Drive wheel.

Shakey, developed at the Stanford Research Institute in 1969, was one of the first computer-controlled mobile robots. Although it was a machine that physically ran trials, one of its principal functions was to act as research tool in the nascent field of Artificial Intelligence. Its working environment was an uncluttered room containing a few solid objects of simple shape. Shakey was controlled by an innovative problem-solving program called STRIPS (Stanford Research Institute Problem Solver), and although very slow in operation, it proved itself a "reasoning machine" by being able to work out methods of doing simple tasks, such as "pushing the block".

maximum efficiency are preferred to more expensive general methods that deal with a wide range of circumstances that rarely arise, while performing less well on the common cases.

Shortly after cameras and arms were attached to computers, experiments with computer-controlled mobile robots began. The practical difficulties of instrumenting and keeping operational a remote-controlled, battery-powered, camera and video-transmitter-toting vehicle compounded the already severe practical problems with hand-eye systems, and conspired to keep many potential players out of the game.

The earliest successful result was Stanford Research Institute's Shakey (c. 1970). Although it existed as a sometimes functional physical robot, Shakey's primary impact was as a thought experiment. Its creators were of the first wave "reasoning machine" branch of AI, and were interested primarily in applying logic-based problem-solving methods to a real world task. Control and seeing were treated as system functions of the robot and relegated mostly to staff engineers and undergraduates. Shakey physically ran very rarely, and its "block world"-based vision system, which required that its environment contain only clean walls and a few large smooth prismatic objects, was coded inefficiently and ran very slowly, taking about an hour to find a block and a ramp in a simple scene. Shakey's most impressive performance, physically executed only piecemeal, was to "push the block" in a situation where it found the block on a platform. The sequence of actions included finding a wedge that could serve as a ramp, pushing it against the platform, then driving up the ramp onto the platform to push the block off.

The problems of operating a mobile robot, even in such a constrained environment, required the development of a powerful, and as yet unmatched, computer program—STRIPS—that constructed plans for robot tasks. STRIPS' plans were constructed out of primitive robot actions, each having preconditions for applicability and consequences on completion. It could recover from unexpected glitches by incremental replanning. The unexpected is one of the major distinguishing features of the world of a mobile entity and is one of the evolutionary pressures that channels the mobile towards intelligence.

Mobile robots require the development of an intelligence that is different from that suitable for fixed manipulators. Simple visual shape recognition methods are of little use to a machine that travels through a cluttered, three dimensional world. Precision mechanical control of position cannot be achieved by a vehicle that traverses rough ground. Special grippers do not pay off when many different and unexpected objects must be handled. Linear algorithmic control systems are not adequate for a rover that often encounters surprises in its wanderings.

The Stanford Cart

The Stanford University (as distinct from Stanford Research Institute) Cart was a mobile robot built at about the same time as Shakey, on a lower budget. From the start the emphasis of the Cart project was on low level perception and control rather than planning, and the Cart was used as a physical experimental testbed to guide the research. Until its retirement in 1980, it (or rather the large mainframe computer that controlled it remotely) was programmed to:
1. Follow a white line in real time using a TV camera mounted at about eye level on the robot. The program had to find the line in a scene that contained a lot of extraneous imagery, and could afford to digitize only a selected portion of the images it processed.
2. Travel down a road in straight lines using points on the horizon as references for its compass heading (the cart carried no instrumentation of any kind other than the TV camera). The program drove it in bursts of one to ten metres, punctuated by 15 second pauses to think about the images and plan the next move.
3. Go to desired destinations about 20 metres away (specified as so many metres forward and so many to the left) through messy obstacle courses of arbitrary objects, using the images from the camera to servo the motion and to detect (and avoid) obstacles in three dimensions.

Above: The Stanford Cart gained its knowledge of the world entirely from images broadcast by an onboard TV system. It negotiated an obstacle course at c3ft (1m) every 15 minutes.

With this program the robot moved in metre-long steps, thinking for about 15 minutes before each one. Crossing a large room or a loading dock took about five hours, the lifetime of a charge of the Cart's batteries.

The vision, world representation and planning methods that ultimately worked for the Cart were quite different from the "blocks world" and specialized industrial vision methods that grew out of the hand-eye efforts. Blocks world vision was completely inappropriate for the natural indoor and outdoor scenes encountered by the robot. Much experimentation with the Cart eliminated several other initially promising approaches that were insufficiently reliable when having to deal with voluminous and variable data from the robot. The product was a vision system with a different flavour than most. It was "low level" in that it did no object modelling, but by exploiting overlapping redundancies it could map its surroundings in 3D reliably from noisy and uncertain data. The reliability was necessary because Cart journeys typically consisted of twenty moves each a metre long punctuated by vision steps, and each step had to be accurate for the journey to succeed. The Cart research is being continued at Carnegie-Mellon University (CMU) with (so far) four different robots optimized for different parts of the effort.

Pluto, the first robot, was designed for maximum generality—its wheel system is omnidirectional, allowing motion in any direction while simultaneously permitting the robot to spin like a skater. It was planned that Pluto would continue the line of vision research established for the Cart and also support work in close-up navigation with a manipulator (a model task is a fully visually-guided procedure that permits the robot to find, open and pass through a door). The real world has changed the plans. The problem of

Below: Pluto (aka the CMU Rover) was designed to support a wide range of research in perception and control. Currently problems with the steering system have halted development.

controlling the three independently steerable and driveable wheel assemblies of Pluto is an example of a difficult, and so far unsolved, problem in control of overconstrained systems. It is being worked on, but in the meantime Pluto is nearly immobile.

When the difficulty with Pluto became apparent, a simple robot, Neptune, was built to carry on the long-range vision work. Built like a tricycle, powered and controlled (by a large computer) through a tether and seeing through a pair of television cameras, it is now able to cross a room in under an hour, five times more quickly than the Cart. Neptune has also been used to navigate by room maps inferred from measurements made by a

Above: The Terregator is Carnegie-Mellon's largest mobile robot. Unlike the others, which are electrically driven, Terregator is powered by a gasoline engine.

Below: One of the most distinctive features of Neptune is the ring of 24 wide-angle sonar ranging devices sited beneath two TV cameras. The cable leads to a DEC VAX 11/780 computer.

Above: This is JPL's conception of an intelligent Mars Rover. To help plan its route, it would have been equipped with stereo TV cameras, laser-ranging instruments and proximity sensors.

ring of 24 wide-angle sonar ranging devices. This sonar method is not as precise as vision, but requires about ten times less computation.

Uranus is the third robot in the CMU line, designed to do well the things Pluto has so far failed to do. It will achieve omnidirectionality through curious wheels, tyred with rollers at 45 degress, that, mounted like four wagon wheels, can travel forward and backward normally, but that screw themselves sideways when wheels on opposite sides of the robot are turned in opposite directions.

The fourth mobile robot at CMU is called the Terregator (terrestrial navigator) and is designed to travel outdoors for long distances. It is much bigger than the others, almost as large as a small car, and is powered by a gasoline generator rather than batteries. It is designed for long outdoor trips, and has so far travelled short distances along roads, visually tracking the road edges to stay on course. It should in time avoid and recognize outdoor obstacles and landmarks. The earlier work makes clear that in order to run at reasonable speeds (a few km/h) it will need computer speeds about 100 times faster than its medium size mainframes now provide. The regular machines will be augmented by a specialized computer called an array processor to achieve these rates.

Throughout the 1970s the Jet Propulsion Laboratory of the California Institute of Technology conducted research with a tethered mobile robot, called the RRV (for Robotic Research Vehicle), equipped with a laser rangefinder, a stereo pair of TV cameras and a robotic arm. The intent was to develop a system that would permit a robot operating on the surface of Mars to travel moderate distances without human supervision (which requires control from Earth and suffers from a time delay of about 30 minutes for the round trip). The project demonstrated programs that could locate rocks in front of the vehicle, drive around them, and pick them up. The work was suspended in 1978 when funding for a mission to follow the Viking Mars landings was cancelled.

Walking Machines

Above seventy per cent of the earth's land surface is inaccessible to existing vehicles, although much of it can be visited on horseback. The problem is one of footing. Wheels are a wonderful invention, but a wheel is only half a system—it requires smooth ground to work well. In comparing wheels with legs, one observes that a wheel makes no attempt to control its points of contact with the ground; it puts load on each section of ground in its path. A legged organism, on the other hand, can choose its points of contact, and adjust for irregularities in the terrain. On smooth, hard surfaces wheels are the most efficient form of locomotion. On more typical rough, natural terrain wheels can be arbitrarily inefficient, and the contest goes to legs.

Many toys that seem to walk have been invented, but these move their limbs in an automatic way, and do not exploit the potential advantages of controllable interactions with the ground. To walk in actuality requires a high order of knowledge of the immediate environment. Machines that walk in this latter sense have existed only since computers have become available to manage the massive measurement and decision-making processes needed.

A pioneer walking machine was the Quadruped Transporter or walking truck demonstrated by a research group in the General Electric company in 1968. Resembling an aluminium elephant, it

Below: Unlike wheeled vehicles, walking machines can intelligently adapt their gait to the terrain. This quadruped was created by Profs. Umetani and Hirose at the Tokyo Institute of Technology.

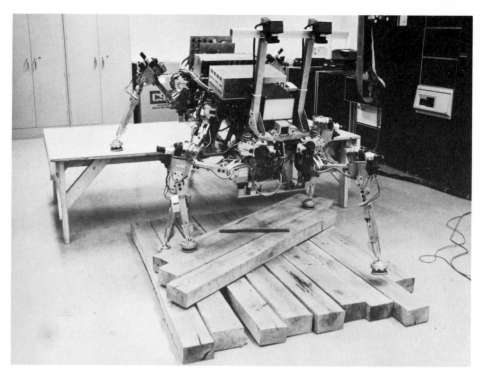

was powered by a gasoline engine driving a hydraulic compressor, and was controlled by a human strapped into an onboard assembly that amplified the motion of his arms and legs into the motion of the four legs of the vehicle. It was difficult to control, but at its best provided some very impressive demonstrations: building a platform and then climbing on it; moving a truck; not crushing an egg. It encouraged much later work in the field of more automatic legged machinery.

In the mid-1970s a group at the University of Moscow demonstrated control algorithms for six-legged walking machines that chose footholds given an incremental map of the forward terrain. The work proceeded to the construction of small tethered working models. Several small robot walkers have been constructed by Japanese researchers. One of the most successful was built at the Tokyo Institute of Technology. It looks like a

Above: The Hexapod shows off its paces in the lab at Ohio State University, where it was developed by Dr Robert McGhee. Current research into a more advanced vehicle is funded by DARPA.

breadbox-sized, four-legged spider. Each leg is a pantographic mechanism driven by three motors in the body, and it is controlled and powered through a tether. It walks slowly and only senses its environment through contact switches in its footpads. It is able to climb stairs and over obstacles and rough terrain by raising its foot until it no longer encounters a barrier, and conversely traverses depressions by lowering a foot until it contacts the ground.

The longest continuous line of walking machine research has been conducted since the late 1960s at Ohio State University. The OSU group has studied four-legged locomotion, but has worked primarily with six-legged machines. They have addressed problems of gait planning, force co-ordination, static and dynamic stability, foothold selection and a constellation of related problems. Their testbed for most of this work has been a six-legged, tethered, electric vehicle about the size of a desk but half as high, called the OSU Hexapod. The group is now working under a large DARPA (Defense Advanced Research Projects Agency) contract to build a much larger machine, dubbed the Adaptive Suspension Vehicle, or ASV, designed to traverse rough outdoor terrain, which will carry one passenger up front. Its six legs will be hydraulically actuated, with power coming from an onboard gasoline engine. DARPA hopes to merge a vehicle resulting from this line of development with the results of research into visual navigation and planning techniques that they also support, for a vehicle that can automatically move around in rough and hostile terrain. Further information about this programme will be found in the following chapter.

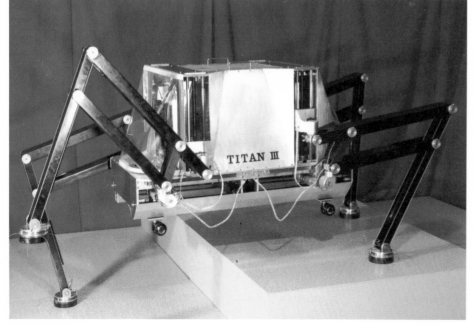

TITAN III

DARPA also supports a project at Carnegie-Mellon University, the principal researcher being Dr Marc Raibert, that is studying the problem of dynamic stability, or balance. The testbeds for this work have been a pair of one-legged hopping machines, powered by compressed air and small hydraulic actuators. The work has thus far concerned itself only with the problems of hopping from place to place and balancing on flat ground. The vision is to produce multi-legged machines that gallop and leap instead of just crawl.

The walking machine closest to commercial application was built by an engineering team at Odetics Inc., a California company best known for manufacture of tape recorders for spacecraft. The Odex-1 stands about 6·6ft (2m) tall, although its height varies depending on the configuration of its six spider-like legs. Each leg is controlled by three electric motors, two driving screws that control the leg's extension and height, and a third to swing the leg forward and back. With a few key positioning commands from a human via a radio remote controller, programs on computers onboard this impressive machine cause it to climb out of the truck in which it is delivered and then walk about a room. Odex-1 uses a tripod gait, alternately raising three legs (the translators) to advance, while the other three (the strokers) remain on the ground. It is strong enough to lift and drag its delivery truck, and dextrous enough to pick up, place and then stand on a hatbox-sized platform. Odetics hopes in time to produce an autonomous walking machine suitable for a wide range of applications; these are explored in greater detail in the following chapter.

Perception and Thought

The significance of mobile robot research may be much greater than the sum of its applications. There is a parallel between the evolution of intelligent living organisms and the development of robots. Many of the real-world constraints that shaped life by favouring one kind of evolutionary change over another in the contest for survival also affect the viability of robot characteristics. To a large extent, the incremental paths of development pioneered by living things are being followed by their technological imitators. Given this premise, there are lessons to be learned from the diversity of life. One is that mobile organisms tend to evolve in the direction of general intelligence, immobile ones do not. Plants are an example of the latter case, vertebrates an example of the former. An especially dramatic contrast is provided in an invertebrate phylum, the molluscs. Most are shellfish, like clams and oysters that move little and have tiny nervous systems and behaviours more like plants than

Right: Odex-1 was built as a technology demonstrator for a future generation of versatile, mobile "functionoids". It is impressively agile, its maximum step up or down being some 33in (100cm).

How Odex-1 Walks
1 Vertical motor.
2 Swing motor.
3 Extension motor.

Odex-1 has 18 motors onboard, three associated with each leg. The largest of the three causes vertical leg motion, while the other two control extension and swing, the latter enabling Odex to change course in mid-stride. The sequence of diagrams (right) shows the range of postures and extensions that Odex can achieve under this system. As well as climbing steps, Odex can change its profile to adapt to a variety of environments. Standing "tall" with articulators fully extended it is 78in (2m) high; in the squat position it is only 36in (91cm) high, and although this makes the distance between the legs 72in (1·8m), Odex can still walk in this position. In the tucked posture for minimum exposure, it is 48in (1·2m) tall, and 27in (69cm) wide.

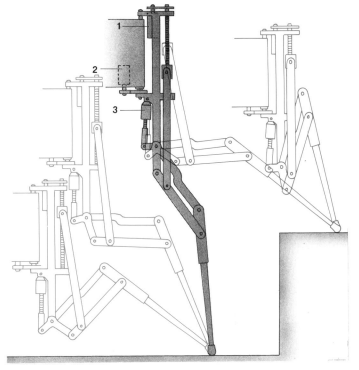

like animals. Yet they have relatives, the cephalopods, like octopus and squid, that are mobile and have developed independently many of the characteristics of vertebrates, including imaging eyes, large nervous systems and the behavioural ability to solve problems.

The twenty-year-old modern robotics effort can hardly hope to rival the billion year history of life on Earth in richness of example or profundity of result. Nevertheless the evolutionary pressures that shaped life are already palpable in the robotics labs. The following is a thought experiment that we hope soon to demonstrate with a physical machine. We want robots to be able to execute general tasks such as "go down the hall to the third door, go in, look for a cup and bring it back". This desire has created a pressing need—a computer language in which to specify concisely complex tasks for a rover, and a hardware and software system to embody it. Sequential control languages successfully used with industrial manipulators seemed a good starting point.

Paper attempts at defining the structures and primitives required for the mobile application revealed that the linear control structure of these state-of-the-art arm languages was inadequate for a rover. The essential difference is that a rover, in its wanderings, is regularly "surprised" by events it cannot anticipate, but with which it must deal. This requires that contingency routines be activated in arbitrary order, and run concurrently. One answer is a structure where a number of specialist programs, communicating via a common data structure called a blackboard, are active at the same time, some operating sensors, some controlling effectors, some integrating the results of other modules, and some providing overall direction. As conditions change, the priority of the various modules changes, and control may be passed from one to another.

Robot "Psychology"

Suppose we ask our future robot, equipped with a controller based on the blackboard system, in fact to go down the hall to the third door, go in, look for a cup and bring it back. This will be implemented as a process that looks very much like a program written for the arm control

languages (that in turn look very much like Algol, or Basic), except that the door recognizer routine would probably be activated separately. Consider the following caricature of such a program:

```
MODULE Go-Fetch-Cup
Wake up Door-Recognizer with
   instructions (On Finding-Door
   Add 1 to Door-Number Record
   Door-Location)
Record Start-Location
Set Door-Number to 0
While Door-Number < 3 Wall-Follow
Face-Door
IF Door-Open THEN Go-Through-
   Opening ELSE Open-Door-and-
   Go-Through
Set Cup-Location to result of
   Look-for-Cup
Travel to Cup-Location
Pickup-Cup at Cup-Location
Travel to Door-Location
Face-Door
IF Door-Open THEN Go-Through-
   Opening ELSE Open-Door-and-
   Go-Through
Travel to Start-Location
End
```

So far so good. We activate our program and the robot obediently begins to trundle down the hall counting doors. It correctly recognizes the first one. The second door, unfortunately is decorated with some garish posters, and the lighting in that part of the corridor is poor, and our experimental door recognizer fails to detect it. The wall-follower, however, continues to operate properly and the robot continues on down the hall, its door count short by one. It recognizes door 3, the one we had asked it to go through, but thinks it is only the second, so continues. The next door is recognized correctly, and is open. The program, thinking it is the third one, faces it and proceeds to go through. This fourth door, sadly, leads to the stairwell, and the poor robot, unequipped to travel on stairs, is in mortal danger.

Fortunately there is a process in our concurrent programming system called **Detect-Cliff** that is always running and that checks ground position data posted on the blackboard by the vision processes and also requests sonar and infra-red proximity checks on the ground. It combines these, perhaps with a high a-priori

Left: CMU researcher Kevin Dowling having set up an obstacle course for Neptune (foreground). The robot can cope with finding its way round static objects, but not a moving presence like the lab mascot, Truck the dog!

Below and right: These pictures show how Neptune views the world and plots its path across a cluttered room. Its twin video cameras scan the scene (below) and the computer assesses how far away are numerous "points of interest" in the room by stereoscopic comparison of the images, rather in the manner of human binocular vision. The computer then maps the scene, draws a circle around obstacles (right) to show minimum miss distances, and charts a safe path. The robot will then move, pause, and repeat the process.

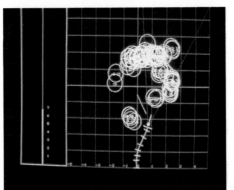

expectation of finding a cliff when operating in dangerous areas, to produce a number that indicates the likelihood there is a drop-off in the neighbourhood.

A companion process **Deal-with-Cliff** also running continuously, but with low priority, regularly checks this number, and adjusts its own priority on the basis of it. When the cliff probability variable becomes high enough the priority of **Deal-with-Cliff** will exceed the priority of the current process in control, **Go-Fetch-Cup** in our example, and **Deal-with-Cliff** takes over control of the robot. A properly written **Deal-with-Cliff** will then proceed to stop or greatly slow down the movement of the robot, to increase the frequency of sensor measurements of the cliff, and to back away from it slowly when it has been reliably identified and located.

Now there is a curious thing about this sequence of actions. A person seeing them, not knowing about the internal mechanisms of the robot might offer the interpretation: "First the robot was determined to go through the door, but then it noticed the stairs and became so frightened and preoccupied it forget all about what it had been doing". Knowing what we do about what really happened in the robot, we might be tempted to criticize the observer for using such sloppy anthropomorphic concepts as determinination, fear, preoccupation and forgetfulness in describing the actions of a machine. We could criticize, but we would be wrong.

The robot came by the emotions and foibles indicated as honestly as any living animal—the observed behaviour is the correct course of action for a being operating with uncertain data in an dangerous and uncertain world. An octopus in pursuit of a meal can be diverted by hints of danger, in just the way the robot was. An octopus also happens to have a nervous system that evolved entirely independently of our own vertebrate version. Yet most of us feel no qualms about ascribing concepts like passion, pleasure, fear and pain to the actions of the animal.

We have in the behaviour of the vertebrate, the mollusc and the robot a case of convergent evolution. The needs of the mobile way of life have conspired in all three instances to create an entity that has modes of operation for different circumstances, and that changes quickly from one mode to another on the basis of uncertain and noisy data prone to misinterpretation.

Among the natural traits on the immediate horizon for roving robots is parameter adjustment learning. A precision mechanical arm in a rigid environment can usually have its kinematic self-model and its dynamic control parameters adjusted once permanently. A mobile robot bouncing around in the muddy world will probably always suffer from problems like dirt build-up, tyre wear, frame bends and small mounting bracket slips that mess up accurate a-priori models. Existing visual obstacle course software, for instance, specifies a camera calibration phase where the robot is parked precisely in front of an exact grid of spots so that a program can determine a function that corrects for distortions in the camera optics. This allows other programs to make precise visual angle measurements in spite of distortions in the cameras. The present code is very sensitive to miscalibrations, and we are working on a method that will calibrate the cameras continuously just from the images perceived on normal trips through clutter.

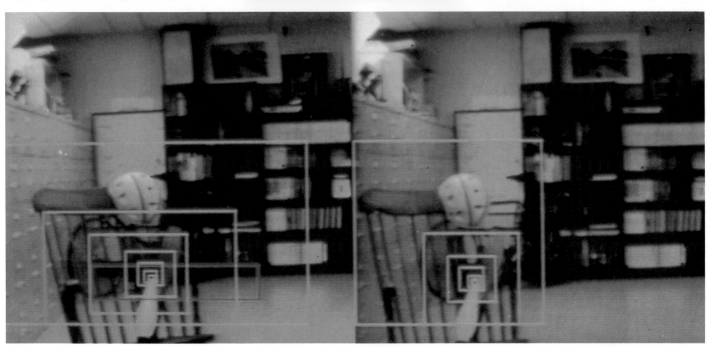

With such a procedure in place, a bump that slightly shifts one of the robot's cameras will no longer cause systematic errors in its navigation. Animals seem to tune most of their nervous systems with processes of this kind, and such accommodation may be a precursor to more general kinds of learning.

Perhaps more controversially, the beginnings of self-awareness can be seen in robots. All of the control programs in more advanced mobile robots have internal representations, at varying levels of abstraction and precision, of the world around the robot, and of the robot's position within that world. The motion planners work with these world models in considering alternative future actions for the robot. If the programs had verbal interfaces one could ask questions that might receive answers such as "I turned right because I didn't think I could fit through the opening on the left". As it is, the same information is often presented in the form of pictures drawn by the programs.

So What's Missing?

There may seem to be a contradiction implicit in the various figures that describe the speed of computers. Once billed as "Giant Brains", computers can do some things, such as arithmetic, millions of times faster than human beings. "Expert systems" doing qualitative reasoning in narrow problem-solving areas run on these computers approximately at human speed. Yet it takes such a computer an hour visually to guide a robot across a

large room. How can the discrepancy apparent in such numbers be reconciled?

The human evolutionary record provides the clue. While our sensory and muscle control systems have been in development for millions of years, and common sense reasoning has been honed for probably about a million, really high level, deep thinking is little more than a parlour trick, culturally developed over a few thousand years, which a few humans, operating largely against their natures, can learn. As with Samuel Johnson's famous aphorism comparing a woman preaching to a dog walking on its hind legs, what is amazing is not how well it is done, but that it is done at all!

Computers can challenge humans in intellectual areas where humans perform inefficiently, because they can be programmed to function less wastefully. An extreme example is arithmetic, a function learned by humans with great difficulty, which is instinctive to computers. These days an average computer can add without error a million large numbers in a second, which is more than a million times faster than a person. Yet one hundred millionth of the neurons in a human brain, if reorganized into an adder using switching logic design principles, could sum a thousand numbers per second. If the whole brain were organized this way, it could do sums one hundred thousand times faster than the computer.

Computers do not challenge humans in perceptual and control areas because these functions, which have evolved over many million years, are carried out by a large proportion of the nervous system operating as efficiently as the hypothetical neuron adder above. Present day computers, however efficiently programmed, are simply too puny to keep up. Evidence comes from the most extensive piece of reverse engineering yet done on the vertebrate brain, the functional decoding of some of the visual system by D.H. Hubel, T.N. Weisel and colleagues.

The vertebrate retina's 20 million neurons take signals from a million light sensors and combine them in a series of simple operations to detect things like edges, curvature and motion. The image thus processed is transmitted to the much bigger visual cortex in the brain. Assuming

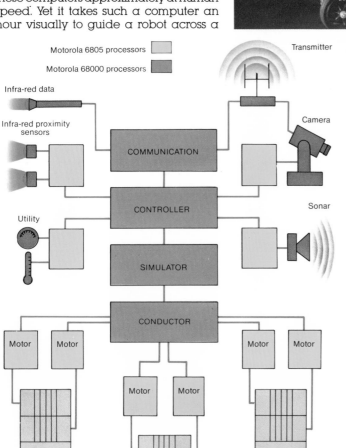

Motorola 6805 processors
Motorola 68000 processors

Infra-red data

Infra-red proximity sensors

Transmitter

Camera

COMMUNICATION

CONTROLLER

Utility

SIMULATOR

Sonar

CONDUCTOR

Motor Motor Motor Motor

Motor Motor

Pluto Onboard Processors
This block diagram shows the interrelationship of the processors that control a mobile robot, in this instance CMU's Pluto. Pluto is moved by 3 independently steerable wheel assemblies, each consisting of a drive motor and a steering motor with associated shaft encoders. The motor sequencing signals come directly from onboard microprocessors (one for each motor) which servo the motor to produce the desired motion, as instructed by the *conductor* processor. Another processor, the *simulator*, monitors the shaft encoder outputs and torques from all the motors to maintain a dead-reckoned model of the robot's position. The results are compared with the desired position as defined by the *controller* processor, and the conductor tries to adjust the rates of single motors to bring the simulator in line with the controller. The other processors are as follows: *communications*, to maintain an IR link with the main VAX 11/780 controlling computer; *sonar*, to control collision-avoidance sonar ranging devices; *camera*, to control TV camera pan, tilt and slide motors; *proximity*, to monitor short-range IR proximity sensors; and *utility*, to check conditions such as motor temperature and battery voltage.

Above left: Another CMU machine – Jim Crowley's Intelligent Mobile Platform is a prototype of an intelligent navigation system. The "horn" is a rotating sonar ranging device.

Below: One advantage of mobility is that it will enable a robot to work in a hostile environment; this is a Japanese design for a robot to decommission nuclear power stations.

the visual cortex does as much computing for its size as the retina, we can estimate the total capability of the system. The optic nerve has a million signal-carrying fibres and the optical cortex is a thousand times deeper than the neurons which do a basic retinal operation. The eye can process ten images a second, so the cortex handles the equivalent of 10,000 simple retinal operations a second, or 3 million an hour.

An efficient program running on a typical computer can do the equivalent work of a retinal operation in about two minutes, for a rate of 30 per hour. Thus, seeing programs on contemporary computers seem to be 100,000 times slower

than vertebrate vision. The whole brain is about ten times larger than the visual system, so it should be possible to write real-time human equivalent programs for a machine one million times more powerful than today's medium-sized computers. Even today's largest supercomputers are about 1,000 times slower than this desideratum. How long will it be before our research medium is rich enough for full intelligence?

Faster Computers

Since the 1950s, computers have gained in speed by a factor of 1,000 per constant dollar every decade. There are enough

developments in the technological pipeline, and certainly enough human determination, to continue this pace for the forseeable future. The processing power available to AI programs has not increased proportionately. Hardware speed-ups and budget increase have been dissipated on convenience features: operating systems, time sharing, high-level languages, compilers, graphics, editors, mail systems, networking, personal machines, etc. and have been spread more thinly over ever greater numbers of users. I believe this hiatus in the growth of processing power explains the disappointing pace of AI in the past 15 years, but nevertheless represents a good investment. Now that basic computing facilities are widely available, and thanks largely to the initiative of the instigators of the Japanese Supercomputer and Fifth Generation Computer projects, attention worldwide is focusing on the problem of processing power for AI.

The new interest in "crunch" power should ensure that AI programs share in the thousandfold per decade increase from now on. This puts the time for achieving human equivalence at twenty years. The smallest vertebrates, shrews and hummingbirds, are capable of interesting behaviour employing nervous systems one ten thousandth the size of a human's, so we can expect fair motor and perceptual competence in less than a decade. Robot programs now are similar in power to insects' control systems.

Some principal researchers in the Japanese Fifth Generation Computer Project have been quoted as planning "man capable" systems in ten years. I believe that this more optimistic projection is unlikely, but not impossible. The fastest computers now in use or in development, notably the Cray X-MP and the Cray 2, compute at 1,000 million operations/ second, only 1,000 times too slowly. As the computers become more powerful and as research in this area becomes more widespread, the rate of visible progress should accelerate. I think artificial intelligence via the "bottom up" approach of technological evolution comparable to the evolution of mobile animals is the surest bet, because the existence of independently evolved intelligent nervous systems indicates that an incremental route to intelligence does actually exist. It is also possible, of course, that the more traditional "top down" approach will achieve its goals, growing from the narrow problem solvers of today into the much harder areas of learning, common-sense reasoning and perceptual acquistion of knowledge as computers become large and powerful enough, and the necessary techniques are mastered. Most likely both approaches will make enough progress that they can meet effectively somewhere in the middle, for a grand synthesis into a true artificial sentience.

Left: The Cray 1-S/2000, here being tested for hot spots, is an example of today's high-speed supercomputers. Does AI depend upon even greater crunch power for its evolution?

A major stimulus to the "emancipation" of the robot from the factory floor is its ability to work in a hostile environment, be it ocean bed, nuclear power plant, or even battlefield.

OUTSIDE THE FACTORY

The fact that virtually all the robots so far produced have been set to work in factories should not blind us to their other potential applications. As robotics technology improves—and as people become more familiar with such devices—robots will become accepted in many everyday areas of life outside the world's workshops. The robots of this generation will be markedly different from those that toil away painting or welding in factory applications. They will be mobile (using wheels, tracks or legs) and will contain efficient sensor mechanisms so that they can react instantaneously to external events. While industrial robots usually mount just one arm and associated gripper, the machines that become common outside engineering plants may well be multi-armed to permit greater flexibility of manoeuvre.

According to a report issued by SRI International, an R&D company in Menlo Park, California, potential applications for this kind of robot exist in many diverse industries. They include mining, nuclear power, agriculture, cargo handling, forestry, medicine, fire fighting, commercial surveillance and police work. The study was commissioned by Odetics Inc, a Californian firm that has developed a six-legged robot that it hopes could be adapted to serve these kinds of industries.

Japan, which has come from behind the US and Western Europe to take over the mantle as the world's top robot-using country, is particularly keen on novel applications for robots. The country's Ministry of International Trade and Industry has started several schemes to encourage the development of such machines. Prof Yukio Hasegawa, a robotics expert at Waseda University and an adviser to MITI, has attempted to forecast when robots of this type will start to find their way into certain industries. In a paper in 1981, he suggested that 1985 would see the entry of robots into areas such as oceanography, atomic energy, medicine and fire-fighting. Robots in the construction and mining industries might start to appear two years later.

In 1983 the Agency of Industrial Science and Technology (AIST) of the Japanese government started a £63m, eight-year programme to develop advanced robot technology. The project is designed to

Right: Scorpio, an underwater remotely operated vehicle designed for drill rig support, illustrates how a machine can relieve man of dangerous tasks in a hostile environment.

Below: In a Japanese research project, students and trainee nurses monitor the heartbeat, respiration and blood pressure of an android "patient" which responds to correct resuscitation and artificial respiration techniques.

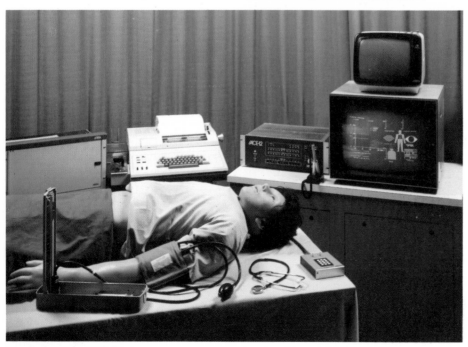

develop advanced robots that "perform tasks in place of man in hazardous working environments such as in nuclear plants, deep sea environments and disaster stricken areas." Dr Shogo Sakakura, the AIST councillor for technological affairs, pointed out in 1984 the benefits that the Japanese hope the programme will provide. "In hazardous areas such as nuclear plants, people can often work in jobs such as maintenance only for one hour a day. A robot would be able to work 24 hours a day, seven days a week. As for activities deep in the sea, people cannot work in such environments at all."

A key group of workers in the Japanese project are at the Ministry of International Trade and Industry's Mechanical Engineering Laboratory in Tsukuba City, near Tokyo. The researchers are working on four- and six-legged walking machines that can function in rough terrains.

A forecast in 1981 by Survey Japan, a company of consultants in Tokyo, produced this detailed list of areas into which the novel kinds of robots would enter (which echoes SRI's findings):

1. Agriculture: spraying of chemicals, fruit harvesting, farming, milking, disposal of animal excreta.
2. Forestry: felling, trimming, gathering and moving timber, fertilizing, planting.
3. Mining: underground pitwork.
4. Civil engineering: drilling, blasting, work at heights.
5. Social welfare: assisting and guiding blind people, rehabilitation of physically handicapped, assisting nurses, firefighting, rescue work, cleaning.
6. Public services: loading/unloading of ships, cleaning windows of public buildings.
7. Nuclear power stations: maintenance, disposal of radioactive waste.

8. Marine development: exploring deep-sea resources, rig construction, observation above or below sea.

A common theme in all these applications is that the jobs to be done by the robots are either difficult or extremely dangerous for people. Take, for example, the cleaning of the hulls of ships. This is a task which is essential to keep the fabric of vessels free from encrustations of dirt or of sea creatures, such as barnacles. For a person, the job is highly unpleasant and can be risky. As a result, people who clean hulls in this way command high wages; there is thus a corresponding economic reason for engineers to develop machines that will do the same job and so save on overheads that would otherwise by incurred by shipping fleets.

Down the Tubes

Outside the nuclear business, the scope for the introduction of mobile robots in general industry has been limited. Underground or pipeline operations are one fairly obvious area for operation of such machines. British Gas has, for instance, developed systems known as "intelligent pigs" that inspect gas transmission pipelines while they are in service. The devices are propelled by gas pressure along the insides of pipes, typically on a 50 mile (80km) run. They record data about the pipes' integrity and are afterwards retrieved and sent for analysis of the information in a laboratory. Two types of instruments are used: magnetic probes to detect loss of metal in pipe walls and ultrasonic devices to locate cracks in the structure of the pipes.

In areas of military work, it often goes without saying that a task is unpleasant or dangerous, and thus it would be prefer-

Above: Engineers in Japan are among the world leaders in development of remote-controlled vessels that move along the sea bed, eg. to collect information for geological surveys.

Below: This Japanese-built self-propelled machine performs a useful job in crawling over a tiled surface to sense where tiles are becoming detached from a building's exterior walls.

The "Intelligent Pig"
1 Cleaning bristles.
2 Pressure vessel for data acquisition unit.
3 Vehicle coupling.
4 Distance wheels.
5 Support wheels.
6 Pressure vessel for tape recorder and battery pack.
7 Drive cup.
8 Drive cup.
9 Sensor rings.

10 Magnets under bristles (to collect any ferrous debris in the pipeline).

This drawing shows the basic configuration of the robot device that British Gas has developed to carry out on-line inspection of its 10,000 miles (16,000km) of gas transmission pipeline in the United Kingdom. The pig is propelled down the pipe by gas pressure; a typical run being 50

miles (80km). As it moves, complex on-board equipment transmits magnetic and ultrasonic signals at the pipeline walls, and sensors detect and record any anomalies that might reveal the presence of a structural defect. A typical run will produce some 500 million individual inspection readings, the whole process being controlled by on-board computers. After retrieval, the recorded tapes are taken to the laboratory for computer analysis.

Below: British Gas has developed a series of vehicles—"intelligent pigs" —for on-line inspection of pipelines. This is a 24in (600mm) diameter vehicle about to be launched down the pipeline at a pig trap installation.

able for a machine (if it can be given the skills and sensitivity of a man or woman) to do it. A machine would not be predominantly concerned with attempting to preserve its "life" when going about tasks such as mine sweeping or surveillance behind enemy lines. If the military robot were destroyed, it would be a relatively simple matter for its masters to replace it with another. Furthermore, it would probably be far easier to shield such a machine with protective devices than it would a person.

Some jobs are not hazardous, so much as arduous or boring—to such a degree that there are simply not enough people to do them properly. One example is the assistance that people who are physically handicapped require. Such men and women may require constant help if they are unable to exercise proper control over their limbs. It would be possible to employ a human helper to be continually on call, but the job would be physically and psychologically demanding in the extreme. A mechanical creation which could provide a second (or third, or even fourth) pair of limbs to help a handicapped person would be an invaluable invention. If the machines could be produced sufficiently cheaply, they could be made available as a matter of course to all people who suffered from severe physical handicaps, such as cerebral palsy.

The more sophisticated robots to be considered in this chapter will not become common until at least the 1990s. Development of the machines will require advances in five key areas of technology:
Sensors. Devices such as TV cameras or touch sensors will relay detailed information about what is taking place around the machine to the master computers.

The sensors will discriminate between "background" data that is of only limited interest, and more specific information that is of use to the machine in plotting its next action. A mobile machine, for example, would need to know the shape and position of obstacles in its path. The sensors, in the form of high-resolution cameras or range finders, would have to supply the information quickly enough for the machine to take avoiding action.

End effectors. These are the devices that respond to signals sent from the machine's supervisory computers in order to carry out a specific sequence of actions. The end effectors might be grippers on the end of arms (as in today's factory robots) or propulsion devices such as wheels or (for underwater applications) flippers and thrusters. The hardware would have to be capable of very sensitive actions. For example, when fruit picking, harvesting, or assisting handicapped people,

Left: With an unmanned inspection vehicle called SCORPEE, marine engineers can obtain TV pictures of the sides of ship's hulls and other inaccessible undersea objects.

Below: The COBRA end effector, developed by the UK Atomic Energy Authority's Culham Laboratory, can perform inspection tasks inside nuclear power station reactor vessels.

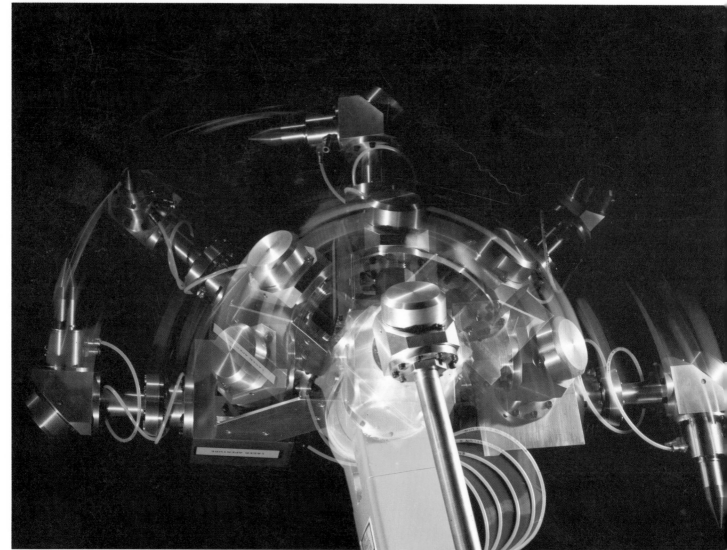

Right: Taylor Hitec and Vision Engineering, two British companies, have developed this stereo TV system for use in the nuclear engineering industry.

the end effectors would have to perform extremely delicate operations that require some skill on the part of a human.

Computers. The machines would be controlled not just by one computer but by a hierarchy of electronic systems, each of them responsible for some specific element of the robot's activities. Today's industrial robots usually undertake pre-determined tasks according to a fixed program of instructions written into the memory of the robot before it begins its operations. The robots that work outside factories might contain similar sets of instructions but these programs would be activated not by commands from human operators but by signals sent from computers near the top of the supervisory hierarchy. These computers would work out campaigns of action on the basis of information from the outside world supplied by the sensors. In this way, for instance, a machine at work in a fire-fighting application could calculate (using information supplied by heat-sensing devices) the location of the centre of a blaze and direct jets of water at it.

The computers in the system would differ from the electronic systems common today in two main ways. First, they would process information extremely rapidly to assess the value of data channelled from perhaps tens, or even hundreds, of sensory sources before sending the results of this evaluation to end effectors. The computers would probably work by what is known as parallel processing; they would simultaneously process dozens of streams of data (rather in the fashion of the human brain which can "think" about several different matters at once). In contrast, the computers available in the mid 1980s generally process data serially: just one stream at a time. The second innovation is that the computers would contain in their memories information equivalent to the general knowledge that human beings carry around in their brains. This information would help the machines to work out what to do in specific circumstances. To return to the example of the fire-fighting robot, the machine would have to know the differences between tackling a blaze in a car and one in a house. It would therefore have to know, in terms of their rough dimensions and layout, general information about cars and houses. In a discipline of computer science known as knowledge engineering, researchers are drawing up mechanisms for introducing into computer memories this kind of information.

Control strategies. It is not enough for computers to draw up strategies for coping with specific sets of circumstances. Some way must be found of translating the strategy into an effective response. Furthermore, the delay in transmitting messages in the right sequence to the robot's end effectors must be negligible. If this is not the case, by the time the instructions for the response have been transmitted and received, events in the outside world will have changed to such a degree that a new batch of instructions would be required. The robot would run the risk of reacting to information that is always slightly out of date. So engineers are faced with having to formulate techniques to transmit information not only quickly, but also efficiently. The data would be required to travel along internal message channels (analogous to the nerves in people's bodies) to the correct end effector to carry out a specific programme of action. Researchers would also have to work out the correct form of instructions to initiate a programme of

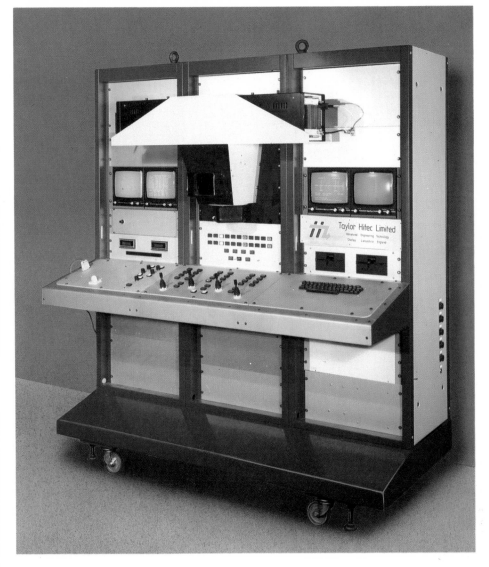

Left: In a system devised by Taylor Hitec to inspect the interior of a nuclear plant, an operator employs stereo TV to guide a remote manipulator from this control unit.

action that involves several end effectors. In a walking machine, for example, the different legs of the hardware must act in coordination to make the robot move in the required direction at a specific speed.

Ease of application. The sort of "extramural" robots that we are considering will not be totally autonomous. Operators will have to be able to intervene, at least intermittently, to change a pattern of activity or to give new instructions that might override whatever the machine is working out for itself. There will, therefore, have to be straightforward ways in which a human controller can communicate with the machine. The conventional way in which people interact with a computer is by a keyboard, but quicker and more accessible techniques will be required in the future if robots are to become useful in wider areas of application. For example, it may become possible for people to give broad instructions to machines simply by talking to them. This would require computers to be able to respond to voice recognition programs which would enable electronic mechanisms to translate spoken messages into sets of binary digits that computers can understand.

Full development of the technologies described above will take at least a decade to accomplish. In many cases, more immediate non-factory applications of robots will come about by experimentation with teleoperator systems and their associated manipulator arms. Such a teleoperator may be on wheels or tracks, and could be capable of moving with great precision to do just the kind of jobs performed by robots. What sets teleoperators (also called telechirs) apart from robots is that each action of the manipulator is controlled by a simultaneous action performed by a human operator. While a robot can be left to

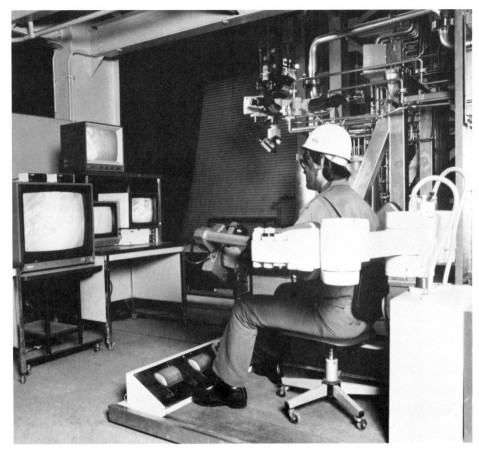

perform a set routine in the absence of a human controller, a teleoperator needs a person continually to control its actions.

Teleoperators have been put to work in some areas of industry (in nuclear power plants for example) for over three decades. They are usually activated by one of three types of master control:

Replica master. The operator moves a master arm through a sequence of movements which is replicated by a slave arm. It is the latter that carries out a job of work, perhaps a maintenance operation in a hazardous environment such as a chemical plant.

Switch box control. The slave arm moves in response to electrical signals sent from a simple control unit. For instance, move-

Above: Operating a telechir under remote control is a skilled task. Here a technician at the Tokai Reprocessing Plant in Japan works a two-armed bilateral servomanipulator

ment of one switch would cause the arm to move to the right or left; another would control speed of action; a further switch would adjust the position of a gripper located at the end of the arm. This form of control is relatively inflexible and would not be suitable for jobs in which great precision of movement is required.

Joystick control. Here the operator controls the telechir in a similar way to a pilot operating the control surfaces of an aeroplane—by a series of movements with a small stick. This is superior to switch box control because coordinated motions can be made using computer guidance to accomplish movement.

A vital element of teleoperator systems is the communications link, be it a cable, radio or fibre optic, between the person in control and the machine itself. As important as the downlink signals are those coming back the other way. These relay to the human operator information about the immediate surroundings. Normally they derive from one or more TV cameras that send pictures of objects near the machine to the human controller. Other signals can be sent—for instance, sounds or X-ray images. In theory, it is possible to provide the operator with enough information to enable him to visualize the situation as though he were actually at the scene where the manipulator is functioning. Such a state of affairs is very much a current research goal: workers in the US are particularly interested in providing such "telepresence"

Below: Engineers at the Harwell laboratory of the UK Atomic Energy Authority developed a machine called ROMAN that trundles on caterpillar tracks around hazardous areas. ROMAN is joystick-controlled by a supervisor

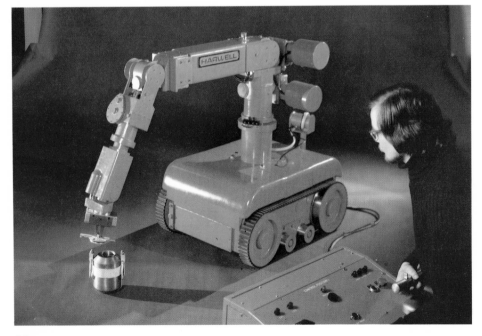

to the people in charge of teleoperators used in future space activities (see also chapter 7).

Apart from nuclear work, the main applications of teleoperators are military (such as bomb disposal), undersea operations, and activities in outer space. In all these cases, people require machines to perform difficult tasks in locations that are unpleasant or hazardous for human operators. Significant research is now taking place to develop teleoperators endowed with some form of autonomy. Examples include underwater craft that relay TV pictures to shore about, for

instance, pipelines or shipwrecks. With this sort of internal control, a teleoperator begins to resemble a true robot.

There may, indeed, be some advantage in blurring the division between telechirs and true robots. Machines that can switch between autonomous operation and direct human control may actually turn out to be more useful than either of the two pure kinds of device. Such items of hardware are called hybrid robots. They would operate in a manner analogous to sheepdogs, spending large amounts of their day working independently by using their own senses and instincts, yet still

Top: CURV III is an underwater recovery vehicle developed by the Naval Undersea Center, San Diego. It is here being hoisted aboard a cable repair ship in readiness for its attempt to rescue the submarine Pisces III disabled with two men aboard in August 1973.

Above left: The rescue of Pisces III, stranded 1,450ft deep, is underway and CURV III is about to attach a line.

Above: CURV III (cable-controlled underwater recovery vehicle) is seen aboard a launch/recovery platform.

under the supervisory control of a human master who at specific moments may give his charges broad instructions on strategic matters—for example, on which flock of sheep to attend to, or the general direction in which he wants the animals to be herded.

Robert Frosch, a former administrator of NASA who is now in charge of General Motors' research laboratories in Michigan, is one of the champions of hybrid robots. He is chiefly concerned with the potential of these machines to work in space but his remarks apply equally well for other robot tasks. Frosch wrote in the September 1983 issue of "Spectrum", the journal of the Institute of Electrical and Electronic Engineers:

"There is a kind of schism, a schizophrenia, in the space community about people and machines. There has been a split historically between those who insist on doing everything in space with people and those who insist on doing everything with machines. But there has been remarkably little work done on how people can work with machines in space ... It is not necessary to assume that the machines one uses are either perfectly intelligent or completely unintelligent, and it is not that people are necessarily more reliable or less reliable than machines. However, the human-machine combination is more reliable than either of them alone. We have in fact the hybrid possibility of a few intelligent people working with a very large number of moderately clever machines."

Military work is one key area in which teleoperator and hybrids are already being used. And military engineers are hard at work developing true robots that will have applications both on battlefields and in behind-the-scenes activities such as surveillance. A special segment of military work where such machines have applications concerns bomb disposal.

These devices have been developed in the past decade in response to one of the banes of late 20th Century life: urban terrorism. Until unmanned vehicles came on the bomb disposal scene, the job had to be done solely by hand—an especially hazardous job. However, IRA terrorist

Below: Scout, a British unmanned vehicle for bomb disposal, can wheel up to a terrorist device and destroy the detonator with a shotgun.

activity in Northern Ireland greatly stimulated the development of technologies to deal with bombs remotely. The British Army has developed expertise in using teleoperators to reduce the hazard to bomb-disposal officers. This experience, in turn, has spawned several companies in Britain and Eire that sell bomb-disposal hardware of this kind—not only to the British Army but to police and military forces all over the world that have to deal with similar types of explosive device.

Common to all the machines is that they carry TV cameras and manipulators, and are controlled by an operator via cable or radio link. In a typical incident, a bomb is discovered and its location plotted. Before the advent of such machines, a bomb-squad officer would advance and attempt to defuse the bomb by hand by removing items manually, perhaps lifting off a cover shielding the device, and then destroying the detonator.

Left: Wheelbarrow, a bomb-disposal vehicle made by Morfax, has seen extensive use in Northern Ireland. The equipment used with it (below) includes a closed circuit TV monitor, shotgun for explosive detonation, a variety of booms and grab mechanisms, coils of tow rope and cable, and the hand set by which it is controlled (centre left).

This last task is usually accomplished by one of two methods. The officer either attempts to disconnect the detonator, which involves him in delicate and dangerous manipulative operations, or he destroys the whole device in a controlled explosion.

Bomb Disposal

Using a teleoperator, the task becomes less hazardous. The bomb-disposal operator remains at a safe distance from the explosive device, normally around 100 metres. The machine, whether wheeled or tracked, is driven towards the location of the explosive. It is normally powered by electricity, either from a mains supply, a generator, or on-board batteries. Once at the scene, the machine transmits via a TV camera pictures of the bomb to the operator, who can instruct the robot to lift parts of the explosive device with manipulators or, alternatively, to remove coverings that might be in the way. Once the machine has a clear sight of the detonator of the bomb, the operator can manoeuvre it into the correct position such that it can destroy the mechanism with a shotgun or similar means.

The dominant company in the world in bomb-disposal teleoperators is Morfax, based in London. Since 1975, the company has sold a teleoperator called Wheelbarrow which was developed originally by the British Army for use in Northern Ireland. The invention was a joint effort by the Military Vehicles Experimental Establishment, a Ministry of Defence research base in Chobham, Surrey, and the Royal Army Ordnance Corps. As an established MoD contractor, Morfax gained a licence to make Wheelbarrow. It has sold about 500 of the machines, including about 100 to the British Army and the Metropolitan Police (the London police force, which has its own bomb squad). The remainder of the devices have been sold to army and police departments in some 40 countries. The

biggest customers are in Western Europe and the Middle East.

Wheelbarrow has no ability to act autonomously; every action must be initiated by the human operator. Morfax says there is no necessity to build into the machine any element of computer control. This is because terrorists' devices always differ from one another, even in the smallest detail. It is better to let the bomb-squad officer decide how to tackle a specific explosive device, rather than to instruct the machine in a set routine for dealing with bombs.

Wheelbarrow travels on tracks and is mobile enough to go up stairs and turn round tight corners. It sells for about £23,000 ($25,000), including a set of standard equipment such as manipulators. Several other companies have emerged as competitors to Morfax in this area. Their offerings are all basically similar, though the machines may travel on wheels and (rather than carry electric batteries, as is the case with Wheelbarrow) receive electric power via the control cable. Among the competitors to Wheelbarrow is Hunter, made by the Sas Group of Beaconsfield and Hadrian, made by Monitor Engineers of Wallsend. Hadrian and Hunter were both on duty at the Los Angeles Olympic Games in 1984, where they were on stand-by to deal with any terrorist bombs.

Two other machines are Scout (made by Vale Security, a Wantage company) and Ro-Veh, which is sold by Analytical Instruments of Cambridge. Both machines are smaller and lighter than Wheelbarrow and more easily transportable—they can fit into the boot of a car. Hobo, sold by Kentree of County Cork in Eire, operates on wheels (as do Hadrian and Hunter).

Odetics Inc, a company in California, is one of the leaders in efforts to build military robots that are truly autonomous. The company has in mind a range of applications for its machines—they include bomb disposal as well as other

Left: Another type of remote-controlled machine, called HOBO, is operated by a bomb-disposal expert who remains well out of harm's way.

Below: HOBO deploys an extensible arm and gripper with which it can grab suspicious-looking objects, taking them away for disposal.

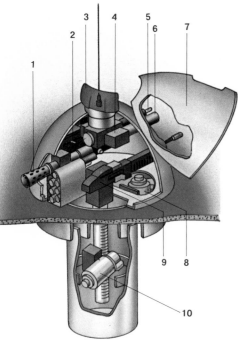

Robot Gun Emplacement
1 Recoilless anti-tank weapon.
2 Communications and control.
3 Target acquisition radar.
4 Target discrimination black box.
5 Laser rangefinder.
6 40mm grenade launcher.
7 Ordance access door.
8 Azimuth control.

9 7·62mm machine gun.
10 Turret elevation control.

In a document entitled *AirLand Battle 2000* the US Army has outlined its operational concepts for 21st Century warfare. Robot weapons, such as this unmanned anti-tank/personnel battle station, are envisaged.

activities such as sentry duty, the placing and detection of mines and general work on a battlefield.

The philosophy of designing machines to work under fire in military conflicts was outlined by Daniel Leonard, a US Navy researcher, at a conference in 1981:

"The violent nature of future conflicts naturally leads to the idea of getting somebody else or some other thing to go in harm's way, and that thought leads to remotely controlled devices, teleoperators and robotics, or what might be called remotely located weaponry (RLW). This combat role represents a different type of role for RLW which requires a different kind of approach to the design problem. Industrial robots are generally designed to operate in a benign environment to perform those jobs which are physically demanding, either from the standpoint of strength or precision required, or those jobs which are extremely boring or tedious... Battlefield RLWs should be built with the expectation that they will be destroyed, which says the cost is a major design consideration. These robots should be rugged but not necessarily superhardened."

Odetics has listed a number of types of robot that could operate on a battlefield:
1. Vehicle Recovery Aid: this would be a highly mobile, dextrous system capable of ground movement to travel to the scene of damaged vehicles and tow them to safety.
2. Multi-Purpose Manipulators: handling support systems, for use in jobs such as moving ammunition, transfer of bridge sections in engineering work.

Above: The Canadair CL-227 is a small VTOL remotely piloted vehicle designed for military target acquisition and reconnaissance. Its sensors include daylight and low light TV, laser designator, thermal imager, radiation detector and decoy equipment. Mission duration is 3 hours.

3. Mine Emplacer: to plant mines.
4. Mine Clearer: to remove them.
5. Smoke Layer: mobile machines to move to predetermined positions and emit smoke to confuse enemy forces.
6. Infantry Precursor: would move ahead of human forces to spot opposing infantry divisions, draw fire and report back.
7. Combat Porter: small cargo transportation duties, for example the removal from the battlefield of injured soldiers.
8. Heavy Fighting Sentry: robot would have weapons and sensors necessary to engage enemy armour and light weapons for close-in fighting.
9. Infantry Robotic Grenade: the machine would be given brief instructions from a soldier, move rapidly to a target and detonate an explosive payload.
10. Ground Observer/Designator: to observe areas of battlefield activity and alert commanders when enemies appear.
11. Tactical Reconnaissance Robot: for autonomous surveillance missions behind enemy lines.
12. Street Walker Scout: to check ahead of army units in urban areas.

All these machines, Odetics suggests, could be developed from the basic framework of Odex-1, a six-legged walking machine that the company has

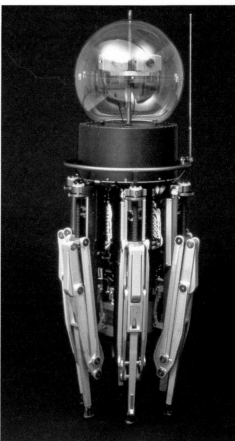

Above: Odex-1 could have a variety of military applications; the US Army has asked Odetics to research how it might be used for materials handling, while the US Navy wants a design for a shipboard firefighting system.

Above: A USAF Ground Launched Cruise Missile on test. It is in effect an unmanned bomber that relies on self-contained guidance systems.

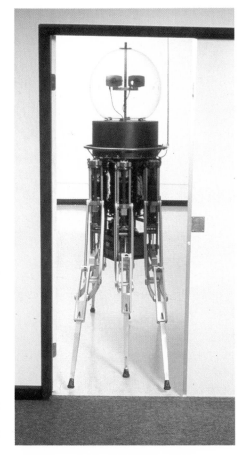

Above: A robotic battlefield vehicle must be able to traverse rough terrain, and Odex-1's six-legged design has demonstrated great stability. Here it is in its "thin" profile which lets it squeeze through narrow openings.

built at a cost of $1m. Odex-1, about as tall as a person, can walk up steps 3ft (1m) high and lift a tonne with a manipulator. It runs on a 24 volt battery and is controlled by seven computers, one for each of the machine's articulated legs and one to supervise the walking action by coordinating the limbs. Odex-1 can "walk" at about the same speed as a man, "squat" to gain access through narrow openings and change direction in mid-stride. It is half way between teleoperator and true robot. The machine has some autonomy but must be controlled by a human operator who keeps in touch with a radio link. Odetics has christened it "a functionoid".

Walking to Battle

Odetics plans to develop the machine so it has sensory abilities. For example, with TV cameras the device would receive images of objects and so "see" where it is going, transferring instructions about obstacles in its path to the computers that control the machine's six legs. The Californian company is working with RCA, the US communications and electronics concern, to develop new generations of walking hardware based on Odex-1 that could have uses in military projects.

Walking hardware for military applications was pioneered in the late 1960s by General Electric, which built what was

called a quadruped transporter for the US Department of Defense. The machine was about the size of an elephant and was steered by a person who rode on top of the contraption in a cab. The vehicle displayed animal-like mobility and overcame obstacles beyond the capability of conventional mobile machines. But the technology of the time did not permit the use of an on-board computer. So coordination of the hardware was achieved solely by the human operator using a master-slave manipulator technique. In this, the hands of the "pilot" controlled the front legs of the vehicle with two three-degree-of-freedom levers. The person's legs, meanwhile, were attached to other actuators to control the rear legs of the vehicle. The control mechanism worked reasonably enough but was excessively tiring and difficult for the operator. As a result, the research programme came to an end in the early 1970s.

The Department of Defense has not, however, given up its plans to develop walking machines for military applications such as troop transportation or the laying of mines. The main motivation is that this kind of walking hardware could function in difficult environments, such as deserts, swamps or mountainous terrain, where wheeled or tracked vehicles would break down.

In a project for the Department of Defense, Dr Bob McGhee of Ohio State University has developed a series of what are called adaptive suspension vehicles. These require a driver, as did the General Electric machine. The difference is that sensors and computers provide the vehicle with some rudimentary ability to work out actions for itself; as a result, the operator does not have to tell the machine every last detail of what he wants it to do. This makes the job of guiding the vehicle less time consuming and complicated.

Dr McGhee's latest machine, built with a grant of $3·4m from the DoD, has six legs. It is 16ft (5m) long and can climb steps some 6·5ft (2m) tall. A person controls the machine (called Adaptive Suspension Vehicle, or ASV-84) from a cockpit, using a steering device similar to a joystick. The device "sees" obstacles in front of it with a scanning mechanism. This sends instructions to the chain of computers that control the vehicle's legs. The instructions ensure that the contraption moves in the right direction and avoids rocks or other obstacles in its path. Each of the machine's six legs has its own computer and is jointed in three places. The nine other computers built into the device are responsible for sorting out information from the scanning mechanism and for ensuring that the six legs move in a coordinated fashion.

Dr McGhee sums up the philosophy of the vehicle's control strategy by pointing to the way in which people ride horses. He says that the pilot will generally tell the machine (using his joystick) which way to travel, but will leave to the hardware the details of formulating specific movements. "People on horses point the animal in the right direction", observes Dr McGhee, "but they do not tell it how to trot."

In a highly ambitious project announced in 1984, the DoD is to try to adapt the walking machine of Dr McGhee to produce an unmanned vehicle that can perform totally autonomously. The complete project, to be managed for the DoD's Defense Advanced Research Projects Agency (DARPA) by the aerospace and defence company Martin Marietta, will cost $50m and last until 1990. A dozen or so different contractors are working on parts of the project, which aims to produce a walking machine that will have the ability to work out for itself how to traverse

12 miles (20km) of difficult countryside at speeds up to 12mph (20km/h).

The programme has two main components. First, engineers will work on the design of the walking machine itself. They will probably start from Dr McGhee's ASV-84 machine and strip it of two of its legs to produce a quadruped. Six-legged machines, though highly stable, would be unable to reach the kinds of speeds specified in the design requirements for the 1990s version of the vehicle.

Working on this part of the project will be Dr Marc Raibert, a computer scientist at Pittsburgh's Carnegie-Mellon University, who is a specialist on the control theory of four-legged hardware. Dr Raibert started in this area with work on a one-legged machine, called a "pogo stick" robot, that hopped around a room. Dr Raibert learned from this development

some of the control theories needed to keep such a contraption on the move without tumbling over. To control a one legged device was much easier than he thought. Just three factors were important: the speed of the "pogo stick" over the ground; the height of the "hops"; and whether the body of the hardware remained upright. He found he could drive his hardware by giving it instructions affecting just these three elements. The machine obtained information about its surroundings with force sensors, a gyroscope and a compass.

To develop further strategies to control a four-legged vehicle will probably be more difficult, though Dr Raibert thinks the task is not insurmountable. He says that in designing the limbs for his hardware he has learned from the world of biology. For example, the legs of his machines

Above: Engineers at the Ohio State University created this model of the six-legged ASV-84 under contract to the US Department of Defense.

Above right: Martin Marietta has won a 5 year DARPA-funded contract to develop an autonomous land rover as a test bed for the military use of AI.

Right: RUM III is under development by the University of California; it is a remotely operated work vehicle to aid study of the deep sea floor.

Left: General Dynamics makes its F-16 aircraft with the aid of a $7·9m energy monitoring system which uses a mainframe and 108 "field" computers to control heating and lighting levels.

Below: An engineer at General Dynamics Fort Worth plant monitors equipment controlling energy levels in the factory. The hardware is intended to save $1·4m annually.

contain springs to make them resemble the compliant muscles of animals.

In the second part of the DARPA unmanned vehicle programme, engineers will attempt to give a mobile machine the power to work out from its surroundings information about how to avoid obstacles. Initially, technical workers will try out navigation techniques on conventional wheeled rather than legged vehicles.

The Environmental Research Institute of Michigan, a company in Ann Arbor, is developing a laser scanner that will provide a vehicle with a three dimensional picture of its surroundings up to 330ft (100m) away. The information will be supplemented by images from colour TV cameras. The data from these sensors will be compared with digital images of maps of the terrain that the machine is covering. In this way, vehicles should be able to work out for themselves exactly where they are at any time. To translate this kind of information into data that instruct a vehicle's steering mechanism is a daunting task. The steering devices must receive comprehensive information very quickly so that they can move to take any necessary evasive action. In the DARPA project, Texas Instruments is to build some

of the high-performance chips that will form elements of the navigational computers. Three further groups are designing the parallel processing computers (machines that work particularly quickly by working on several chains of data simultaneously) to analyse information from sensors and send instructions to steering devices. These groups are workers at Carnegie-Mellon University; BBN, a company in Boston; and the Thinking Machine Corporation of Cambridge, MA.

DARPA plans that the finished vehicle—which will be an amalgam of the work on legged machines and on computer navigation—will be powered by a gas turbine engine. This would differ from Dr McGhee's ASV-84, which runs on a converted motorcycle engine fuelled with petrol. DARPA has a detailed timetable for the development of the vehicle. By May 1986, a prototype wheeled vehicle should be able to travel at 6mph (10km/h) along a road studded every 100ft (30m) with obstacles 6·5ft (2m) high. In May 1987, the wheeled machine will see action in rough countryside such as the Arizona desert. The high spot of the programme should be in 1989 when engineers attempt to fuse the two elements of the project, the work on walking hardware and that on navigation. If it works as expected, engineers will be able simply to give the vehicle rough instructions as to where to travel, and leave it to the machine to calculate a strategy for making the journey.

Robot Submersibles

Robots that operate under water are another brand of unmanned machine for which many applications suggest themselves. Hitherto, engineers have devised teleoperated submarine vehicles linked by cable or sonar links to human operators. These perform tasks such as inspection of pipelines or location of shipwrecks. Several groups of technical workers around the world are attempting to extend the capabilities of these devices so they can operate autonomously.

Above: RUM III will operate up to 3 miles (5km) below the surface at the end of 6 miles (10km) of coaxial cable that transmits power to the vehicle.

Design Requirements for Submersible Robots

Type of robot	Octopus	Crab	Shark
Operational field	Structures	Seabed	Midwater
Max sensor range	33ft (10m)	330ft (100m)	6mi (10km)
Min sensor accuracy	0·004in (0·1mm)	4in (10cm)	0·4in (1cm)
Max vehicle range	0·6mi (1km)	60mi (100km)	600mi (1,000km)
Min effector accuracy	0·004in (0·1mm)	4in (10cm)	0·4in (1cm)
No of manipulators	more than 3	more than 1	more than 0
Manipulator min DoF	more than 5	more than 4	more than 2
Manipulator max strength	220lb (100kg)	220lb (100kg)	4·4lb (2kg)
Manipulator design	Exchangeable end effectors	Exchangeable end effectors	Specialized end effector

Table adapted from Scott Harmon's paper, "Autonomous Robot Submersibles", prepared for the 2nd International Computer Engineering Conference 1982.

Scott Harmon, an engineer at the US Navy's Naval Ocean Systems Center in San Diego, California, analysed the potential of these mechanisms in a paper prepared for the 2nd International Computer Engineering Conference in 1982. He particularly emphasized that unmanned robot submersibles could help engineers to recover minerals and other material resources from the sea bed. This is significant because of the discovery in recent years that large sections of the ocean floor, for example in deep parts of the Pacific, contain nodules of important metals such as cobalt and manganese. Various forecasters have predicted that if the world could mobilize its resources to collect the minerals from the bottom of the oceans, mankind would have available an ample stock of industrial materials for the next couple of centuries. Further to this, robots will continue to play a useful role in the exploitation of undersea resources, such as oil and gas.

Harmon pointed out: "Present undersea drilling and mining practices are highly human intensive. The hostility of the environment imposes great risk on those who must directly work in the water. There is considerable surface support required for each human used in the work site. The elements of risk and support make the cost of exploiting these resources very high. In some cases, humans can be removed from the hostile environment by using teleoperated or remotely controlled devices. However, teleoperated systems are dependent on a high-bandwidth communications link between the master unit and the slave ... In addition, teleoperated systems have proven most successful in relatively simple tasks. Very little experience has been gained in using such systems in complex tasks. Interfacing a human operator to a teleoperator system performing a complex but tedious and lengthy task is a very difficult challenge as yet unmet. These factors support the existence of the crying need for an ARS (autonomous robot submersible) capability, the component technology to support near-term implementation for certain applications and the research interest to advance the technology still further."

According to a classification devised by Harmon, robot submersibles will have five main applications: inspection, tool guidance, navigation, search, and communication. The machines themselves will come in three different configurations: a crab-like structure for crawling along the ocean floor to bury cables, or mine sea-bottom minerals; an octopus shape with several manipulators to inspect, maintain and repair complex three-dimensional ocean structures such as drilling rigs or even shipwrecks; and a shark form to move at speed midway between the sea bottom and the surface on such tasks as surveying, mapping and surveillance. Details of the different applications and types of robot are shown in the table. Common to all systems is that they contain various

Above: The Naval Ocean Systems Center in San Diego has developed a free swimming submersible for inspecting underwater structures such as pipelines. The craft can operate to a depth of about 2,000ft (700m) and sends TV pictures by fibre-optic link.

Below: Pioneer, a remote-controlled submersible built by SubSea Offshore, can detect leaks in oil pipelines and bring to the surface samples of cement or metal for analysis by engineers. It can also cut or untangle wires with a set of manipulators.

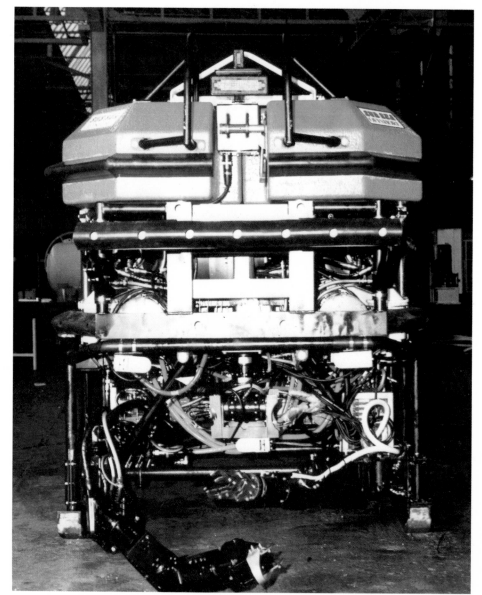

Dolphin Undersea Vessel
1 "Natsushima" mother ship.
2 Tether cable.
3 Direction finding sonar.
4 Responder.
5 Foam blocks.
6 Up/down thruster.
7 Forward/reverse thruster.
8 Side thruster.
9 Telemetry control canister.
10 Hydraulic power unit.
11 Still camera.
12 Rate control grabber/cutter (5 DoF).
13 Sample basket.
14 Colour TV camera.
15 Master-slave manipulator (7 DoF).
16 Stereo TV camera.
17 Light.
18 Light.

The Dolphin-3K is one of a series of remote-controlled submersibles to be developed at the JAMSTEC in Yokosuka. The vehicle, due to be completed in 1986, is the largest and deepest diving (10,800ft, 3,300m) robot underwater craft so far built in Japan. Its tasks will include inspection of underwater structures, sample return, and geological survey. It is also planned to use it as a pathfinder for the manned submersible Shinkai 2000.

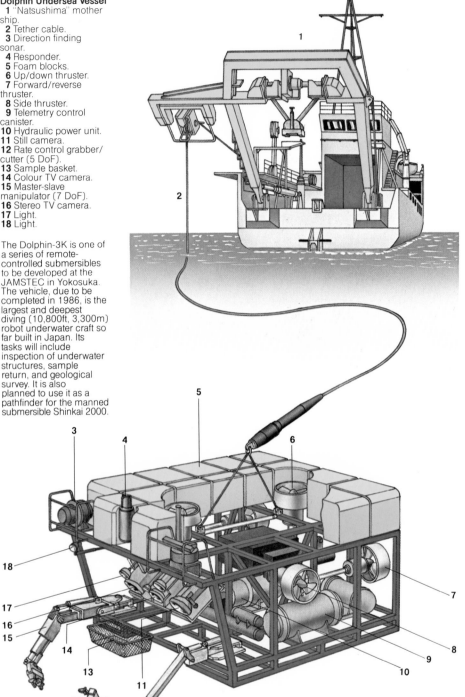

manipulators, sensors to provide details of their surroundings, and on-board computers to process information from the sensors.

Japanese Designs

Teleoperated undersea vehicles, in contrast to autonomous underwater robots, are used routinely in oceans around the world. In Japan, for example, workers at the Japan Marine Science and Technology Centre (JAMSTEC) in Yokosuka and various Japanese companies have joined forces to build undersea vehicles linked to the surface by a tether. These move underwater, propelled by thrusters, and receive commands via the umbilical link. JTV-1, an early prototype of such a vehicle, underwent trials in the early 1980s. It can swim at depths of 660ft (200m) at about 2·5mph (4km/h). It weighs 95lb (43kg) and is not much bigger than a large TV set. The machine carries two TV cameras, a depth meter, a magnetic compass and a still camera. Information about the surroundings of the vehicle is relayed back to a support crew via the tether.

Using this machine, researchers have surveyed fishing grounds off the coast of Japan and inspected an underwater pipeline off Nauru. JTV-2, a commercial model of JTV-1, was built in 1982 by a company called Q.I. in conjunction with JAMSTEC. Vehicles of this series have inspected underwater telephone cables and seen service in the Antarctic in studies of marine creatures which live at great depths beneath ice cover.

JAMSTEC has also built an underwater vehicle called Mosquito that can travel up to 330ft (100m) below the surface. The research centre is working on two more vehicles: Hornet, a larger and deeper version of JTV-1, which should be able to operate at a depth of 1,640ft (500m), and Dolphin-3K, which is designed to dive to

Below: Hornet-500, another of JAMSTEC's fibre-optic-tethered undersea survey vehicles, is powered by four thrusters which are controlled by micro-computers. After launch (below left) it can dive to a depth of 1,640ft (500m).

Right: Here seen running trials, the Marine Robot RM3, developed by Normed Shipyards, is a three-legged amphibian designed to clamber over the hulls of ships, cleaning them of barnacle growth as it goes.

10,800ft (3,300m). The latter two vehicles will use fibre-optic cable to receive instructions and to send messages to the surface. This form of cable has a higher bandwidth, or information-carrying capacity, than conventional copper telecommunications wires. JAMSTEC is also engaged in long-term research aimed at perfecting an autonomous undersea craft.

Hydro Products, a US company based in San Diego, is also working towards this goal. The company sells a range of hardware for undersea work that are conventional teleoperators, but it is working on vehicles that can operate independently. Among Hydro Products' hardware for inspection and observation of underwater objects is RCV-225 a small, roughly spherical vehicle—nicknamed "the flying eyeball"—that relays TV pictures to a control station. It has numerous applications in the fields of underwater surveying, and observation work. A more advanced vehicle, RCV-150, incorporates manipulators, which an operator on the surface can instruct it to cut cables or repair faulty equipment.

Among other types of teleoperated devices that work under water are remote controlled trenching equipment that automatically buries sub-sea pipelines in waters up to 1,650ft (500m) deep. These have been routinely used in the oil and gas field developments in the North Sea. One such automatic trenching system was designed and built by Kvaerner Brug of Norway in the late 1970s. Two other companies, Brown & Root of the US and Volker Stevin of Holland, have joined this enterprise to form a new organisation called KBV that has improved the hardware. The trenching system was used in 1983 to bury a 2·5 mile (4km) length of pipe in the Brent field in the North Sea.

Trenching is achieved with a mechanical suction cutter while another section of the machine grips a length of pipe and places it automatically in the newly-dug hollow.

Free Swimmers

One of the world leaders in autonomous underwater machines is International Submarine Engineering, based in Van-couver, Canada. The company has experimented with two classes of such hardware for work up to 990ft (300m) beneath the surface. The company also sells underwater hardware of the conventional tethered type, but it reasons that independent computer-controlled vessels, which can navigate their way around obstacles and return to a base unaided, promise greater versatility. They can travel further and faster because they are not restrained by attachment to a heavy cable. The absence of a cable also removes the possibility of entanglement with underwater obstructions. The new vehicles, furthermore, are likely to be less expensive to operate because they do not need a skilled engineer to guide them for every minute that they function.

The computer-controlled machines made by the Canadian company cost $1m to $2m each. They detect the presence of objects by means of acoustic sensors. These send guidance information to the computers controlling the propulsion thrusters. Before the vessel starts its journey, engineers program into the computer's memory the coordinates of

Left: VELPO is another Normed Shipyard machine; it is designed to protect submarine pipelines on the ocean floor from damage by wrapping material around them. This 120-tonne, hydraulically powered prototype can operate at a depth of 1,000ft (300m).

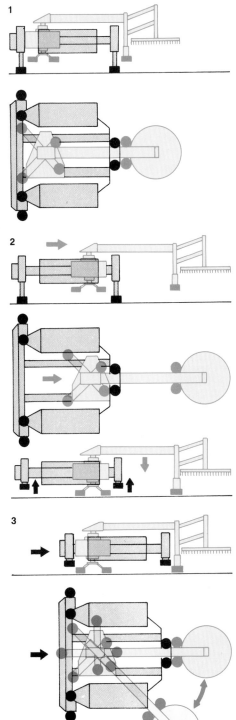

the path along which it is to travel, so that, for instance, it could follow the line of a pipe to spot cracks. Alternatively, the device could sweep a wide area of ocean, searching with TV cameras for material on the sea bottom such as metallic nodules.

ISE's autonomous hardware comes in two types. Both are about 3·3ft (1m) in diameter and some 33ft (10m) long. The ARCS (for autonomous remote controlled submersible) vessel travels up to 990ft (300m) below the surface, powered by batteries. It sends back information via an acoustic data link. The second vehicle, a survey vessel called Dolphin (Deep Ocean Logging Platform Instrument for Navigation), travels only about 16ft (5m) below the wave tops. It keeps in touch with an operator via radio waves, transmitted via a snorkel that pokes above the surface. The snorkel also collects air from the atmosphere to help power the device's diesel engine. ARCS is designed to travel at 5mph (8km/h), while Dolphin should scythe through the water three times faster.

Automatic machines for underwater applications have been developed to an interesting stage in France. The Normed Shipyards, in conjunction with the French atomic energy commission (CEA), have experimented with using robots to clean ships' hulls. The devices operate under the water line and scrub away growths such as barnacles that impede the smooth passage of the hull through the water. The RM3 system devised by Normed is

Above: RM3's land-based counterpart, RGH1, can be used to clean the exterior of fuel tanks. Note the cable between robot and remote unit which carries the optical fibre communications link.

controlled by an operator either on the ship being cleaned or on another vessel. The machine itself moves using an ingenious form of legged locomotion (see diagrams at right) and has one manipulator. The latter may hold a cleaning brush or alternatively another kind of device such as a deburring tool, inspection camera or even a paint spray. The operator sends signals to the machine via a fibre-optic link. A land-based version, RGH1, is being developed to clean fuel tanks and similar large structures.

The Nuclear Workplace

Teleoperators have been used for years in the nuclear industry for jobs such as maintenance of fuel rods in places that experience high levels of radioactivity. Taylor Hitec of Chorley, Lancashire, has developed a range of systems for use in British nuclear power stations. In a recent move, the company has devised an articulated robotic arm—the links system (see operational diagram overleaf)—that slides through a hole in the casing of a reactor. Once into the heart of the reactor, the arm unfolds like a telescope with joints. The mechanism can

RM3 Locomotion
The Marine Robot RM3 consists basically of two functional units: the 3-legged main structure (black) and the mobile structure (red) on which the arm is mounted. The two units use magnetic and vacuum cups to achieve grip, and they alternately advance and catch up to make the robot walk. In the initial action of making a step, the mobile structure is raised while the main structure has its three legs extended (**1**). The mobile structure then moves forward (**2**) up to 18in (40cm), this being the step length. The legs of the main structure then retract leaving the robot supported by the mobile structure. This latter

then "withdraws", causing the main structure to move forward (**3**). It then lowers its legs, and one step has been achieved. The whole process is then repeated. In order to change direction, the mobile structure can be rotated up to 90° away from the centre line (blue). The main structure's legs retract, the mobile structure bears the weight, and it drives the main structure into alignment with the new heading, ready to take the next step forward. Walking speed is 500ft (150m) per hour and cleaning rate is 53,800 sq ft (5,000m²) per day. RM3 can also be used for painting, video and X-ray inspection, and grinding.

then operate according to set programs, for example to weld pieces of metal or inspect parts of the reactor with TV cameras.

Several nuclear utilities around the world use tracked teleoperators for jobs inside power stations and related plant. The UK Atomic Energy Authority has developed two such contraptions, Spider and Roman, which have seen service in the Sellafield (formerly Windscale) reprocessing plant in Cumbria. The CEA in France has also developed similar hardware. The Electric Power Research Institute in California, a research organization funded by the US power utilities, is investigating how walking machines could patrol nuclear plants to do routine jobs such as maintenance or inspection. Engineers attempting to repair the disabled nuclear power station at Three Mile Island, Pennsylvania, have examined the use of wheeled, teleoperated hardware to do jobs in parts of the reactor where radioactivity levels are high. A Remote Reconnaissance Vehicle (RRV) specifically designed to undertake missions at Three Mile Island has been developed by the Civil and Construction Robotics Lab at Carnegie-Mellon University under the direction of William Whittaker. Technical workers at the Joint European Torus, a mammoth research project in Oxfordshire, UK, which is a base for experiments into the provision of

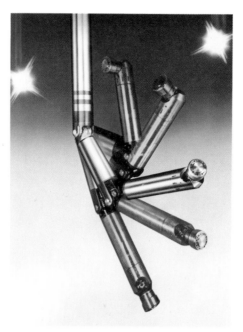

Above: This advanced manipulator, built for the Central Electricity Generating Board by Taylor Hitec, carries out in-reactor tasks, such as remote welding.

Below right: Engineers at Carnegie-Mellon University have devised this remote reconnaissance vehicle to operate in the contaminated buildings at Three Mile Island power station.

energy by nuclear fusion, plan to employ similar mobile machines to patrol the torus when it starts full operation in the late 1980s.

In mining, engineers are working on several fronts to develop tunnelling machines that will be self-guiding. The systems use sensors such as gyroscopes to ensure that they cut away rock in the correct direction. In one development in the UK, engineers at the National Coal Board are experimenting with a company called Dosco. The result is roadheading equipment fitted with sensors that steers itself for short distances without the need for supervision by an operator. In coal mining itself, Prof Meredith Thring, formerly of London's Queen Mary College (now retired) has published designs for a series of telechiric devices that would dig out coal. But so far such work has had little practical application.

Leading the Blind

Perhaps the most novel application of robots outside the factory is represented by the work in Japan on a mobile machine to help blind people. Called Meldog, the wheeled device has been under development at the government's Mechanical Engineering Laboratory in Tsukuba City since 1977. The machine moves along directly in front of its blind owner. It sends out sonic pulses that locate

Taylor Hitec "Links System" Manipulator
1 Exchange container bellows.
2 Links scroll drive.
3 Viewing window.
4 Glove port for tool change.
5 Control panel.
6 Links storage drum.
7 Slewing ring.
8 Standpipe.
9 Concrete shield.
10 Gas baffle dome.
11 Serving shoe.
12 Steering camera.
13 Links.
14 Powered manipulator.

Engineered by Taylor Hitec in cooperation with the Central Electricity Generating Board in the UK, this is a design for a manipulator system that could be used to deploy inspection equipment or maintenance tools in an Advanced Gas Cooled Reactor. The primary element is a semi-articulated chain, known as the links system. The links are stored coiled in one direction on a drum, but when extended they form a beam, this being the deploying limb on which tools or cameras are mounted. In the system illustrated, the manipulator can be deployed to a depth of 50ft (15m) from the charge face, and up to 20ft (6m) out from the axis of reactor entry. The payload at full reach is 66lb (30kg), and positional repeatability is ±1mm. The device is guided by a supervisor who monitors its position and performance on a television screen, receiving pictures from a steering camera mounted at the foot of the mast.

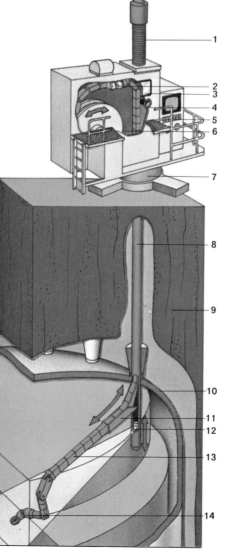

and identify objects in its path. A computer in the machine compares information so obtained with a digital map of the area being traversed. In this way, the machine builds up a representation of what is taking place in the immediate surroundings. It would be able to work out, for example, if a car or other road vehicle were travelling near an intersection that the blind person wanted to negotiate. The machine also has an optical sensor to gather landmark information that is then passed to a computer for analysis.

The Meldog system communicates with its human owner by an electrical connection that sends pulses to electrodes attached to the skin. The pulses are sent in a special code which the user has to learn in order to be able to use the hardware. For example, the code can tell the blind person to step either to the right or the left to avoid a collision with an object in the Meldog's path. The Japanese have still to prove that Meldog is more than just an expensive stunt, and that it will be of real use to blind people. They have also still to demonstrate that the system is easier to use than the tried and tested mechanism of the guide dog. But if the Meldog experiment produces useful results, that will be a sure indication that robots have emerged from the factory with a vengeance and are establishing themselves significantly in the world outside the shop floor.

Above: Meldog Mk IV guiding a blind person; the robot navigates using a map that is stored in its memory, and relies on a battery of ultrasonic sensors to detect and avoid obstacles.

Below: This view of the UKAEA's Spider clearly shows the operator's panel with twin TV monitors, manipulator controller (right), joystick, and attitude indicators (top centre).

Following on the heels of the microcomputer, small robots are rapidly finding their way into schools and homes around the world; what is the potential for these diverse new systems?

THE RISE OF THE MICRO

The reaction of many people on first seeing an arm-type micro-robot is to compare it with the amusement arcade game in which a small crane is made to grab for prizes. The manipulation of control knobs moves the crane backwards and forwards and opens and closes the scoop-like grippers. It can grab a handful of sweets from the bottom of the case if you are adept, and then tip them down a chute to the delight of the young operator. The shape of the crane resembles the small robot and there is a mechancial similarity between the two machines. The main difference is that small boys turn the knobs of the machine on the pier. The robot's knobs are turned by motors controlled by the computer.

The computer is capable of directing and moving the robot very accurately, returning it to the same spot time and time again, without tiring or making a mistake. The small boy will be excited, inaccurate and will tire of the game easily. However, what the young operator will be able to do is to judge a situation, and turn the knobs to take advantage of it, in a way that a small computer could never do. In these situations, the capa-

bilities of the live intelligence exceed those of the computer, while conversely the computer can do some things better than the fallible human hand and eye.

The use of the micro-robot and the microcomputer together has led one of the leading authorities in the field, Dr John Billingsley, to say that "robotics is a computer with muscles"; that is an excellent description. It might be more accurate, however, to say that a robot is a computer with motors, because it is the computerized control of those motors which is at the centre of robot technology. The gears, levers and other mechanisms that work the machine are secondary to the drives, so it is the motor that is the crux of the matter. The fact that one or

Right: After the unmanned factory, could the unmanned laboratory be next? Repetitive tasks, such as the weighing of chemical samples, can be undertaken by micro-robotic arms.

Below: Micro-robots are educational and fun! Tomy's Armatron Robo 1 is a sophisticated piece of engineering that sells for the price of a toy.

Left: Robots are valuable promotional aids, attracting crowds at trade fairs and commercial events. This character was built by Namco in Japan, its function being to hand out leaflets to passers-by, using a simple vacuum gripper built into its hand.

Most of all, the media have discovered robots. There are two magazines in Britain, one in the USA and one in France specifically concerned with micro-robots, and the press and television are currently full of robot stories. The market is beginning to show signs of maturing and a clearer picture of the possibilities for the technology and economics of micro-robots is now emerging.

The technology is not viewed as such a "black" science now, as it was previously. The technician who is considering using a robot is more aware of its limitations and possibilities, and so to a lesser extent is the general public. Much of this is due to the emergence of the micro-robot as a teaching and experimental tool. Micro-robots can be bought in kit form, and the breaking-down of the technology into its constituent elements that this implies is of considerable educational value; nobody who has put together a robot kit feels as "in awe" of the mechanics of robots as before. The programming of movement sequences is also more easily understood if the operator runs them from his own program. The 1980s have seen the birth of the micro-robot and the pace of development has been fast if erratic. In the following pages we trace the present "state of the art" in small robots, both mobile and static, and also indulge in a little crystal ball-gazing into the future.

Micro-robotic Arms

Britain leads the world in the development of arm-type robots. The arm or anthropomorphic (i.e. imitating the human body) type of robot has more developers in the UK than the rest of the world put together. This follows on quite naturally from the fact that the United Kingdom also leads the world in ownership of microcomputers. The static working of the arm-type micro-robot establishes it as a form of computer peripheral. The USA, as you will see later, is much more concerned with mobile robots. The teaching capacity of the arm has been appreciated by Britian's educational authorities, and about 7,000 units have been sold in the last couple of years.

The range of robotic devices which are available is very wide, not only in size and price but also in the types of mechanics and drives employed. This category of robot includes some with hydraulic drives, but most have some form of electrical motor drive. The stepper-motor servo device and direct current motor are all used in one or another of the machines listed. They come in all shapes and sizes as well as exhibiting considerable variations in lifting capacity. Lifting from a few grams to a couple of kilograms, the price tends to go up in line with the available "muscle", although

several motors can be driven and controlled by a microcomputer makes the whole technology more "transparent" to the understanding of the hobbyist or student. But first things first, what exactly is a micro-robot?

Most people recognize an industrial robot when they see one, but a micro-robot is more difficult to define. It generally comes in one of three forms. It might be an amusement robot with a novelty or entertainment value such as is used at exhibitions and trade fairs. It might be a hobbyist and educationalist's robot which often comes in kit form. This ranges from the Fischertechnik kit which enables us to build several robots from the same parts, to a dedicated machine which can be bought either assembled or in parts for approximately £1,000. Lastly, there is the device which is a serious tool for use in laboratories and possibly in industry. This development is still emerging as a technology, and the applications have yet to be properly established.

The evolution of the micro-robot really started in 1980 as an outgrowth of the

widespread availability of microcomputers. The development of the robot market as a whole, however, began in the 1960s when a few companies started a lonely crusade to persuade industry of their worth, in much the same way that big computer companies came into being in the late 1950s. As was explained in Chapter 2, by the 1970s robots were well established performing jobs such as spray painting, and welding, and were becoming generally accepted. At the same time their price was coming down and the machines were getting smaller. This is comparable to the period of the introduction to the market of the mini computer. Finally, the micro-robot came into being and it is going through many of the development patterns that the microcomputer experienced in the 1970s and early 1980s.

Small robots are now being made by a number of manufacturers with a fair amount of software to drive the machines, and the manuals and literature are steadily improving as the makers understand the needs of their customers better.

Above: Simulation of full-scale industrial robots can be achieved by micro-robotic arms such as Feedback's Armover SSA 1040 which is here directly interfaced with an Apple II computer.

Below: Colne Robotics' Armdroid 1 is a continuous path machine that has five axes of motion. Somewhat unusually, it features a 3-fingered gripper.

there are exceptions. A specific application design is more expensive. The Swiss Microbo device, which is made to assemble watches, is an example of this. The fine accuracy that this needs has led to such a high level of engineering that it costs in the order of £8,000. This is way out of the price bracket that we expect for these machines. They generally cost from £100 for those lifting ten grams or under, to a figure around £1,000 for those lifting one or two kilos.

The configuration, geometry or any other buzz word that technicians use to describe how the machine moves is the same as that of industrial robots (see pages 20-23). The only established robot movement configuration that is not found in micro-robot arms is one with cylindrical coordinates. That form of movement is typical of production robots using moving belts, and the small robot is not used in that way, at least not yet. The other important aspect of movement is the degrees of freedom (D of F) that a machine possesses. This is again similar to the principles exhibited by an industrial robot. Many of the small robot arms have six degrees of freedom in the same way that your arm has. The shoulder has two freedoms, rotation and extension, the elbow has one. The wrist has three, rotation and pitch and yaw (up and down and side to side). These movements enable a human or a robot to handle most tasks. However, some things we have to do need two hands; well that is all right! Patcentre's robot, Yes Man, has

two arms and hands.

The main movements of the machine are certainly significant, but, like the human arm, the most important part is the hand or gripper. Most of the machines available have a two-fingered gripper, although the Colne Armdroid has three. None of the machines has the capability of changing one gripper or tool for another, as some industrial ones have,

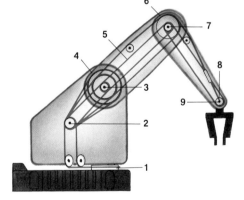

Microbot Alpha II
1 Base drive pulley.
2 Common drive shaft.
3 Shoulder axle.
4 Shoulder drive pulley.
5 Stainless steel drive cables.
6 Elbow drive pulley.
7 Elbow axle.
8 Wrist differential drive.
9 Wrist axle.

The Alpha II, an improved version of Microbot's Alpha system, moves mechanically using the sort of precision cable technology that operates aircraft controls. It is powered by six electrical stepper motors housed in the base of the robot, and the torque of these motors is transmitted, via timing belts coupled with metal pulleys, to the cables that control arm motion. The system comprises a five axis arm plus cable-operated gripper; the arm's reach is 18·4in (467mm); max payload is 3lb (1·36kg).

Above: This Fischertechnik robot, which comes in kit form, is controlled by an inexpensive microcomputer through an MRS analogue-to-digital interface.

Below: Androbot's Topo is a 3ft-tall mobile personal robot that receives signals from a home computer via an infra-red data link.

Another new appearance on the scene is probably the smallest, cheapest, most flexible kit yet produced. The Micro Robotic Systems interface with the Fischertechnik kit can build six or more robots from the same box of parts. The ability to construct several robots, a tracking machine, a sorting machine etc makes this one of the best value educational systems yet devised. Micro Robotic Systems, who build complete systems for specific tasks using existing small robots, make the point that a certain amount of modification in any arm is necessary to fit it into a system to perform a particular task. The purpose-built robot, such as the Swiss Microbo machine, is very expensive and we are now beginning to get enough variety of choice in machines, drives, electronics and grippers to be able to choose the best for modification for a particular application in laboratory, factory, shop, hospital or home. The trend in industry seems to be away from large industrial robots; if the micro-robot can get away from the current "string and pulley" design image, it might be that a

but there are a few that are supplied with a choice of tools. The Rhino enables you to slot on to its arm a pneumatic sucker or a two- or three-fingered gripper. The Smart Arm also uses several alternative methods of holding or manipulating workpieces. An important development in micro-robots will have to be the improvement of grippers. Both static and mobile robots have their own distinctive uses and virtues. The main virtue of the arm is that it works from a fixed base and is therefore potentially more accurate in its positioning and repeatability, and thus the anthropomorphic device will probably have more useful applications in the short term than the mobile one.

The development of the small robot manipulator technology since its first appearance in the early 1980s has been dramatic. The first of the arms to become available was the American Microbot Alpha System. This is still one of the best machines for the money, as was proved by long tests by The UK Atomic Energy Authority at Harwell in 1982. Since then, there have been newcomers, of course, but Microbot's products remain good value. The next on the scene were Feedback's hydraulically-driven Armdraulic robot and Colne Robotics' steppermotor-driven kit. Both of them were launched in August 1980. At the same time came The Smart Arm: a small industrial training device. This last product was unusual, because the emphasis of this small machine, plus other machines from the same stable, was in envisaging micro-robots in the context of the production line. It uses DC servo motors and the instruction books, software manuals and promotion kits underline how the machine can simulate robots in factory production layouts. The concepts of integration with other machine tools, how the machines interact, and the way they function within a work cell, form the basis of their demonstration and explanation by sales and technical staff.

major market awaits the arm-type robot in industry and commerce in the relatively near future.

Mobile Robots

The popular image of the robot is of an intelligent man-like machine which trundles or even walks around in order to carry out tasks of varying complexity. The essential features of this image are mobility and intelligence. The ability to move around enables the worker, robot or human, to go to the task rather than vice versa as is the case with static arm robots. The fact that the robot moves around, however, creates problems in itself. The raison d'être for robots is to interact with the environment (this is essentially what work is), but how can you accomplish this if you are mobile but never quite sure where you are, let alone where everything else is? Well that is where intelligence comes in, the ability to sense and react to obstacles, workpieces, people and all the things that crowd the outside world. The ability to cope with the problems which this entails is essential for a good robot servant or worker.

How advanced is the technology that is applied to the current generation of mobile robot? First of all, none of them walks. The ability to walk like a human is an extraordinarily difficult mechanical task to achieve: the sequence of lifting one foot off the floor, moving it forward and then transferring weight on to it and lifting the other is not nearly as simple as rolling on wheels or tracks. Moving on wheels, however, makes going upstairs, and indeed traversing any rough terrain very difficult. All the presently available machines roll on wheels or tracks, mostly wheels.

The initiative for the development of mobile robots comes mainly from America; they come in two forms—turtle type and free-style type. The turtle type of robot has a trailing wire attached to the computer which controls it. It is described on page 109. The purposes of this device are mainly educational. The machine that is the ancestor of what may turn out to be the universal manservant is the free-style device complete with "onboard" computer, power, sensors of many kinds, and a clever program to run it all. Hobbyists with the urge to create their own robots have been particularly active in the USA for some years. The American Robot Association knows of over two hundred individual robot designers who have made their own machines. They range from Shakey, one of the first mobiles designed by the Stanford Research Institute (described in Chapter 4), to many others built in laboratories, workshops and garages across the nation. The main initiative in the UK comes from British Petroleum Ltd, who are running the world's largest robot-building competition. Pupils at over 100 schools are busy designing and constructing robots which will serve a specific number of drinks to people seated at tables (dressed in waterproofs?) in defined positions in the competition area.

These machines, however, are not the ones that will serve the general public as personal robots; the latter come from commercial manufacturers. There are roughly half a dozen makers who offer various devices, but leading the field is the Hero 1 robot. Produced by Heathkit Corporation, who have made a business out of electronic construction kits, it comes in kit or assembled form with probably the best and most effective manual yet produced in the robotic field. Aimed principally at the educational market, the manual is probably the most important aspect of Hero's commercial success. The explanation and instructions form the basis of lessons, which are presented in such a way that teachers can readily use them. Heathkit has sold several thousand Heros, almost entirely in the USA, which gives them about 80 per cent of the whole market. The sales are still not very exciting

Above: In 1984 Tomy introduced a range of high technology toy robots. They are: (back) Omnibot, a radio-controlled electronic "butler" with onboard cassette recorder; Verbot (front left) who responds to 8 individual voice commands; and Dingbot who bumps into obstacles, chatters and then moves on.

when compared with their expectations, and, according to the executive in charge of Hero, Mike Bosworth, they are not expected to grow significantly in the next few years. The reason (he says) is that the customer constantly asks "What does it do?". The answer is, not enough to make it an essential piece of equipment for the householder at £1,600 a time.

What, in fact, does it do? Some of its functions are pre-programmed "modules" which plug in and are called up on a keyboard on the "head" of the machine.

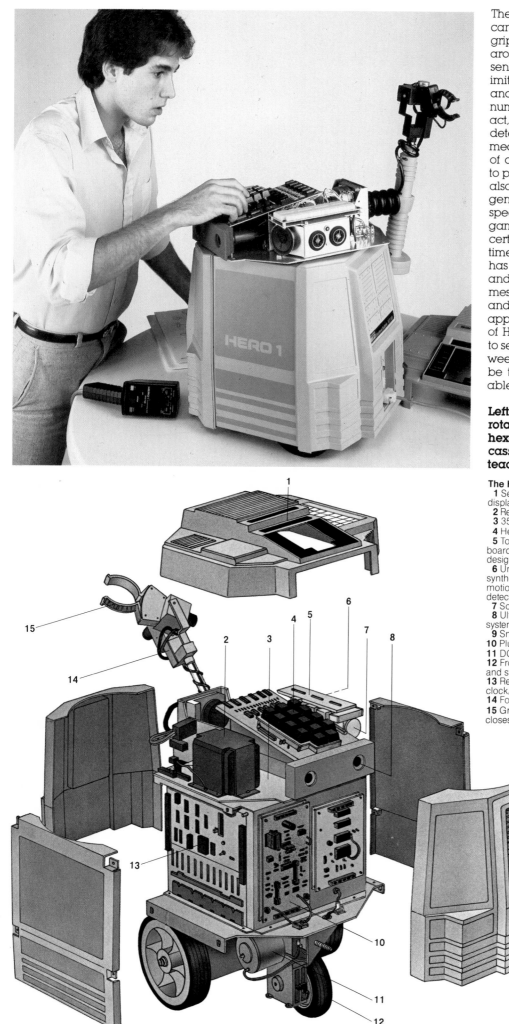

The 19in (48cm) high, 21lb (9.5kg) robot can carry a load of 1lb (0.45kg) using the gripper on its retractable arm, and moves around the home on wheels. It contains sensors within its body which attempt to imitate human senses. It hears sounds and recognizes such things as a limited number of commands on which it can act, i.e. start, stop, left, right etc. It can detect light and use ultrasonic sensors to measure distance and sense the presence of obstacles. It can use its built-in clock to perform programs at a specific time. It also contains a voice synthesizer that generates 64 sounds to simulate human speech and sound effects. It sings; plays games; you can instruct it to patrol a certain area, wake you up at a particular time, or remind you of a special event. It has an arm with which to pick things up and put them on its head to carry as a messenger. The arm extends 5in (127mm) and has 4 axes and a simple gripper. To appreciate the possibilities and limitations of Hero, it would be necessary not only to see it work, but also to use it for several weeks. The general reaction to it seems to be that it is a sophisticated talking toy, able to bring you your pipe and your

Left: This view clearly shows Hero 1's rotating head which mounts the arm, hexadecimal keypad, and sensors; the cassette interface is lower right. The teach pendant is on the table (left).

The Heathkit Hero 1
1 Seven segment LED display.
2 Rechargeable batteries.
3 350° rotatable head.
4 Hexadecimal keypad.
5 Top-mounted bread-board for interfacing user-designed circuits.
6 Unit housing voice synthesizer, ultrasonic motion detector and light detector.
7 Sound detector.
8 Ultrasonic sonar system.
9 Snap-off side panels.
10 Plug-in circuit boards.
11 DC gear motor.
12 Front wheel (drives and steers).
13 Real time clock/calendar.
14 Four axis arm.
15 Gripper (opens and closes).

The Hero 1 personal robot, and the associated educational course that is sold with it, has rapidly established itself as the standard against which competitors measure themselves. Heathkit claims that Hero can demonstrate every major concept that a student needs to learn about robotics, and that it is thus an ideal training aid. Hero is a mobile, programmable robot with arm, gripper, voice, and sensors. The arm and gripper provide a total of five axes of motion: wrist pitch, wrist roll, arm pitch, arm extension, gripper open and close. Maximum payload (arm retracted) is 1lb (0.45kg). The voice synthesizer is a phoneme-based system that generates 64 sounds to simulate human speech and sound effects. The sensors detect sound, light and motion, which allows Hero to be used, for instance, as a domestic night watchman. An ultrasonic ranging system is also included. The head unit, which can rotate 350°, houses the sensors, and also a breadboarding area, which is an experimental circuit board which allows direct access to a user input/output port. The single drivewheel is steered using a stepper motor, while the drive motor is monitored by an optical encoder that measures distance travelled. Hero is controlled by a 6808 microprocessor and can be programmed through its onboard keyboard, a teach pendant, or an external cassette tape recorder.

slippers if they are in the same room. Just the thing for an interesting gimmick at cocktail parties, but when evaluated as a household servant, hardly competition for a washing machine, to take one example.

It is, however, a small step forward in the development of a mechanical helpmate around the house. A burglar alarm, fire alarm, fetcher and carrier it may be, and while it is not yet the perfect manservant, even at the present level of development it is also a great deal of fun.

Robots for Fun

The robot figure that entertains us in fact and fiction has a long line of ancestry. Storytellers and performers realized that a human image, however small, could charm audiences as much and more than a live performer. The marionette or Punch and Judy-type stick puppets were to some extent the forebears of the science fiction robots with which we are now all familiar.

There have been a number of "metal supermen" to amuse us since film-making began at the turn of the century. One of the first of these, as noted in Chapter 1, was the robotic woman in the film "Metropolis" made in 1926. It says more about the nature of human love than of robotics that the image of the robot is generally masculine or non-sexual, and

Above: Dr Who's K-9 is typical of a recent trend in television and cinema that identifies robots as man's friends and helpers, rather than as enemies.

Below: The message that robots are fun has been heeded by toy manufacturers worldwide. This is the Movit range of build-them-yourself mobile robots that originated in Japan.

has very rarely been pictured as being involved in love-making. The stories of Isaac Asimov, however, do increasingly have undertones of a sense of loyalty which the robot feels for its human master. The figure of the robot in the early days was generally associated with images of annihilation and destruction, and while to some extent that still applies today, many other fictitious robots take a more benign view of the human race. One thinks of R2D2 and C3PO in the "Star Wars" films, or the television characters, Metal Mickey and K-9. This generation of robots have personalities of their own. One of the latest of these is Marvin, the robot with permanent mental depression, from "A Hitchhiker's Guide to the Galaxy". The fun robots are beginning to develop genuine characters: not only do their bodies simulate our own, but also their personalities and mental states.

If this is the state of robots on the film or TV screen, is an equivalent development apparent in the real world? Certainly contemporary amusement robots are not as clever as those of the world of make believe, but there is still a lot of fun in them. The main use for the microcomputer in the home is to play games; this may well turn out to be the chief function of the micro-robot in the near future as well. Certainly robotic game concepts are beginning to evolve, and the first will probably be comparable to Space Invaders and will make just as much money for their (no doubt young) inventors. Such games seem a natural progression from the computer games which are so popular now, and no doubt the element of competition will also be an integral feature of them.

The best known robot competition is Euromouse, more popularly called Micromouse. Created by the fertile imagination of Dr John Billingsley of Portsmouth Polytechnic, it is an event which takes place wherever there are gatherings of computer-oriented people. The competition tests the ability of a number of small robots, built by hobbyists, to find their way to the centre of a maze. The board on

which the maze is constructed is several metres square. The walls of the corridors are only a few inches high, and can be demounted and replaced in different ways to vary the route to the centre. The robots, which come in all shapes and sizes, express not only their owners' technical abilities but their highly individual personalities as well. One of the champions, that has negotiated the course in seconds, talks to you as it goes. Another has the wings of a biplane and furry mouse as a pilot! This, however, does not detract from the technical achievements of the hobbyists from all over the UK and Europe who build these pieces of miniature robot technology.

The more that these robots learn about the maze that they are wandering around, and the more they can use that knowledge to guide their wanderings, the more likely they are to win. One of the computer algorithms which has been developed for the guidance of robots has shown a positive step forward in the general field of robotic learning. Another game under development comes from France. The magazine "Micro et Robot" is building a course in which two robots compete against one another to transfer objects from one end to the other. It is not quite as simple as that, however, as they can impede one another's progress as they play. Competition is again seen to be the nub of almost any computer or robot game, and the most fascinating idea is another brainchild of Dr Billingsley: Robot Ping-Pong!

The outline rules have been drawn up specifying the size and shape of the table, methods of serving the ball, lighting etc. All the hobbyist has to do is to build a device to play table tennis — that's all! This sophisticated notion has stimulated tremendous interest in many quarters. The problems of seeing the ball, judging its path, and hitting it at the right time are complex, to say the least. So complex that some suggest it cannot be done. John Billingsley, however, has dismissed the doubters, pointing out that they said that

Below: The rules of Euromouse require a microprocessor-controlled robot mouse to find its way to the centre of a maze within 15 minutes. This is Thezeus competing in Copenhagen in 1984.

the Micromouse contest was not possible at the beginning. The first round is scheduled to take place at the 1985 Computer Fair which is held at Earls Court arena in London, and encouragingly Dr Billingsley already has over 100 applicants to build a device.

Robot games therefore show great promise of being a major development in the field of micro-robotics. We may yet see a gladiatorial contest of life-size robots fighting to the "death" in some science park Colosseum. The element of competition in pitting robots against human beings is also going to be a major facet of this sort of games-playing. It brings to mind the film "Westworld" in which Yul Brynner played a robot gun-slinger who went out of control. Maybe it would be better to make all our fun robots in the shape of Brigitte Bardot or Bo Derek. That, of course, is a different kind of fun!

Robots in Education

If we turn from amusement robots to consider educational robots, it can be observed that robots of all kinds, arms and mobiles, large and small, were and still are being bought by schools, colleges and universities. Such institutions take the view that learning skills are best developed by actual, rather than textbook experience, particularly if the student has an opportunity for "hands on" practice. Programming the robot to go through a sequence of movements using your program compels you to think through the creative process and encourages learning. The fascination for children, and indeed for all of us, is that a robot is like a mirror in which we can see ourselves.

To make a robot perform certain functions, you must first imagine the sequence of actions; then you describe what you are doing; having done that you transcribe that description into a complete program. You may well find that the robot does something that you had not anticipated. You then have to go back and check your description and the way you programmed it. All this promotes a sense of awareness, a more accurate use of language, and of course leads to better computer programming with its attendant mathematics and algebra. It is an ideal educational tool. To say "Bend your arm like this" to a

child is easy enough, but it is necessary to translate that into "a 45° bend" for the robot. This provides a graphic demonstration of the concept of an angle, and thus a visual and personal understanding of simple trigonometry.

Much of what we have to teach children, particularly in the field of mathematics, is abstract. The main reason for the failure of elementary education in maths and even arithmetic is that children are not learning about ideas that they can relate to their own experience. The computer provides a way for them to get actual experience of computation, formulae and numerical abstractions of many kinds. These are powerful techniques for learning, and this follows a tradition in teaching, particularly in Britain, which uses concrete objects to demonstrate abstract principles.

Because the control and programming of robots is a growing part of the technique of teaching, a simple cost effective robot for the schoolroom had to be devised. This is "the Turtle". It is a mobile vehicle attached to the computer by a flexible wire, and is, therefore, directly programmable from the computer keyboard. Because the Turtle is simple both mechanically and electronically it is often sold in kit form. The construction of a kit is in itself an educational experience which expands the pupils' understanding of the capabilities of the Turtle robot, its control and movement. Thus the mechanical and electronic components of a device are supplied, and its construction explained in the manual and assembly instructions of the manufacturer.

The other dimension of the Turtle lies in the software used to control it. This is often used by pupils in primary schools, and must be simple enough for them to understand. For this reason it needs to have two capabilities. Firstly it must be able to trace its steps for its "master". This is easily done — the Turtle is equipped with a built-in pen or pencil with which it draws a track. When the operator chooses, it will lower its pen to leave a line on the paper or table top to show where it has been; sometimes the control can even alternate between differently coloured pens. Secondly, the Turtle requires a simple computer language to control the movements and tracking of the machine.

Robot Ping-Pong
The drawing shows the dimensions of the table specified for robot ping-pong. The playing area for each robot is a half metre square frame at the end of the table. Bat size must not exceed a 12·5cm diameter circle. As in table tennis, the robot must strike the ball so that it bounces once on the opponent's side of the table before emerging through the playing frame, when it may be returned by the opposing robot. Rallies are started by a simple mechanism at the top of the centre frame which projects the ball towards the server. The area of the centre frame is restricted to prevent any unscrupulous robot

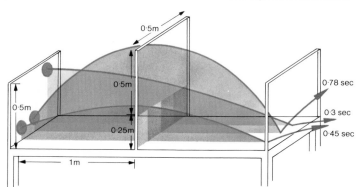

lobbing the ball out of the sight of its opponent's sensors. The three trajectories show the transit time of the lowest possible drive over the net, a

permissible lob, and a smash from higher in the playing frame. To prevent interminable rallies, an opponent is deemed to have won the point when it has returned the ball

20 times. It is hoped that, apart from being fun, the competition will encourage the development of low-cost sensor techniques capable of tracking the ball.

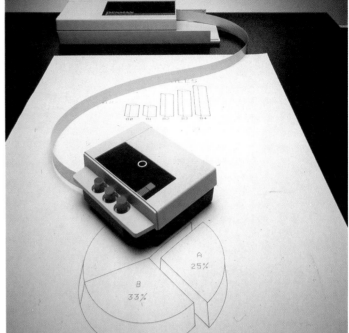

Above: Feedback's Armadillo turtle is propelled, under computer control, by two independently driven wheels. When directed, it can lower a pen to chart its course on paper.

Above right: Penman is three-colour plotter that also functions as a desktop turtle. It has optical and tactile sensors to help find its position on the paper and to avoid obstacles.

Right: The BBC Buggy is specifically designed as an educational tool to familiarize children with the ways in which computers are used as controlling devices in industry.

This language is LOGO, the brainchild of educationalist Seymour Papert of the Massachusetts Institute of Technology. He started with a few words and rules of grammar—much simpler than other computing languages such as BASIC. To these words and their grammar, he added a core of simple commands, called primitives, built into the language. These primitives perform such operations as addition, subtraction, multiplication and division, as well as manipulating words and lists of words. LOGO is a language for quick, easy learners who are able to build on initial programs to construct more complex ones. In other words the young pupils of elementary and secondary school age.

At the other end of the educational spectrum the micro-robot is being used to instruct the more advanced student in abstract mathematics, geometry and calculus at a much higher level of proficiency. The syllabuses which are being developed in the UK for "A" level students of computer control, notably by Essex University, lean heavily on the use of micro-robots to show the flexibility of the maths and geometry within their working envelope. This technique has been taken up with enthusiasm by Britain's Open University. A

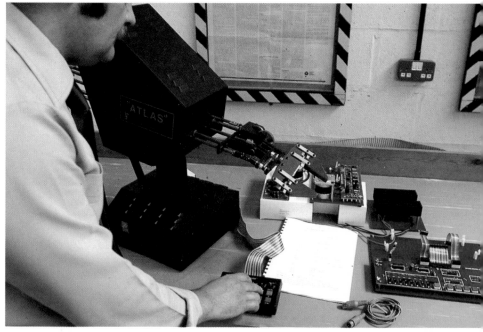

Above: Students involved with the robotics technology programme at Vincennes University, Indiana, obtain "hands-on" experience in the lab with the Rhino XR educational system.

Below: In this system, an Armdroid picks up and places chemical samples on a balance. Their weights before and after treatment are automatically recorded by a microcomputer.

Above: An instructor at the Telford Information Technology Centre in Shropshire demonstrates an Atlas arm as part of a vocational training course in electronics for school leavers.

robot has been specifically developed for them with two new robotics courses in mind. The first course is concerned with the mathematics and geometry of movement and position. The second, which is supported by the Department of Industry, is a much more practical syllabus, designed for production engineers working in factories. The course package is directed at the problems and solutions posed in the applications of robots to everyday manufacturing requirements. These courses provide not only notes, papers, and both verbal and video-taped instructions but also a worthwhile robot. It has six axes of movement and a gripper with DC servo motor drive with a reach of 20in (50cm). It can lift 2·2lb (1kg) with a repeatability of 0·08in (2mm), and is supplied with an experimental kit of tools that enables industrial tasks to be simulated. In such an instance the micro-robot can be clearly seen to be a useful adjunct to its big industrial brother. The provision of a small but sophisticated teaching robot, which has enough muscle to do a worthwhile industrial task, is a world first.

In the United States, one of the most widely used instructional robots is the Rhino XR. This has an open construction which permits the student to observe the internal mechanisms in operation, and also a completely accessible controller and teach pendant. Because of its flexible design the robot has been used to teach a wide variety of subjects including robot design, robot control, work cell layout and management, industrial electronics, and computer programming. The system has been adopted by many educational establishments, while industry has also taken up the XR for in-house training of robotics personnel, and to retrain workers who want to change their careers. At Tufts

New England School of Medicine, the XR has even been adapted for use with a joystick to turn the pages of a book for handicapped patients. Truly, the educational robot has come of age.

Further Applications

So, as we have seen above, while many micro-robots were originally developed for educational purposes, technicians and businessmen soon began to think of other worthwhile uses for the small robot. Most manufacturers also supported this diversification. The first establishment that developed a project for the evaluation of micro-robots was The UK Atomic Energy Research Establishment at Harwell. A test programme carried out by Dr Brian Pierce and Trevor Huddlestone measured and compared the accuracy and performance of all micro-robots on the market. The tests included trials of a work station for handling small radio-active isotope samples, carried out over many months. In those early stages of development of the technology the results were disappointing. Only one machine came up to the standard established by Dr Pierce

and that was the American Microbot Alpha system, which was virtually the first robot to be introduced onto the market. It has generally proved the most accurate and reliable both in tests and use.

As the first practical effort to establish objective standards, the results of the Harwell tests were somewhat discouraging, but not a total failure. The world saw that a reputable establishment had taken notice of the "toy" robot and had made tests of a scientific nature. These results were equivocal, but these were early days for the robot. Since then there have been modifications, new models and a general improvement in microcomputer technology. However, the really important development is not so much the technological advance, although that is essential, it is the imaginative vision of the potential of micro-robots that has arisen. Significant applications take some time to establish, but some of them are now clearly apparent and other trends are discernible.

One of the most obvious areas of application for micro-robots is in the laboratory. The preparation and analysis of samples for pharmaceutical, chemical and food testing is often a repetitive and boring process. The laboratory staff who perform much of this repetitive work are relatively highly paid, and a high level of mechanization and even automation already exists in such situations. Furthermore, laboratory managers are accustomed to investing heavily in expensive, sophisticated equipment, and therefore they understand the principles of payback for machine installations. This market has obvious promise for micro-robot technology.

A prime mover in the development of robots for laboratory use has been the Laboratory of the Government Chemist in

Above: This system in the Office of the Government Chemist in London uses a vision sensor to identify letters on the tops of sample bottles to assist in categorization and transfer operations.

London. Much investigatory work has gone on in their laboratories under the supervision of Derek Potter, Head of Administration Services, who has made robotic handling his special study. Automatic machines already carry out all sorts of specific tasks. Chemical titrations (mixing two liquids until they go bang or change colour) are carried out for samp-

ling. Other machines weigh samples on delicate balances, accurate to a ten thousandth of a gram. A laboratory technician often has to transfer samples in the form of files or flasks of liquids or chemicals between weighing, titration, or other work stations. Experiments concerning the transfer and handling of these samples by robots have been going on for some time. Now we are beginning to see some results from that experimentation. One of the most repetitive tasks in chemical analysis is the weighing of samples to the fine limits already described. A work station to carry out this task

with a small robot was one of the first projects investigated by research teams in the oil, chemical, food, pharmaceutical and other industrial laboratories, and the results were encouraging. Automatic placing of samples on the balance and the recordings of readings on a microcomputer, before and after treament, is now a routine procedure in laboratories. The introduction of small robots into the preparation and analysis system is going to make the concept of the unmanned laboratory as real a prospect as the unmanned factory is on a larger scale.

Another quite different application envisages the use of a robot as a bartender. A waitress wearing a lightweight microphone can communicate with the robot-controlled bar and place orders which the robot dispenses. Such a bar has been in operation in the USA for some time, and the robot recognizes speech and is able to "talk back". The "voice" can be changed so that it is a feminine one during the day, and a man's in the evening. The waitress can order a round of drinks directly from the customer's table which could be several hundred feet from the bars. The customer would hear his order being given so he would know that it was correct. The drinks are then poured and mixed automatically, while the waitress attends to the other tables. The bar is

Below: The world's first robotic bar was introduced in San Francisco by Scarab Robotics Corp. The waitress relays orders to the bar via a headset, and the robot automatically mixes the drinks and has them ready by the time she gets back to collect them.

programmed to dispense up to 150 drinks or mixers. The costing of the bar which is done by a microcomputer, can accurately assess the price to the proprietor of adding even a slice of lemon to the drink. Stocktaking and cash control are also performed by the computer, and the customer sees his order displayed on a screen with cost of drinks, money offered and change given also indicated. The system would seem to leave very little room for inaccuracy as money changes hands between customer and proprietor. All the "bartender" needs to do now is to be able to listen sympathetically to its customers' problems.

Problems of a different kind are being solved for the disabled by using small robots. Dr K. S. Gill of Brighton Polytechnic in the United Kingdom is one of the several researchers looking into the aid that the small robot can offer those unable to help themselves. His project, aimed at developing voice-controlled arms which can react to the commands "Up, Down, Forward, Back" etc, can provide partially or wholly paralysed patients with the handling ability that they so badly need. One young girl, almost totally paralysed, has been taught to control a small robot using whistles and grunts. The spectacle of such a young woman, previously practically helpless unless aided, controlling a robot to feed herself a spoonful of food is incredibly moving. Other projects which mount small arms onto wheelchairs are being carried out in the Veteran's Disabled Center in Palo Alto in California. These enable patients who can move around in their chairs to reach and hold objects that their paralysed limbs cannot grasp. These few illustrations of the use of micro-robots, ranging from the light-hearted to the deeply serious, show the wide range of applications to which the micro-robot can be put as a flexible tool in the hands of industry, commerce and medicine.

Sense and Sensibility

As we have seen, there are many tasks that a micro-robot can undertake in its present form. What would it not be able to do if it were smarter? More to the point, how can it be made a cleverer machine? Quite simply, in the same way as its larger industrial brother, by adding sensors and also by programming intelligence into the controlling computer. The only difference with these sensors is that, because the micro-robot is much cheaper and smaller than the ordinary robot, the cost

Above left: Dr Funakubo of the University of Tokyo developed this robot to assist bedridden patients. The two manipulators are capable of cooperative motion, and they can be commanded by voice, whistle or keyboard, depending on the patient's abilities.

Left: Mobile robots may make life easier for the disabled. This home-produced model was exhibited at the first International Personal Robot Congress in Albuquerque in 1984.

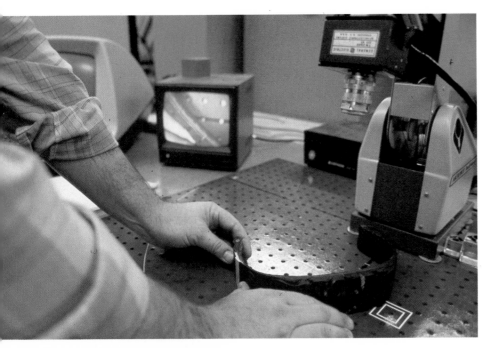

Above: A Microbot TeachMover fitted with a General Electric vision system scans the constituents of radial tyres in this research programme conducted at Pennsylvania State University.

of the different kinds of sensor and intelligence will have to be commensurately lower.

If you think of a robot as a person, then sensors represent that person's senses, such as sight, touch, hearing etc. It has been said that the contemporary robot has the capability of a blindfold man, seated on a chair with one hand tied behind his back. This is not entirely true because man has a sense of touch, which the robot may not possess. The tactile sense can be given to a machine in a number of ways. The most simple is a touch switch or limit switch, so called because it represents the limit of travel of an arm or work-piece. The switch can, of course be programmed: it can be made to stop the machine or even reverse its path. Other sensors, or transducers as they are sometimes called, are force transducers which sense the mechanical pressures which are exerted on them. These sensors on the end of a gripper's claws enable the robot to know how tightly it is holding an object, so the machine can judge how to handle and hold an egg as opposed to a tough object like a brick. The feedback of signals and information about the pressure that the gripper is exerting enables the computer to increase or decrease the pressure of its grip. The nature of feedback and its relation to robotics was introduced in Chapter 3.

Vision systems in particular depend on feedback and there are a number of low cost systems which are available for use with small robots. They include a wide variety of devices using different techniques. One of them simply looks at a single spot on the image and tells the computer if what it sees is black or white. It would be necessary to scan the field of vision with this device in order to look at a whole picture, in the same way that you might look at the horizon with a telescope. Such black and white images are called binary, because they can only be either of two states: light or dark. The more complex images which include shades of grey are much more difficult to compute and process. The more complex devices needed to capture shaded images, such as those received by video cameras, are able to translate that image into a digital picture for the computer. The ability of the robot to see, and more importantly to be able to make sense of what it sees, is the most significant step towards making the robot more clever. A number of small vision devices costing only a few hundred pounds are available for use with most small robots. The most critical element that allows the interpretation and use of information from images is the intelligence of the software that drives the robot's controlling computer brain. The recognition and perception of patterns needed to interpret images is a part of that intelligence.

Artificial Intelligence, or AI as it is called, will require a machine to recognize all sorts of patterns beside visual images. The sense of hearing and of touch both use different methods to recognize and process the signals in order to render them intelligible to the computer. They have to be interpreted very quickly because they all need a swift reaction. The master's voice requires an immediate answer. The perception of an obstacle requires rapid messages to the wheels to take evasive action. The touch of the gripper requires different pressures to be exerted if it is holding an egg, or if it is grasping a brick. All these take a calculating mind and, in the case of a robot's computer brain, one which has a large memory to cope with these calculations. The mechanics of AI and the techniques for coping with those large numbers of calculations is complex and explained more fully in Chapter 8. However, one can say that the increasing numbers of programs containing AI techniques are getting cheaper all the time. Intelligent chess programs, expert systems and pattern recognition and perception programs are now available for a few hundred pounds each.

Robot control is more and more achieved through high level languages such as one created specifically for the purpose called FORTH. The developers claim that the structure is ideal for computer control techniques of many kinds. Another computer language called LOGO has been developed by educationalists for young children and students. Its keynote is simplicity and it is designed to drive such basic devices as the Turtle and Fischertechnik kits as had been explained earlier. The sensors which give a picture of the outside world and the programs which enable the robot to use that picture are an integral part of the way that robots act and react. The sensor aspect of robot technology has been to some extent neglected in the effort to make the basic machine mechanically more accurate and more reliable. However, experimentation shows that accuracy can be achieved more easily by a "seeing eye" checking the position and correcting it than by concentrating on a high level of mechanical accuracy. The advances in sensor development in the last few years, particularly in the low cost applications associated with micro-robotics, have been considerable. The potential that this gives to the robot of tomorrow is a gateway to the future.

The Robot of the Future

The future for such a volatile, fast-moving technology as micro-robotics can equally be discussed in the light of likely near-term developments—say, the next two years—or likely long-term development—over the next twenty years. In twenty years, which brings us to the beginning of a new century, we can contemplate an electronic machine which has the capability, structure and complexity of some of the robots of science fiction. Its physical form will be of secondary importance to its intelligence, although it is fairly certain that there will be mechanical bodies to carry the computer brain around. Whatever shape they take, there is little doubt that robots, both great and small, will have a major social, economic and physical impact on our world. In the nearer term, the micro-robot will begin to exploit the additional technology, applications and markets open to it, to fill an important technological niche by the end of the century. What are those markets and applications likely to be? In the near future the structural environment of the factory and the laboratory will allow further utilization of micro-robots along the lines already discussed. Work places will probably not be entirely unmanned, but exist with a skeleton staff to run the production facilities of tomorrow. Commercial and domestic areas of labour will also see robots doing more chores, a few of which are already apparent.

As regards retailing services offered to the public, you have already read about the robot bar. There are already plans for robots to prepare food behind the counters in fast food shops. One hamburger shop in Los Angeles had developed its own specification for such an installation. The purpose is not mainly to save on staff and thus payroll (although that will happen), it is a marketing ploy for the attraction of custom and publicity. Robot installations with suitable cosmetic appearances will make their appearance in many fast food restaurants and other shops and kitchens in the relatively near future.

The big market opportunity, however, must lie in the home. Present day domestic robots are little more than clever toys, although they are able to act as a domestic or even commercial security guard in homes or offices. This application is not far off, and as a wandering watch-dog a robot will be more flexible than the wired-in burglar alarm which secures all windows and doors. Even using existing technology, a robot can challenge all-comers and recognize only specific people nominated by the user. The development of a robot to provide a realistic home servant that could serve the home owner both in the home and in the garden is now technically (if not economically) possible. This has always been the dream of the small robot enthusiast, and to some extent machines such as Hero can be considered as prototypes of such mechanical servants.

Architects have defined the house as a machine in which to live. Already many machines are available to help us: vacuum cleaners, washing machines, dishwashers etc. On a secondary level, machines such as food processors, weighing machines and microwave or ordinary cookers help us prepare and process food for cooking. Just like laboratory or factory appliances, these machines have to be switched on, loaded, operated and unloaded, in this case by human beings. A great deal of housework is therefore similar to repetitious factory work, and many of the robotic solutions can probably be as well applied in the home as in the factory. The fact that some people enjoy parts of domestic work and may want to step into the working system to produce the sauce for their favourite dish is a complication, but not a serious one. The average home then has all the ingredients for an automated domestic system built into it, but the integration of the elements has not yet been perfected. What will the house of the future need to support us all in the idleness of which we dream? It is fairly certain that the system will be built into the structure of the house, and not added on by the use of a mobile "butler type" robot. Such mobile helpers may be called upon to carry out occasional tasks, but the mechanical servant will not be the principal functionary in the robotized home.

The elimination of dust from the house is already partly possible through the use of draught-proof double glazing and sophisticated air-conditioning filters. Dusting the furniture is unlikely to become a thing of the past, but it will not be the regular pastime that it is now. The mud from the boots of robot-age children can

be dealt with by a cleaner similar to those already designed which will wander the house at convenient times to clean floors. It should not need emptying because it could plug itself into a duct system which would deposit the dirt straight into the dustbin. Laundry will have its own ducting system to carry dirty clothes to one of the cleverest programmable machines that you have in your home at the moment, the washing machine. Ironing is probably the most intractable problem because of the flexibility of cloth, which makes it the most difficult to handle before ironing.

Right: Do robots have a future in the home as domestic helpers? Reekie Research thinks they do, and this is a prototype of the basic home robot that it hopes to sell for under £300.

Below: RB Robot's RB5X is designed specifically for the home. In 1984, financial problems forced RB Robot to file a plan of reorganization with the US Bankruptcy Court—is this an omen for the home robot market in general?

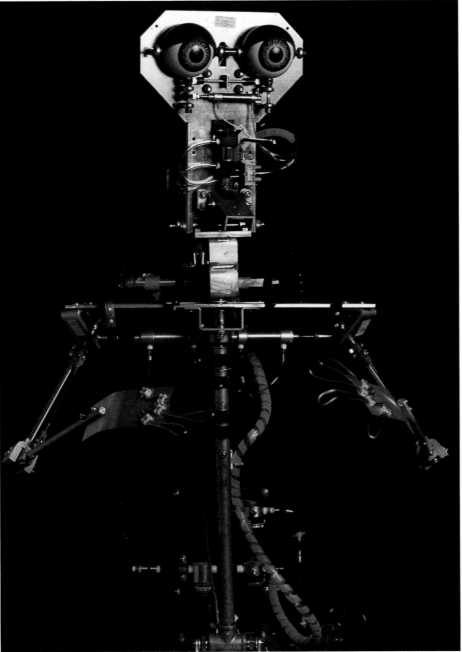

Above: The future for micro-robots with educational applications looks assured. Feedback's Armsort PPR 1030 can be programmed to test and sort resistors according to resistance values.

Left: Chuck E. Cheese Pizza Time restaurants use robots like this to entertain the customers; one day they may also be making the pizzas.

The laying out of clothes on an ironing machine is not an easy thing for a robot to do; work is going on in the field, however, and at least one university hopes to offer a solution soon.

The main problem in fully automating the home, however, is to develop robots which can cook in an automated kitchen. Food mixers, processors and other machines already exist, but cooking is a complex task as menus vary, and also the number of meals to be served is small. However, there is no doubt that the technology can cope with cooking simple meals. There are a number of fast food chains in the USA which have developed an automated system for preparing, cooking and serving such items as hamburgers using robotic techniques. The concept of the unmanned kitchen is here now; how long before it becomes cheap enough to be generally available is another question.

This is the robot of the fairly near future. You will notice that it is not doing extremely clever or sophisticated things. There will be intelligent robots using skill and even judgement in industry, space exploration etc, but the larger market in the near term will be for small, safe, reliable robots to serve the public. In the 1990s, the micro-robot will have improved its technology a little, and its applications a lot. The uses and systems are available; we have not yet developed the robotic tools to do the tasks that are needed. The future is here in kit form; all we need to do is put it together.

Robots have already taken their first steps into space, but current plans for future space development envisage an ever broadening role for a new generation of intelligent machines.

SMART SYSTEMS IN SPACE

The use of robots as opposed to man has long been one of the key issues in the debate over how best to explore space. Surprisingly the arguments offered here do not differ greatly from those advanced in the debate on the use of robots in the factory. The key argument is the expense that can be saved by sending a cheap (often expendable) surrogate vs. the gains that can be made by sending a human with unique skills. In truth the space programme has always featured a blend of manned and unmanned explorers and the debate really centres on where man should stop and instead dispatch his surrogates.

Few spacecraft have been launched that can truthfully be considered to fit the definition of a robot although the term is often used loosely when discriminating between them and manned spacecraft. All satellites possess an assortment of automatic mechanisms, but most are little more than devices for extending booms with sensors or rotating solar arrays.

Ewald Heer, program manager for autonomous systems and space mechanics at NASA's Jet Propulsion Laboratory (JPL), in the November 1981 issue of "Mechanical Engineering" that defined the state of and prospects for space robotics, came up with this assessment:

"Future robots and manipulators in space may be put into four general categories: (1) space exploration; (2) global services; (3) space industrialization; and (4) space transportation . . . It is clear that the spacecraft autonomous

capabilities, including automated decision making and problem solving by the onboard computer system, will be major elements in the operation of these systems. The robot spacecraft must be able to implement sophisticated control strategies and manage its onboard resources. It must also be able to assure self-maintenance of its functions and make the appropriate decisions toward achieving the assigned tasks.

"Present and projected developments in machine intelligence suggest that in the future many of the presently ground-based data processing and information extraction functions can be performed autonomously on board the robot spacecraft. Only the useful information would be sent to the ground and distributed to the users. This would imply that the robot is able to make decisions on its own as to what data to retain and how to process them to provide the user with the desired information . . .

"The multitude of systems and widely-varying activities envisioned in space until the end of this century will require

Right: Dale Gardner (left) and Joseph Allen retrieved two "rogue" satellites with the aid of a Canadian-built robot arm (right) during the 51A Shuttle mission in November 1984.

Below: NASA's Viking 1 lander robotically scoops up soil samples from the surface of Mars after its arrival on the planet in July 1976.

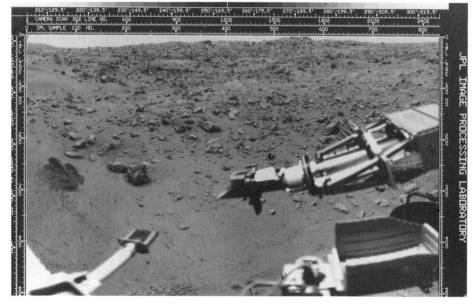

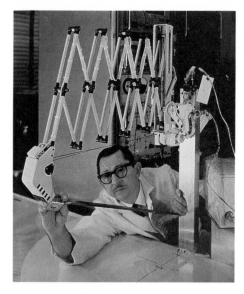

Above: An ingenious arm, part of the Surveyor 3 lunar lander, could dig a trench in the Moon's soil up to 3ft (1m) away from the spacecraft.

Right: The USSR built two Lunokhods to trundle over the lunar surface under the control of operators on Earth who obtained a view of the Moon via two stereo cameras (centre left).

the development of space robots and automation technologies on a broad scale. It is in this area that robot and manipulator technologies will have the greatest impact."

Although generally thought of as being at the forefront of technology, NASA was found by a 1980 study to be lagging in the area of robotics and teleoperators. "Machine Intelligence and Robotics: Report of the NASA Study Group" chaired by Dr Carl Sagan, found that "NASA is 5 to 15 years behind the leading edge in computer science and technology... Although Viking was a brilliant techno-logical success, given its design limitations, Viking's use of robotics technology and in situ programming was rudimentary. Future missions will require great advances in these technologies, and those planned at present are designed for traditional data gathering with little provision for automation. Unlike its pioneering work in other areas of science and technology, NASA's use of computer science and machine intelligence has been conservative and unimaginative." The group recommended that NASA adopt a policy of vigorous and imagina-tive research in these fields along with a number of institutional steps.

The first robots in space were in the US Surveyor series of unmanned lunar landers. Each was equipped with a pantograph-type arm that could be commanded to dig trenches in the lunar soil up to three feet away from the spacecraft. It could yaw through a 112-degree arc and pivot to place the 2 x 5in (5 x 13cm) sample scoop from a maximum of 40in (102cm) above the surface to 18in (46cm) below. A total of 24 square feet (2·2m²) was available to it. Although limited in performance, this arm was

capable of at least one small repair—on Surveyor 7 it was used to nudge loose a soil analysis instrument that refused to drop to the ground.

The Soviet lunar soil samplers had arms that really belong to the actuator class, being nothing more than booms to deploy drills and coring devices, then transfer the sample to a return capsule. The Soviets were the first to demonstrate teleoperation—remote control—with the Lunokhod lunar rovers. These spacecraft carried stereo cameras to provide the human operators with a view of the surface as they drove it around on the Moon. They were also the first to experi-ence the problems of time delay in remote control of space systems (it takes almost three seconds for a signal to travel to the Moon and back).

Vikings on Mars

The first advanced robots in space were the two US Viking landers which arrived on Mars in 1976. Their robot arms were great improvements over the crude pantographs of Surveyor. Each lander had a single spherical coordinate arm that could extend up to 8ft (2·4m) from its base to scoop up soil then drop it into four openings on top of the spacecraft that led to automated analysis labs and growth chambers. The arms were made of two strips of metal that were slightly curved to form an oval cross section. Each strip was rolled lengthwise for storage so that, when extended, the transverse curve and the opposite longitudinal curling of each strip would form a rigid member. The shovel at the end also could be vibrated to shake fine grains through a sieve which excluded pebbles that might otherwise clog the mini-labs. Through

Below: The Viking 1 lander travelled to Mars in this encapsulated form. The unit from which the soil-sampling boom unfurls is centre right, between the two facsimile cameras.

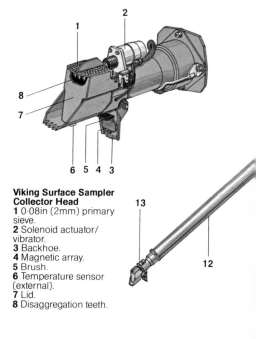

Viking Surface Sampler Collector Head
1 0·08in (2mm) primary sieve.
2 Solenoid actuator/vibrator.
3 Backhoe.
4 Magnetic array.
5 Brush.
6 Temperature sensor (external).
7 Lid.
8 Disaggregation teeth.

Above: This robot arm, called the remote manipulator system and built by Spar Aerospace of Canada, is used for tasks such as retrieval of satellites during Space Shuttle missions.

more than two years of operations, until contact was lost with the landers, the two arms worked without fail.

The most advanced robot to fly in space to date is, of course, the Space Shuttle's remote manipulator system (RMS). Early in the Space Shuttle programme, NASA managers recognized that there would be many payloads that would need to be replaced in the payload bay of the Shuttle and that neither vehicle would be capable of providing the exquisite movements needed to position a satellite within less than an inch of holding mechanisms. Further, there would be satellites that would require deployment by means other than the spring-release mechanisms that send satellites with their attached upper stage motors on their way.

At the same time the Canadian government was seeking a role in the new Shuttle programme. After examining the options available, they chose to develop the robot arm, now called the remote manipulator system (RMS) at no cost to the US Government. In return, the US promised not to fund any competing models and to buy one RMS for each Shuttle after the first model was delivered.

The National Research Council of Canada managed the programme and selected SPAR Aerospace as its prime contractor. SPAR had no space flight experience but did have an extensive background in aircraft motors and transmissions, the sort of mechanisms that would be required to build the robot. The project actually was about one-third American with SPAR developing the arm and its control panel, Rockwell International (the Shuttle prime contractor) the RMS positioning mechanism and retention latches, and IBM, the control software. The combination is known as the Payload Deployment and Retrieval System (PDRS), although most readers will probably have heard it described as the robot arm, RMS, or Canadarm (the project name given shortly before the first flight on STS-2 in November 1981.)

The specifications set for the RMS were that it must be able to deploy and retrieve a full Shuttle cargo—65,000lb (29,485kg), 15ft (4·6m) wide and 60ft (18·m) long. Operating requirements included having a 50ft (15·2m) reach, capturing a payload moving at 0·1 feet per second (0·03mps) past the Shuttle, releasing a maximum-weight payload within 5 degress of a specified attitude and with less than 0·015-degree-per-second motion, stopping within 2ft (0·6m) when moving a 32,000lb (14,515kg) payload at 0·2 feet per second (0·06mps), moving at 2 feet per second (0·6mps) with no payload, positioning the end of the arm within 2in (5·1cm) and 1 degree of a desired position, attaching payloads to another spacecraft, and deploying and retrieving at least five payloads on each mission. Additionally, it was to be outfitted with TV cameras to aid the crew, weigh less than 1,000lb (454kg), and operate through the Shuttle's general purpose computer.

The general design was to be a six-jointed arm with a snare-type end-effector.

Viking Lander
1 S-band low-gain antenna.
2 Facsimile camera No 2.
3 UHF antenna (relay).
4 X-ray fluorescence funnel and spoiler.
5 Biology processor.
6 Seismometer.
7 S-band high-gain antenna (direct).
8 Wind and temperature sensors.

9 Boom magnet cleaning brush.
10 Gas chromatograph mass spectrometer processor.
11 Descent engine (3).
12 Furlable boom.
13 Collector head.

In 1976 the US sent to Mars two Viking landers to find out about conditions on

the planet. Each machine had a robot arm, a great improvement on those previously used in Surveyor space probes, which unfurled from a storage unit, and could extend up to 8ft (2·4m) from the lander to collect soil. The sampler head deposited this material into a series of openings

on the top of the space vehicles that were miniature, automated laboratories for tasks such as chemical analysis. Other instruments on the landers monitored factors such as seismology, the planet's magnetic properties and wind speed and direction.

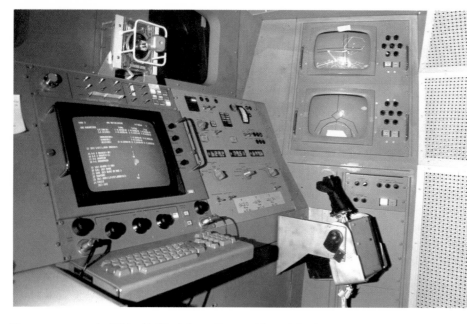

Left: The remote manipulator system is controlled by an astronaut on the Shuttle flight deck. Note the translational and rotational hand controllers (top and bottom right).

The upper arm is 251in (6·37m) from the shoulder to the centre of the elbow joint. The lower arm is 278in (7·06m) from there to the centre of the wrist joint, and the hand is 74in (1·88m) from there to the lip of the end effector. The two arm sections are made of 13in (33cm) wide carbon-epoxy tubing chosen on the grounds of minimum weight and maximum strength.

The shoulder can pitch through a 147-degree arc (2 degrees down into the payload bay, 145 degrees back), and yaw through a full circle. The elbow can rotate through 162 degrees ("backwards", 2 degrees and closed, 160 degrees). The wrist consists of three joints for maximum flexibility in approaching a target: 240 degrees of pitch and yaw, and 447 degrees of roll (more than a full circle). Brushless DC motors with high-reduction gear transmissions are used in each joint.

The end effector works with three wires that are fixed to the end effector "can" at one end and to a rotating sleeve at the other. As the can is rotated the wires close, like the iris of a camera, and trap a small post protruding from the target. The end effector then retracts the sleeve to pull the target snug with the lip of the can, thus providing a firm grip on the target. This design allows for a large degree of misalignment between the RMS and the target spacecraft. A TV camera is fixed on one side of the end effector so the crewman can see the target, and an electrical connector, for instance to power electrical tools, is on the other side (use of the connector is optional). An additional TV camera is sited on the end of the upper arm, just above the elbow joint.

The grapple fixture on a target spacecraft consists of two parts. Firstly there is a circular baseplate with a 10·8in (27·4cm) steel post (the grapple shaft) standing out, which has a small knob at the end of the post. Three guide ramps are mounted around it which match three depressions in the lip of the RMS end effector. Above the fixture is the target, a black bar with a white stripe across its width. A small rod with a white tip extends 4in (10·1cm) from the target. When viewed through the TV camera on the end effector, the alignment of the white dot relative to the white stripe behind it tells the operator the alignment of the end effector relative to the spacecraft.

The RMS is directed by an astronaut working at a station located at the aft port work station on the Shuttle flight deck. There are two hand controllers, left for translation and right for rotation, plus two TV cameras and two aft flight deck windows which provide views into the payload bay. Additionally, there are switches for direct control of each motor and brake on the RMS, warning lights, and readouts of each joint's position.

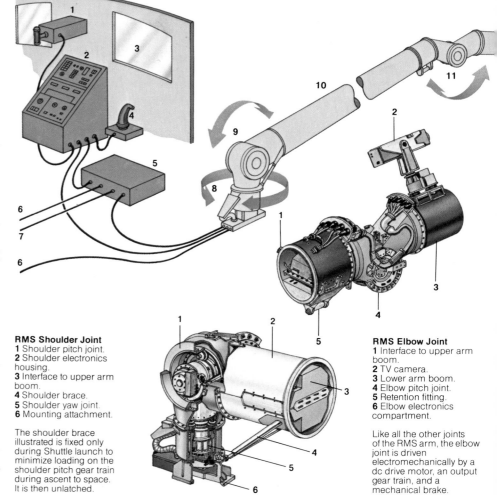

RMS Shoulder Joint
1 Shoulder pitch joint.
2 Shoulder electronics housing.
3 Interface to upper arm boom.
4 Shoulder brace.
5 Shoulder yaw joint.
6 Mounting attachment.

The shoulder brace illustrated is fixed only during Shuttle launch to minimize loading on the shoulder pitch gear train during ascent to space. It is then unlatched.

RMS Elbow Joint
1 Interface to upper arm boom.
2 TV camera.
3 Lower arm boom.
4 Elbow pitch joint.
5 Retention fitting.
6 Elbow electronics compartment.

Like all the other joints of the RMS arm, the elbow joint is driven electromechanically by a dc drive motor, an output gear train, and a mechanical brake.

Below: The RMS as deployed during mission STS-7 in June 1983. A camera on the free-flying SPAS pallet recorded this fine image of the arm parked above the payload bay.

Below: Astronaut John Fabian in front of the RMS grapple fixture on SPAS-01. The target bar and grapple shaft encircled by its three guide ramps are clearly visible.

The arm has five control modes: automatic (computer follows an automatic sequence loaded before flight or by the crew), manual augmented (operator "flies" the end effector and the computer generates the appropriate joint commands), manual single joint (operator commands joints by means of individual switches), direct and backup direct drive (operator commands through switches hard-wired to joints and by-passing computer).

The RMS is able to reach about 90 per cent of the work space in the payload bay. The exceptions are a 7·5in (19cm) buffer zone (defined in software) at the edge of the payload bay, about the last 10ft (3m) of the aft payload bay, and a spherical zone immediately under the RMS shoulder joint.

Testing the RMS

Development of the RMS took place at SPAR's Toronto plant where a full-scale working model was built and operated from a mock-up of the Shuttle aft flight deck. The RMS model was limited, though, because being almost identical to the flight model, it was too flimsy to support its own weight on Earth. It had to ride on air-bearing pads on the floor and most tests were limited to two dimensions. A less-capable mock-up was built at Johnson Space Center in Houston where helium-filled balloons in the shape of spacecraft are lifted in deployment exercises.

The first flight of the RMS was made on the second Shuttle mission, STS-2, during 12-14 November 1981. Despite the mission being cut short to two days, most of the basic RMS checkout tests were completed. These included having the end effector trace the edges of the large Earth-mapping radar carried in the payload bay; the pattern was stored in the computer and the whole sequence was done automatically. Initially the RMS was meant to pick up a contamination monitor, but cautious managers decided to limit the test to grappling only. Even that was scrubbed, though, when the No 2 end effector, undergoing tests in Canada, developed a problem that indicated that the flight model might jam in place. Despite these setbacks, the RMS was successfully berthed with the contamination monitor's grapple fixture.

The STS-3 mission (22-30 March 1982) was frustrated by a different problem when failure of the wrist TV camera meant that the crew would not be able to see in order to grapple the contamination monitor which, on this flight, was obscured by the science pallet. The crew was able to pick up a 500lb (227kg) plasma diagnostics package and use it in a series of experiments in and around the payload bay. In one sequence, the crew positioned the package directly in a stream of electrons emitted by a fast-pulse electron gun.

On STS-4 (27 June-4 July 1982) the arm finally was used to pick up the 1,000lb (454kg) contamination monitor and manoeuvre it around the payload bay to map contamination levels in and around the Shuttle orbiter during thruster firings. The arm was also used in a futile attempt to pop open the lid of an infra-red telescope carried on the secret Air Force cargo.

Progressively heavier cargoes were used to test the RMS on operational Shuttle flights over the next two years. On STS-7 (18-24 June 1983) the arm was used to deploy and then retrieve the SPAS-01 satellite developed by MBB of West Germany, the first time any spacecraft had retrieved something it deployed. On STS-8 it lifted, then returned to its position, the

Space Shuttle Remote Manipulator System (RMS) Components

1 Translational hand controller.
2 Display and controls console.
3 Aft observation window.
4 Rotational hand controller.
5 Manipulator controller interface unit.
6 Power cables.
7 Cable to general purpose computer.
8 Shoulder yaw joint.
9 Shoulder pitch joint.
10 Upper arm boom.
11 Elbow pitch joint.
12 Lower arm boom.
13 Wrist pitch joint.
14 Wrist yaw joint.
15 Wrist roll joint.
16 Standard end effector.

The RMS is the mechanical arm portion of the Shuttle's payload deployment and retrieval system. It is designed to manoeuvre a payload from the cargo bay and release it into space, and also to grapple a free-flying payload and berth it in the payload bay, as it did with the Solar Max satellite during mission 41-C. The basic configuration consists of the manipulator arm, a display and control panel in the Orbiter and a control unit that connects to the Orbiter's computer system. Normally only one arm is installed on the port longeron of the payload bay, but a two-arm installation is also possible. The RMS operator controls the position and attitude of the arm by viewing it through the flight deck observation windows, as well as on closed-circuit TV from both arm and payload bay cameras, and sending commands by means of two hand controllers. In the single-joint drive control mode the operator can move the arm on a joint-by-joint basis with full computer support. A jettison system is also installed in case the arm cannot be safely stowed.

RMS Wrist Joint (top)

1 Wrist forward electronics compartment.
2 Wrist aft electronics compartment.
3 Closed-circuit TV camera.
4 Light.
5 Retention fitting.
6 Wrist roll joint.
7 Wrist yaw joint.
8 Wrist pitch joint.
9 Retention fitting.

The RMS wrist possesses three degrees of freedom, like other robot wrists.

End Effector (above)

1 Extra-vehicular activity (EVA) handhold.
2 Snare cables which open and close around grapple fixtures.
3 Electrical connector.
4 Mechanism to pull snare assembly to back of end effector to "rigidize" contact.

This is the standard snare-type end effector which is fitted to the RMS arm. Special purpose effectors can also be used.

payload flight test article, a space-age dumbbell, if you will, designed solely for testing the RMS. One end was filled with lead shot (to evaluate different inertias) and both ends had 15ft (4·6m) wide screens to obscure the operator's view so engineers could assess the problems involved in berthing large spacecraft.

The heaviest spacecraft yet handled by the RMS is the Long Duration Exposure Facility (LDEF) deployed on STS-41C (6-13 April 1984). It weighs 22,000lb (9,980kg) and is 14ft (4·3m) wide and 30ft (9·2m) long. Before deploying LDEF, the RMS was also used to turn on some of its experiment trays by twisting a special grapple fixture. As Challenger backed away from LDEF, TV images showed that the spacecraft— which has no attitude control system—had no visible motion. The arm had not given it any "tip off" motion that would put it in a slow tumble and make retrieval impossible.

The RMS's biggest test came two days later when it was used to retrieve the Solar Maximum Mission satellite (Solar Max). Astronaut George Nelson, flying a Manned Maneuvering Unit was unable to berth with the satellite and halt its slow spin, so the Shuttle closed on it and attempted to grapple with the RMS. Because the spacecraft now had a mild wobble added to its rotation—caused by Nelson's repeated berthing attempts and a desperate handhold on the solar panels—astronaut Terry Hart was unable

Right: Bruce McCandless remains hooked to the RMS arm by a "cherry picker" type foot-restraint device in tests during Shuttle mission 41B.

Below: The Earth Radiation Budget Satellite is deployed by the RMS as part of the satellite's release sequence on the 41G mission in October 1984.

Below right: Joseph Allen holds the Westar VI satellite while still attached to the RMS during mission 51A in November 1984. The satellite was captured for return to Earth.

to get a clear shot at its grapple fixture. Two days later, though, ground crews had used magnetic torquer bars to slow the wobble and a successful grapple was made on 10 April, followed immediately by berthing the satellite on a special ring so repairs could be made.

This work was done by Nelson and James van Hoften, in alternation, standing in a manipulator foot restraint which turned the RMS into a sort of utility worker's cherry picker; this application had been tested on the previous mission,

41B (3-11 February 1984). A tool caddy and lights in the front of the foot restraint aided this task. There were no controls to let the astronaut command the RMS. Rather, he had to tell Hart where he wanted to be positioned. At the end of the repair work, the RMS was used to pick up Solar Max and hold it above the Shuttle while the satellite was checked out and its data relay antenna deployed; then it was released.

More work for the RMS came on the next three missions. On STS-41D (30 August-

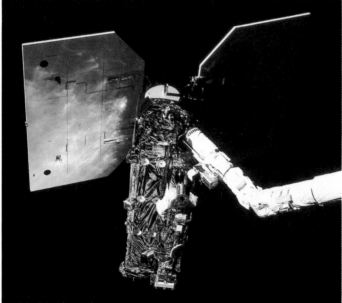

5 September 1984) its wrist TV camera revealed a chunk of ice growing outside the waste water vent and the RMS was used to knock it free rather than risk possible damage to the heatshield when the ice came loose during re-entry. On mission 41G (5-13 October 1984) it deployed the Earth Radiation Budget Satellite (after shaking it and holding it to warm up in the Sun so that stuck solar arrays would deploy). It also nudged a balky Earth-mapping radar antenna into place. And on 51A it picked up the two errant communications satellites that went into incorrect low orbits after deployment from 41B. They were not equipped with grapple fixtures but had them inserted by an astronaut flying the Manned Maneuvering Unit.

A Second Generation RMS

Future missions for the RMS in its current form include retrieval of the LDEF, deployments and retrievals of a number of satellites, on-orbit changeout of the payload modules on Fairchild's Leasecraft satellite and NASA's proposed Proteus satellites (for Explorer-class missions).

A possibility of keen interest to NASA is the Power Extension Package, a 12.5-kilowatt solar array that the RMS would pick up from the payload bay and expose to the Sun to provide electrical power to the Shuttle during extended-duration missions.

A number of upgrades to and second generation variations on the RMS have been suggested. The most immediate change would be in the end effectors to give them more capability. NASA's Johnson Space Center and the California Institute of Technology are working on a "dextrous" end effector that would provide the RMS with some force feedback either in the form of charts on a display in the Shuttle cabin or a restraint that would tighten around the operator's hand. The exact design remains to be worked out at this time, but a first flight is expected around 1987.

Another type of end effector under study is actually a balloon. The sort of aluminium truss beams proposed for use in space construction are quite fragile, so Keith Clark of NASA's Marshall Space Flight Center has proposed using a balloon that would be inflated inside the beam. As it expanded it would press gently and "grasp" the beam, distributing the load across the beam rather than crushing on one or two points. Such a tool could easily be used to grapple anything that had an opening. The balloon would probably be a bladder coated with Kevlar to protect it against sunlight and punctures.

JPL also has outlined a three-digit hand that could be added to the RMS. It would have two fingers and an opposable thumb that would mimic the action of the human hand. The digits would be operated by wire tendons drawn by motors at the base of the hand. Such a scheme would reduce the weight of the hand and moment-of-inertia problems by removing the motors from the digits. It also would give the hand the ability to unfasten bolts, cables, etc without resorting to a series of special-purpose end effectors. Other end effectors might be opposable grippers that would let the RMS pick up flat plates and rods that did not have grapple fixtures.

Spar has studied a Space Crane that would use two arms, each twice the size of the RMS; upper and lower sections would be the length of the payload bay and they would stow by folding over double. A seventh degree of freedom would be provided through upper arm roll to improve dexterity (but also complicating control). The operator would sit in

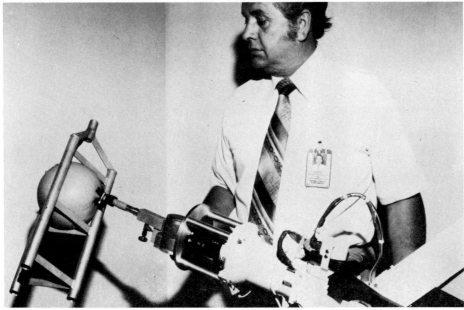

Top: A payload flight test article is held above Challenger's payload bay during tests of the RMS system on the STS-8 flight in September 1983.

Left: Keith Clark demonstrates his design for an innovative end effector which would inflate inside, and so grip, a tubular truss structure.

a pressurized cabin between the two arms. This cabin could be attached to the Shuttle or an unpressurized version could be emplaced at the work site.

More advanced repair platforms for the RMS have been studied by NASA and Grumman Aerospace Corp. The remote work station would resemble the manipulator foot restraint and have controls for the EVA astronaut and a small berthing pin so that the end of the arm could be held firm against the work site rather than wobbling as the astronaut used tools and moved equipment. The next major step would be the manned remote work station, a pressurized module with short manipulator arms. An astronaut could work inside the module, wearing shirt sleeves rather than a space suit, and perform repair work through teleoperator arms extending to the front of the module. Initially the module would be used attached to the RMS, but in time a free-flying version would evolve to give greater flexibility in operations around large spacecraft.

Space Station Robots

The space station era will see the next major developments in the field of space robotics. The space station itself is to have a robot of some sort attached to it. What shape it will have is being decided by US contractors in the so-called Phase B (advanced definition) studies of the space station design. In its request for proposals, NASA stated that the space station manipulator system "shall have reach and dexterity comparable" to that of the Shuttle RMS.

"The manipulator shall be mounted to a mobile platform which provides translation capability to enable the manipulator to reach all critical Space Station elements during both assembly and operational phases." The platform is to provide for movement and operation separate from the station's power supply for up to six hours, and indefinite operation while plugged into the station's power supply. Included in the studies will be

Above: Boeing's concept of the future US manned space station features a rendezvous and retrieval OMV, here seen grappled by the station's RMS arm.

evaluation of controlling the manipulator from the Shuttle during station construction and by astronauts standing on work stations attached to the manipulator. A preliminary drawing shows the robot on a platform that rolls, trolley-fashion, across the station's main structures. An alternative would be to equip the arm with end effectors at each end and use these to "walk" across the station, much as a navigator walks a compass across a chart in marking off distance.

The other space robot will be the Orbital Maneuvering Vehicle, formerly called the

Teleoperator Maneuvering System. The OMV is being developed to operate from the Space Shuttle and to use the space station as its operating base. Initially the OMV will be used to place satellites in higher orbits than the Shuttle can reach and then return, or to bring satellites back to the Shuttle. Project manager William Huber of NASA's Marshall Space Flight Center regards this as "a really significant capacity", one that does not now exist. It will give the space station the capability to service satellites by actually bringing them to the station where spare parts and tools can be stored. Servicing of existing science satellites like the Hubble Space Telescope and the Gamma Ray Observatory has been included as a major goal of the space station programme.

But it is envisaged as more than an unmanned orbital shuttle. "As we go down the road and space station gets into Phase B, we could see mission kits evolving out of that", Huber said. Three such kits are under study now: servicing, refuelling, and tumbling satellite retrieval.

In servicing, "Our approach has been an automated system to exchange modules", Huber said. "We haven't gone into a lot of end effectors, claws and such ... The problem is in designing for servicing. The first likely (customer) is the platform. For most spacecraft it will be easier to bring it back to the station for servicing [because] it would take large spacecraft or large numbers of spacecraft to make servicing economical in place." Despite the promise that is offered, little has been defined beyond the basic techniques described on these pages.

"What we really need is someone who wants a kit", a defined set of tools, Huber said. "It's extremely hard to design a general purpose mission kit." The problem

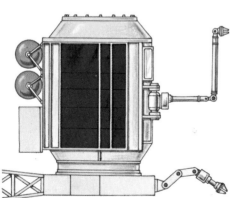

Advanced Repair Platorm
This is Grumman's design for a pressurized manned remote work station. It represents an adaptation of the "open cherry picker" type of platform, and would allow the worker inside to operate in shirt sleeve comfort.

The pressurized capsule would have displays and controls for working the mechanical arms equipped with manipulators that would be used for assembly and maintenance work. The unit is here shown attached to an RMS-type space crane.

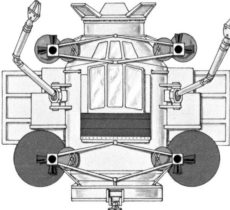

Free-Flier Work Station
The natural development from the work station shown above left would be a free-flying pressurized module, which would allow the astroworker far more freedom to undertake construction work on

large structures in geostationary orbit. This design features two rings of thrusters and propellant tanks which would give the craft the necessary mobility, and again two manipulators which would operate under tele-control.

Above: An OMV leaves the payload bay of a Shuttle to deliver or retrieve satellites in orbits beyond the reach of the Shuttle itself.

starts with the docking interface. That can be made simple enough with a grapple fixture, but then what? How do you arrange the black boxes you want replaced? Where do you put the refuelling ports? How close to the docking area must they be? And how do you design a satellite that still meets its mission while meeting the Orbital Maneuvering Vehicle?

Such a kit was studied by Martin Marietta Aerospace Co for NASA's Langley Research Center as the Remote Orbital Servicing Satellite (ROSS) concept. "The development of a totally autonomous robotic system to accomplish the varied tasks envisioned is currently, and for the foreseeable future, beyond the state of the art, particularly for unplanned or unforeseen contingencies", the study concluded. "However, by retaining man in the control loop, a remotely controlled (teleoperator) system can be developed with today's technology. With man's flexibility and adaptability, the teleoperator system can significantly increase the capabilities to perform space operations."

A key issue in the study was the use of existing technologies and designs, so the ROSS concept relies heavily on the Integrated Orbiting Servicing System (IOSS) and Protoflight Manipulator Arm (PFMA) developed earlier for NASA's Marshall Space Flight Center and discussed below. The design that evolved, weighing 847lb (384kg), would fit on the front end of the Orbital Maneuvering Vehicle. It would have a cruciform structure to hold replacement modules and, slightly above the centre, a pair of robot arms and a stereo TV

camera mimicking human arms and head. Development would take about three years and cost $40 million (1982), Martin Marietta estimated. The Space Shuttle could be used for flight testing of development models that would then be integrated with the OMV for further test and development work.

While this work goes on, the general shape and outline of the OMV and ROSS, and how they might operate, can be seen in three space simulators assembled at Marshall to develop the methods required for "telepresence", or remote manning.

The most extensive telepresence experience is in the nuclear industry where materials in "hot boxes" must be handled. But those always are firmly attached to the ground, in a fixed reference frame,

and with no time delays. In space, commands and data may be delayed by up to two seconds going through communications satellites, and worker and target will be floating free, so there is a great potential for literally blundering around in space and as a consequence damaging valuable satellites.

This is where the simulators at Marshall should be invaluable. They are expected to let engineers and OMV "pilots" simulate a mission from the final phase of rendezvous down to the bumps and wobbles of docking. Three simulators are required for this work, the target motion simulator, the "flat floor" facility, and the six-degree-of-freedom (6-DOF) docking table. There is a degree of overlap among the capabilities that each offers, but that is preferable to a gap.

The target motion simulator is used to duplicate the terminal rendezvous sequence from about 10 miles (16km) out down to docking. In a room, with walls painted flat black, are the OMV—actually a TV camera mounted in gimbals at one end—and its target spacecraft, Landsat 4. The model is mounted on a carriage that rotates it in three axes and moves it lengthwise along a pair of 20ft (6m) long rails. The model is painted in fluorescent paints and the room is bathed in ultraviolet light so the model, on TV, will have the same bright image as an orbiting spacecraft would present in full sunlight.

The OMV pilot sits at a control console left over from the 1970s and which is about to be upgraded. He has a single TV screen, plus some data displays, and two hand controllers, one for rotation (right) and one for lateral motion (left).

Between the two systems is an SEL 3255 computer (which soon will be replaced by a VAX 11/750 mini) that calculates the relative positions and motions of the two spacecraft and converts these into the

Below: This is the OMV control console in the simulator assembled at Marshall Space Flight Center. The operator uses "telepresence" to guide the spacecraft through a docking manoeuvre.

appropriate motions of the camera and spacecraft model. When the OMV fires forward to approach the spacecraft, for example, the model actually slides towards the camera. In the world of simulation this difference is of no importance just so long as the operator sees the same net effect.

The computer also throws in the effects of orbital mechanics. If the OMV moves in too fast it also rises above the target because its greater speed has placed it in a higher orbit. The trick is to aim slightly below the target. Its principal mission is to train candidate OMV operators so the engineers will be able to gauge time and effort required for such work. As an example of how experience builds with the system, this writer "burned" 42lb (19kg) of propellant in flying up to Landsat and still was two feet off the docking target. An experienced operator, though, used only 7lb (3·2kg) of propellant and was right on the mark.

Operations close to the target spacecraft are simulated at the "flat floor" facility where a model of the OMV floats on air-bearing pads across a large epoxy floor, which looks like a smooth pond, and is 44ft x 86ft (13·4m x 26·2m) in size. It was cast on a 12ft (3·6m) deep concrete foundation to assure its stability and is perfectly level to within 1/2,000th of an inch between any adjacent square foot. Such a finish was required because any imperfections would be like hills and valleys that would cause the spacecraft to slide away.

The "spacecraft" is a 2,200lb (1,000kg) vehicle that looks more like a plumber's

Above: A model of an Orbital Maneuvering Vehicle floats on air-bearing pads in the "flat floor" simulation facility at the Marshall Space Flight Center.

Below: Shown here is the IOSS mock-up at Marshall SFC. At the top is the dummy satellite that needs repair, in the centre the IOSS robot arm, below which is the IOSS craft itself.

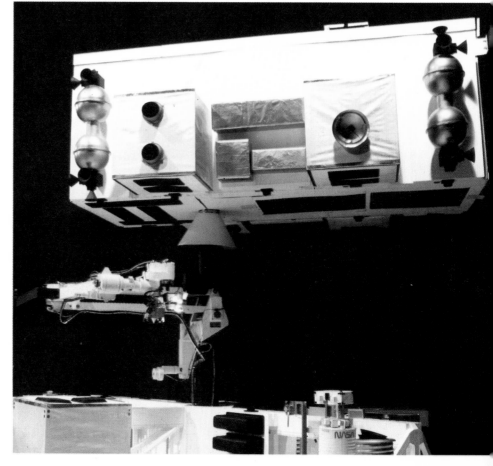

nightmare of airlines and valves. It has six large compressed air bottles to operate the air-bearing pads on which the vehicle rides and the 24 thrusters which make a deafening blast as they push it around the floor. Up to 400lb (181kg) of payload can be placed on the forklift-like end of the spacecraft. Although keyed to the OMV programme, facility manager Fred Roe explained that the facility is generic in order to accommodate a number of spacecraft designs, including an astronaut on a Manned Maneuvering Unit.

The Pilot's View

The pilot's console uses a new design developed by Essex Corp to make flying the OMV less fatiguing. The console has two hand controllers with a keyboard in between. Two TV screens are in front—left for data and right for the OMV camera—and a large-screen projection TV is at the front of the room. The new aspect of the design is that the console top slopes downward to give the operator a more relaxed position while flying the OMV. Stereo vision will be tested soon with a special headset with blinders that darken and clear to present the left and right eyes with the appropriate images on the TV screen. A possible aid to control that will be explored will be to have a computer generate cartoons of how the OMV and target would appear if viewed from a distance, so the pilot will have a better idea of their relative positions. In the works is a six-degree-of-freedom target motion simulator that will hold spacecraft mock-ups and move them as they might be expected to move in space.

Eventually the lab will be able to simulate the rendezvous of the flat-floor spacecraft with another spacecraft, then change video and commands to the Integrated Orbiting Servicing System (IOSS), exchange modules, then switch back to the flat-floor spacecraft and back away. Except for cosmetic differences between the mock-ups, there should be no visible change to the operator. He will dock with the target and repair it, then depart.

The IOSS has the general configuration of a satellite servicing kit that might be mounted on the front end of the OMV; it was used by Martin Marietta in the ROSS study discussed above. It is an X-shaped

Above: Simulation exercises have shown that the IOSS manipulator arm is capable of replacing faulty electronic modules in ailing spacecraft.

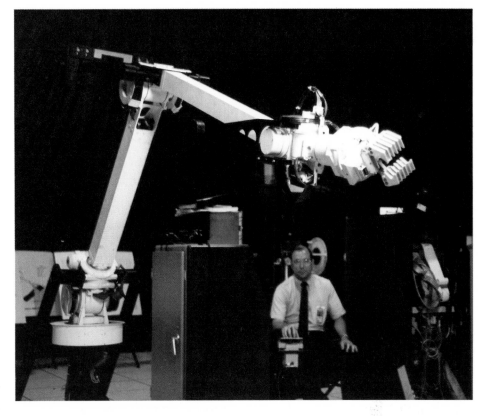

Above: Martin Marietta has developed a Protoflight Manipulator Arm for space operations that can perform intricate jobs, such as reconnection of wires, and opening of doors.

frame with mounting racks for electronics boxes. At the centre is a single robot arm that can latch onto the boxes, remove one, then install it in the satellite mock-up above it. A TV camera is mounted at the end effector which is a simple gripper with a power screwdriver to disconnect the box from its mount.

Gravity will be a problem in space because a robot arm, programmed on the Earth, would be slightly high in its aim when operated in a microgravity environment; the lack of gravity must be compensated for in space. "Because we're in gravity and have to position the arm precisely, gravity enters the equation, and that's why a human needs to be on the orbiter and be able to tweak it a little, then turn control back over to the robot", explained Tom Bryan, one of Marshall's robotics engineers.

Yet another problem with space robots will be that, unlike their industrial counterparts, they will perform many one-of-a-kind tasks rather than repeating the same job may times over. In addition, robots frequently need maintenance on the factory floor. Supervision of machines is important in the factory and it will also be so in space.

The Shuttle RMS can pick up and release satellites, a capability no other spacecraft has. But it can do no more than that. Broader capabilities like opening individual doors, reconnecting small wires, and other tasks are being investigated with the Protoflight Manipulator Arm (PFMA) developed for Marshall by Martin Marietta. The 7-DOF arm uses an intermeshing, jaw-like end effector

that lets it pick up objects in much the same manner that a hand can, and has a 10lb (4·5kg) payload capacity.

Two task boards have been built to give the PFMA a work area similar to the one that might be found in orbit. These include a Fairchild "dripless" fluid connector, a panel with dummy modules behind a door that must be opened and closed, standard electrical connectors, switches, valves, fasteners, etc. The task are simple for a human, but replicating the subtle ways that the human hand can move—including feedback from the end effectors (fingers)—has proved to be a task that is more difficult than bolting the pieces of an erector set.

"One of the real innovative things that we have here is a 6-DOF hand controller," explained Fred Roe. It is ball shaped with a fin on the top so a hand fits comfortably around it. The seventh DOF, the extra roll joint near the shoulder, is used for indexing and must be directly controlled; it is not run by the computer. The hand controller can be rolled or moved laterally in any direction. As one does that, the PFMA moves in response so the end effector moves where you want it.

In developing the robot arm, Roe explained that NASA wants to take a task that a human hand would do and give the operator visual and audio cues "so he will know what kinds of forces he's getting back on the end effector. We want him to think in terms of the job and not the hand controller ... In the nuclear industry individuals no longer think of the mechanical arm, but of their arm. That's what we're striving for."

The lab also will look at what the best design would be for an end effector. "We can't afford the luxury of two-dozen end effectors", Bryan said. "We have to carry everything with us, so we need more variety in our end effectors."

There are many avenues yet to be explored in developing space robots and teleoperators. A two-year study by the Massachusetts Institute of Technology, "Space Applications of Automation, Robotics and Machine Intelligence Systems (ARAMIS)—Phase 2", concluded that it is possible, with technology in hand or available presently, to develop a telepresence servicer capable of handling all orbital maintenance activities for major astronomy satellites now planned, as well as orbital deployment, retrieval and reboosting.

The initial model—described below—could be available when the space station is operating, if development is started soon. "The successful performance of one contingency operation during the deployment and assembly of the station could more than justify the cost of the entire telepresence development program."

The ARAMIS study team defined telepresence as implying that the manipulators at the work site have dexterities approaching those of human limbs, and the humans at the control station have enough sensory information to feel that they are actually present. "The purpose of telepresence is to perform space operations which require human intelligence, control, and dexterity when EVA [extra-vehicular activity] is not possible, not desirable, or when EVA alone cannot accomplish the desired mission."

Initial servicing calls would involve replacing modules much as Nelson and van Hoften did with the Solar Max attitude control system, and like those demonstrated by the servicing simulator at Marshall. Satellite servicing is still exiencing the "chicken or the egg" problem which NASA will have to crack, as it did with Solar Max, by developing the capabilities first.

"Essentially the problem is that almost any servicing function can be performed with low-level or near-present technology, if the spacecraft is specifically designed to accommodate servicing performed by that type of technology", the ARAMIS team wrote. "The end result is that servicing planning is currently limited to either simplistic exchange devices or EVA operations ... In general, the more advanced the servicer, the less impact servicing will have on the spacecraft design."

Improved End Effectors

Going beyond module replacement will require development of more advanced end effectors. In the near-term it will be possible to develop a system with two end effectors, one to grasp the workpiece, the other to change end effectors back and forth as it unscrews connectors and removes wires, and then replaces them when the new unit is installed. Small size and precision placement would be key requirements for such work.

Among the more challenging tasks will be assembly of structures because this "is composed of many unscheduled operations which must be performed sequentially [but which] will not follow exactly a pre-set construction plan." One only need to follow construction of any building to understand that.

The telepresence servicer unit (TSU) outlined by the ARAMIS study team could be flying by the mid-1990s if development work was started now. The general outline is like that of the Manned Maneuvering Unit introduced by the NASA astronauts in 1984; indeed, one almost expects an astronaut to sit on its bench-like front. There are four arms, two manipulator arms on the front side, and two (weaker) anchor arms on the side. A rack of special-purpose end effectors is mounted below the arms, and a rack of spare parts is below that. TV cameras are mounted above the "shoulders" and on the centre-line; there is one on each of the manipulator arms as well. Such a spacecraft would be delivered to the work site by the more powerful OMV which then would stand nearby while the TSU did its work. The OMV could also serve as its data relay point, battery recharger and parts rack for items larger than the TSU normally could store.

One recommendation is for a binocular helmet-mounted display that would command changes in camera position in response to movement of the operator's head. This would allow the operator to see what was below or to the side by looking there rather than by handling camera control switches. LCDs and fibre optics may make this possible by reducing the weight of the helmet displays. Voice

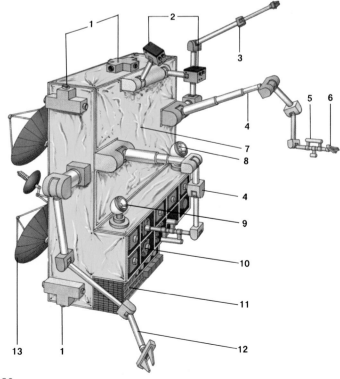

Free-Flying Teleoperator
1 Thrusters.
2 Vision sensors.
3 Anchor arm.
4 Manipulator arm.
5 Vision sensor.
6 Gripper.
7 Thermal insulation.
8 Light.
9 Light.
10 End effector rack.
11 Spare parts rack.
12 Anchor arm.
13 Communications and navigation antennas.

This craft was designed by researchers at the Massachusetts Institute of Technology in association with NASA. It is called the Telepresence Servicer Unit (TSU) and is intended as a remote servicer which would be compatible with several spacecraft, and capable of performing maintenance to the same level as a man could in space. It would employ the concept of telepresence by which a human operator on Earth could direct the robot craft in space as if he were really there. Two arms would grapple the ailing satellite; two others perform repairs.

command would allow the operator to tell the system to zoom or pull back.

Two 7-DOF arms—preferably in an anthropomorphic design—should provide quasi-human dexterity and the capability to reach around small-size objects. A docking device or two grappling arms should also be provided so the spacecraft has a solid grip on the target. These could be unpowered. The manipulators would position them and their own brakes would hold the spacecraft in position. Tendon manipulators would reduce weight while increasing strength by putting the drive motors near the shoulder. Not only would inertia effects (including backlash and positioning error) be elimi-

nated, but the whole system might be lightened by using a transmission to have a few motors drive several joints. Mission flexibility could be assured by carrying additional arms of different sizes.

An early option for the manipulator arms would be to have them follow the motions of a human arm fastened in a similar rig on Earth. To be fully effective, this would require force-feedback so the operator would feel as if he were at the

Below: Anchored in a foot restraint, Bruce McCandless wields a special tool during a mission 41B experiment in orbital maintenance. Future missions may turn to robot arms to do this.

worksite. The advantages of force-feedback would be limited by time delays in the system (although padding the varying time delays to a constant 2- or 3-second delay would give the operator a constant on which he could base his movements). "The more complex the task, the more force-feedback helps the operator...A promising option is to have a master control (either hand or exoskeletal controller) that measures the force applied to it, and commands the spacecraft to apply the same force." This would also require that the control system have a fail-safe capability so that operations will stop if communications fail, and so that actions out of context will not be

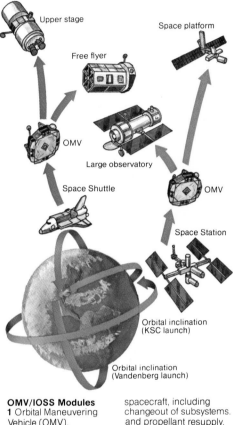

OMV/IOSS Modules
1 Orbital Maneuvering Vehicle (OMV).
2 Integrated Operations Servicing System (IOSS).
3 End effector.
4 Elbow roll drive.
5 Docking probe.
6 Shoulder drives.

The drawing below shows an OMV mated to a modular servicer equipped with one manipulator arm; these craft are intended to provide routine on-orbit servicing and maintenance of

spacecraft, including changeout of subsystems. and propellant resupply. OMV is conceived as a reusable, free-flying spacecraft that would be operated by remote control from a ground station after deployment from Shuttle or space station. The drawings above show the kinds of mission that the OMV might fly after Shuttle launch from either Kennedy Space Center or Vandenberg AFB. Proposed first flight: 1990.

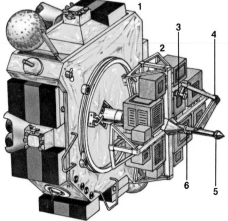

imitated (what happens when the operator sneezes?). With the operator's hand occupied, voice control systems will become attractive for providing additional control over cameras and manoeuvring.

The next step would be tactile sensing. There is a distinct difference between force sensing and tactile sensing. The former is equivalent to pushing a box across a floor or picking up a weight, and thus is easily provided by having drive motors on the operator's arms provide the equivalent resistance. The latter is equivalent to telling the difference between the weave of two materials of identical weight and has greater subtleties.

"From a human factors' viewpoint, the more 'transparent' the system the better for human operators ... A mechanic rarely consciously considers how to position and move his arm while working: the control of his arm is autonomic. If he were forced to plan and think about each movement, his work would be slowed down considerably. A more extreme example is that of a runner. If a runner were to try to control his legs by actually thinking about the kinematics of motion, he probably would not be able to walk, let alone run."

Such a spacecraft could also have applications for planetary missions. Built as a rover—with legs or wheels and using control laws developed for terrestrial robots—it could wander about the surface of Mars or other worlds, with the terrestrial science team directing it. The rover could use its manipulator arms to gather and process appropriate samples for the on-board chemistry lab, and set up (and even repair) remote data stations (which need not have expensive deployment mechanisms since they would be assembled).

"Control technology is the key to telepresence", the ARAMIS team wrote. "A properly designed control system will make up for many errors elsewhere, but an improperly designed control system will render the system useless, regardless of the quality of the other hardware."

Advances in artificial intelligence would be incorporated into the telepresence spacecraft in 1995 and beyond. With the basic unit built, a series of improvements could be made that would expand its capabilities by giving it more independence and authority. This would compensate to a large degree for time lags in the communications system, and do for the human teleoperator what robots are supposed to do for factory workers—eliminate the tedious jobs. It also would provide adaptive control, letting the robot adapt to minor mismatches between the task and the predicted result. If a bolt does not loosen, for example, the robot could apply slightly more torque until it loosens or hits a safety limit, then inspect for other problems or alternatively decide to alert its human masters.

With full telepresence, "the operator actually feels as if he were at the worksite and performs naturally, taking advantage of experience, learned reactions, expertise, and human decision-making capabilities. This type of system should not require training beyond a simple

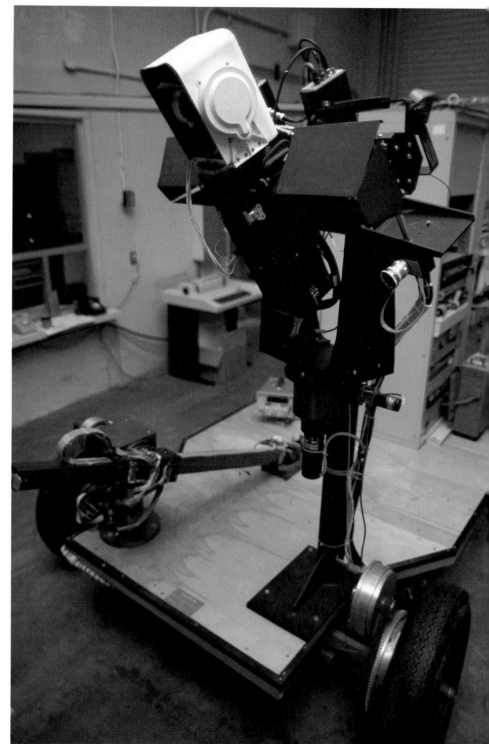

Above: NASA's Jet Propulsion Laboratory built this machine as a research tool to study the design problems associated with a robot Mars Rover.

Right: Bob Cunningham of JPL in front of the Rover Research Vehicle; the battery of sensors include two TV cameras and a laser rangefinder.

introduction to the system, because it will operate in a manner similar to the human. The manipulator arms may not be anthropomorphic, but the system will accept and adapt anthropomorphic input."

As with terrestrial robots, vision will be a tough problem. A near-term solution might be to place bar codes and appropriate corner markers on each component

Above: Planetary rovers would be hybrid vehicles, partially under human supervision from Earth, partially autonomous. This is JPL artwork of their proposed Mars Rover.

so the robot will be able to tell where he is with respect to the workpiece. This might make it possible to reduce the amount of TV sent earthward by just sending data on the orientation of the target. "Pristine" images of the target could be stored on the teleoperator spacecraft and only images of the mismatches would be sent down. Similar technology is being developed for Earth observation spacecraft that will transmit images of areas that have changed since the last observation.

Robots on the Moon

Recently plans have been outlined by a NASA study group for exploiting the Moon by means of robots. Indeed, such an undertaking is seen as a key element in expanding man's operations in space at a minimal initial cost. The first step would be a series of unmanned rovers that would carry science instruments across 1,200 miles (1,930km) of lunar surface for detailed remote assays. Five rovers would be equipped with automated lab equipment to assay the lunar soil. In addition, TV cameras would be mounted atop the rovers to help ground control map the

next moves. The rovers would be solar-powered and spend 75 per cent of the day moving, and the rest of it taking samples. A halo orbiter would be placed at the Lagrange point behind the Moon to act as a data relay station for rovers on the far-side. A sixth rover, probably the last in the series, would be the civil engineer, moving soil and fulfilling other tasks to provide basic data needed for construction plans to be drawn up.

In the third phase — culminating in the year 2007, the 50th anniversary of the Space Age — the manned moonlab would be placed on the Moon with the sixth civil engineering rover as its construction vehicle. Using derivatives of space station designs, a 12-man lunar base would be built. Actually, the people would come second. First on the scene would be an automated factory to produce oxygen from the lunar minerals (hence the importance of detailed analyses of a wide

array of lunar sites). Ilmenite, a black ore made up of one molecule each of iron and titanium and three of oxygen, could be "cracked" to yield the constituents in relatively pure form. Basalts, also common on the Moon, would yield oxygen and silicon. A solar furnace would be the most direct way of supplying the energy for this. The presence of hydrogen in any appreciable quantities on the Moon is unlikely (unless, as some have theorized, there is ice locked in the poles where surface temperatures would not rise). The oxygen would serve two purposes — providing breathing air for the base crew, and a source of propellant to send rockets back to Earth.

In time this modest base could grow from a simple frontier town, if you will, to an advanced factory using all the best of terrestrial robotic and artificial intelligence technologies in order to produce the self-replicating factory first envisaged by John von Neumann in the late 1940s. Here, on a world with no environment or neighbours to be disturbed, one could plant the seed of a mechanical being that would feed on the lifeless planetoid and produce copies of itself which, in turn, would produce copies of themselves. Given the proper instructions and enough time, the robot factory could make specialized robots for "export" to Earth orbit where they would be used to manufacture solar power satellites out of lunar material, or explorer robots that would be launched to the planets to expand our knowledge of worlds still unvisited by man.

Using robots to explore and exploit the Solar System and then the Galaxy, has long been a popular theme in science fiction. Not until the last few years, though, have scientists given it serious thought. The most significant investigation of the

Materials processing and feedstock production   Parts production   Products factory

Mining

EPR

Parts storage (replication)   Parts storage (products)   Product storage

Self-Replicating Lunar Factory
In 1980 two NASA scientists, Georg von Tiesenhausen and Wesley Darbro, published an engineering study for a lunar factory that would turn out replicas of itself, as well as manufacturing a number of useful products. The result would be a mushrooming growth of identical workshops, using materials mined from the Moon's surface, that would rapidly industrialize this planetary body. The key element is the Universal Constructor (UC) which is capable of constructing any system, including a replica of itself. The UC comprises two separate elements: a number of Mobile Universal Constructor units (MUCs) and a single Stationary Universal Constructor (SUC). These would make parts for new factories under the programmed supervision of a Master Control and Command system (MCC) which supervises the total operation. Parts are conveyed to the UC after automatic mining and production (top diagram); other products that could be sold on Earth are stored in the End Product Reception (EPR) area.

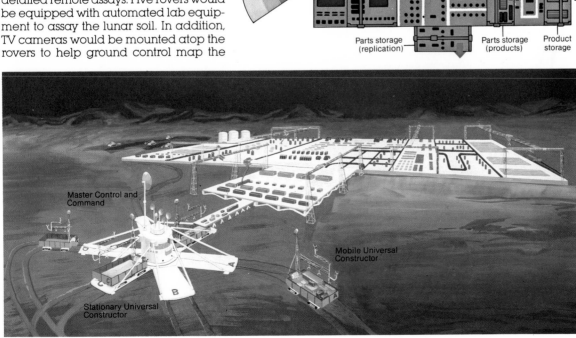

Master Control and Command

Mobile Universal Constructor

Stationary Universal Constructor

ROBOTS

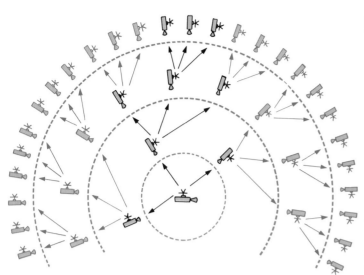

Growth Plan for Self-Replicating Systems
This diagram illustrates how a lunar manufacturing facility might set about reproducing itself. Using materials mined from the Moon, the first lunar factory would make three replicas of itself. Each of these in turn would make three more replicas, until, at the end of the third cycle of reproduction, twenty-seven new factories would be ready to start the next cycle, which would of course result in eighty-one new plants. A single SRS unit is a system that contains all the elements required to maintain itself, self-reproduce, and manufacture products; in this way it is analogous to a biological cell.

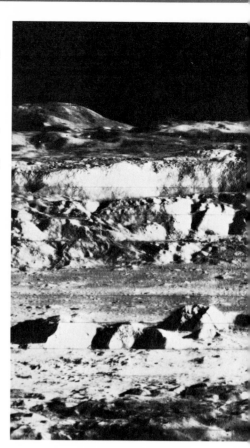

subject was a summer study sponsored in 1980 by NASA and the American Society for Engineering Education and held at the University of Santa Clara, California. Important preparatory studies for this event were conducted by Georg von Tiesenhausen and Wesley Darbro, who produced a technical memorandum, "Self-Replicating Systems—A Systems Engineering Approach". The study team outlined plans for a self-replicating Lunar Manufacturing Facility (LMF) that would grow into what one writer has called a "Santa Claus" machine, one that would be capable of delivering whatever consumer goods one wants for free.

The LMF would go two steps beyond von Neumann's self-replicating machine which he imagined floating in a sea of spare parts, randomly picking up one after the other until it found the one needed for the next step in assembly, then search for the next. The LMF would draw its parts from a well-managed inventory manufactured from stock which in turn had been processed from raw lunar material. As it grew, the LMF, like a living organism, would make copies of itself that would continue this work until they populated the Moon or moved on to other worlds.

For the near term, the study team suggested that robotic self-replication be demonstrated with a set of parts already built and waiting, by a robot already assembled and programmed. Robot 1 would assemble Robot 2 by building it from the circuit cards up to the manipulators. As a final step Robot 1 would insert a blank disk in its own computer, copy its programming then install the copy in Robot 2 and "boot" the computer. This last step was viewed as essential "to make it clear that the generations are truly autonomous" and not just following instructions passed down a common power or data line.

Robot 2 then would assemble Robot 3 to demonstrate that it truly was a replicate of Robot 1—the so-called fertility test. A total of seven robots would be assembled which would then turn to producing some useful product. At the end of the demonstrations they would disassemble themselves. While this might seem simple to the casual observer, it represents an

order-of-magnitude advance over present robotic capabilities. Placing a washer at the end of a bolt requires eight distinct steps. The PUMA 500, a common robot at the time of study, was directed by an LSI-11 computer which could store about 1,000 steps. The PUMA 500 also has 1,500 parts. The study team estimated that it would take about five years to develop a computer, occupying not more than a cubic metre and capable of storing enough commands for a self-replicating PUMA 500.

It still would require a great leap from a lab-sized demonstration (that many critics no doubt would liken to a circus stunt regardless of its complexity) to the 100-ton "seed" that the LMF would need to get started. In addition to developing advanced manipulators, wheeled vehicles, and compact power supplies, there also would have to be a highly-ordered command and control system to bring the LMF to its desired conclusion, and an immense memory to store the complete description of the seed. It is estimated that about 10 million million bits of data would be needed to describe the seed and its replication program—about two orders of magnitude more than are carried in the genetic coding of a single human cell, and two orders less than are contained by the human brain.

Robots Building Robots
The self-replicating Lunar Manufacturing Facility is a robot engineer's dream—it involves robots building other robots. The 1980 study team who met at the University of Santa Clara to investigate self-replication proposed a simple demonstration in which a conventional industrial manipulator would be instructed to build a replica of itself from a set of ready-made parts. When completed, it would then copy its computer software onto a blank disk, and load the second robot's computer with the program. Robot 2 would then have to build a third identical machine to prove that it was a perfect replicate. Robot 3 would then build Robot 4, and the process would continue until seven robots were built.

Above: In 1966 Lunar Orbiter 2— itself a type of robot explorer— returned this picture of the crater Copernicus. Will robots one day build a factory on the Moon's surface?

The third phase of the LMF demonstration would be to supply the robots with industrial-grade feedstocks which would have to be turned into the parts from which the replicates and other products would be made. The fourth phase envisages turning raw material into the industrial stock. This is anticipated as the most difficult step, requiring extensive use of chemical processes and the ability to adapt to changes in the composition of the raw material.

Once these are demonstrated, it will be possible to build the seed for the LMF. The study team estimated that 100 tons as a

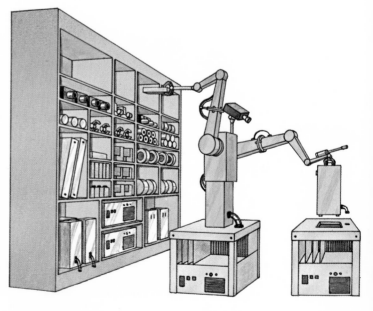

reasonable mass for the seed, based on the payload capability of the US Saturn V rocket (25 tons to the Moon's surface) and on their estimations of available or projected industrial capabilities.

The mission would start with detailed mapping of the lunar surface to select an ideal site. After an automated landing, robots would emerge to erect a "solar canopy" that would generate electrical power and provide some degree of protection for the seed. The robots would then set off to examine the region in detail and, using ground-truth data, make the final selection of the work site. Mobile robots would emplace three radio transponders for precise navigation around the site. Mining and paving robots would grade the surface in the centre of the site so the 395ft (120m)-wide platform could be erected. On this platform the various components of the seed will be deployed as one would lay out tools on a factory floor. When the platform is large enough, the robots would move the main computer into a cellar dug beneath the platform, thus protecting it from solar and cosmic radiation and meteors. Finally the complete solar canopy will be erected and the LMF is ready to go into operation a year after landing.

The LMF would have eight distinct major sections: central control, the chemical sector (turning lunar soil into feedstocks), the fabrication sector (turning the feedstock into parts), the assembly sector (turning parts into working robots), the mining robots (digging out raw soil

and rock), the paving robots (building the platform for the seed and the roads for the miners) and the transponder network. The LMF would be laid out in identical halves, each having chemical, fabrication, and storage sectors that would grow radially from the core. The lunar surface would be mined in front of the sectors to support their growth, and the tailings and slag would be banked to provide a foundation for extending the platform (see picture below).

An early LMF goal would be to make copies of itself so that a disaster would not eliminate the huge investment involved in developing the original. If it only replicated itself, its numbers would grow exponentially. After 18 years, it and its descendants would have an annual total output of 4,000 million tons, "roughly the entire annual output of all human civilization".

Providing the Parts

A key issue in such a scheme is the problem of parts "closure". In the near-term, the study team readily admitted, only 90-96 per cent of the LMF's parts might be made by the LMF. Another 4-10 per cent might be needed as "vitamin parts" just as most human diets need a supplement. These vitamin parts might be precision or miniaturized items like VLSI circuits and precision bearings that require capabilities the LMF would have to "evolve" rather than having at the start. A degree of human control would

Below: This is an artist's conception of the "seed" Lunar Manufacturing Facility might look. In the foreground are paving and mining robots; the control centre is at the hub.

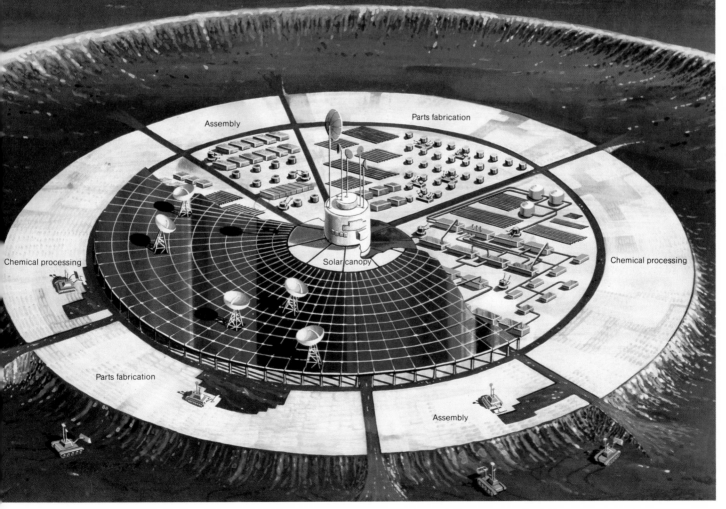

probably also be needed. Even on manned missions today, not all contingencies are foreseen and often require on-the-spot ingenuity to fix.

A wide range of products was outlined for the LMF and its progeny: processed chemicals and elements (including oxygen) that could be used as spacecraft propellants; structural elements, solar cells, and electronic parts for Earth-orbital solar power satellites; computers on a grand scale not now possible; radio and optical telescopes with apertures that dwarf anything now planned. It might even be possible to manufacture factory machinery or, in the longer term, finished products for shipment to Earth.

And the potential for the self-replicating systems (SRS) would not be restricted to the Moon. "It is likely that replicating machines will provide the only 'lever' large enough to explore and, ultimately manipulate and utilize in a responsible fashion, such tremendous quantities of organizable matter", the team wrote. "Lacking this advanced automation capability, most of the more ambitious Solar System applications appear uneconomical at best, fanciful at worst."

Mars and Venus might be rendered habitable by "terraforming", reshaping them to be Earthlike. A seed landed on Mars would use local materials to make 1,000 to 10,000 rovers—wheeled and winged—to explore the planet's resources, and to emplace remote weather and seismic stations. Once the planet was mapped, the seed would replicate itself and, along the way, liberate oxygen from silicon dioxide. After 36 years the seeds would have generated an oxygen atmosphere equivalent to an terrestrial altitude of 16,000ft (4,875m)—thin, but breathable as the Andes Indians will testify. A tougher challenge would be to terraform in the hot-house environment of Venus, freeing oxygen from the carbon dioxide atmosphere. The team concluded that "terraforming times of the order of one century are conceivable using the SRS approach."

On to the Stars

And SRS could also be used, for a time, as assembly lines to produce probes to explore all parts of the Solar System. Seeds could be attached to asteroids bearing rare metals needed at Earth. The SRS would build mass drivers that then would propel the asteroid, over a period of decades, into a high terrestrial orbit, thus making it accessible to the Earth-Moon factory system.

The potential raised by the SRS could be extended beyond our Solar System in the form of automated probes built by automatons that would replicate themselves at each solar system they visited. The British Interplanetary Society in 1978 issued its "Project Daedalus" study which outlined plans for building (largely with human labour) a giant unmanned spacecraft to travel to Barnard's Star in the hopes of finding life there.

Such a spacecraft, operating 50 years in the depths of space, would require a high degree of automation. Indeed, the

last pre-encounter instructions would have to be sent seven years before the event because of the time delay. The spacecraft ". . . must carry a hierarchy of computers with executive authority for the control of all experiments and supporting systems. The computer software, also in hierarchical form, must be capable of varying the operational goals embedded within itself so as to exhibit adaptive behaviour. Not only must the computers control full on-board repair facilities, but must themselves be designed for repair while continuing to operate, i.e., for fault-tolerant fail-soft operation." The Daedalus study team envisioned having two free-flying robots, called wardens, that would roam the giant fusion-powered craft and make whatever repairs were needed and even build small radio telescopes that would be deployed at a distance for interferometric studies.

Following the general plan of Daedalus, in 1980 Robert Frietas outlined how an unmanned starship, Repro, might be launched on a journey of exploration

Above: Venus is also eyed hungrily by space engineers who are keen on the principles of terraforming. This picture was taken by a camera on the Mariner 10 space probe.

Below: Mars, seen here in a picture captured by Viking Orbiter 1, might be robotically "terraformed" to re-shape its climate and conditions to make the planet habitable.

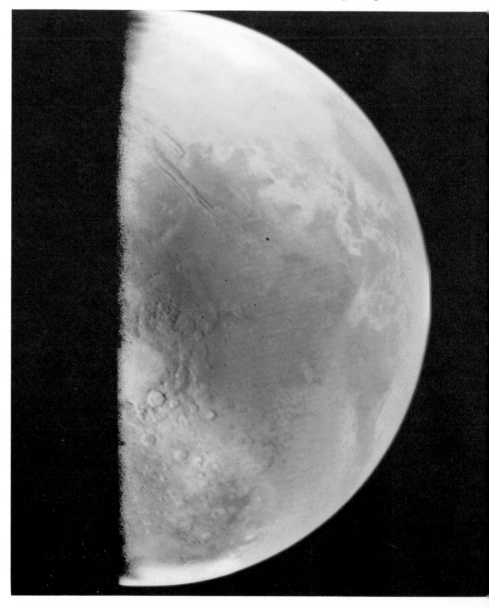

and self-replication. The 23,590 million lb (10,700 million kg) mass would be far greater that that of Daedalus in order to accommodate the space factory and the fuel for deceleration at the target star.

Upon arrival at the target star system, Repro seeks and orbits a Jovian-type planet from which it mines 22,266 million lb (10,100 million kg) of fusion fuel and 1,234 million lb (560 million kg) non-fuel mass. About half the payload, the seed, is landed on one of the Jovian planet's moons. It weighs 977 million lb (443 million kg) and is designed to build and launch planetary probes over the next 500 years. Most importantly, it is to replicate itself in that same period. A variety of robot "species" would be deployed and replicated on the planet's surface—chemists, aerostats, miners, metallurgists, computers, fabricators and assemblers, warehousers, crawlers, tankers, wardens, etc. These would assemble a factory that would assemble new Repros there.

The Unpluggable Robot?

A key to the success of this scheme is the durability of an "ultra-secure Cache" memory which would be used as the master template for all data in the system. A 62 mile (100km) wide moon would

provide enough material for production of 40,000 Repros. The author also considered that rather than launching a Repro as soon as it is built, it could stay at the new world and start manufacturing right there. This could lead to production of a new Repro every 2-3 years and consumption of the moon in 35 years. He even went so far as to suggest "sexual" reproduction—periodic rejoining of the Repros so memories and adapted designs could be compared and edited to produce newer optimal designs. "Niche specialization is possible, and there is a remote possibility that a simple machine ecology might have time to arise, complete with predators and prey.

"A number of ethical issues are raised by the possible existence of Repro-like vehicles in the Galaxy. Is it morally right, or even fair, for a self-replicating starprobe to enter a foreign solar system and convert part of that system's mass and energy for its own purposes? . . . [the mass loss would be negligible]. Nevertheless, it is highly unlikely that humanity would take kindly to an alien starcraft landing on one of the Jovian moons Himalia and Elara and reproducing itself without at least first asking our permission. Probably we would regard it as one of [the particle physicist Freeman] Dyson's 'technological

cancers loose in the galaxy' and attempt to destroy it or disable it."

Ultimately there is the matter of controlling one's creation, a theme as old as Genesis. As the complexity and numbers of the self-replicating robots grow, they will outstrip the ability of humans to comprehend and control. "If there is even the slightest possibility that this is so, it becomes imperative that we learn exactly what constellation of machine capabilities might enable an SRS to cross the subtle threshold into theoretical unpluggability", the study team warned. It might even be necessary to build predatory robots to attack outdated or surplus species, reducing them to spare parts for other machines. The SRS's might be designed to become "infertile" after a period of years or generations, then report to a central depot for recycling, "or even resorting to cannibalism or duelling when crowding becomes too severe."

The key question in all this is not whether self-replicating robots and factories will be built. The history of man shows that new technologies are inevitably developed and exploited. The key question is whether we will attempt to solve the problems of command and control—the master-slave relationship—now, or after the event.

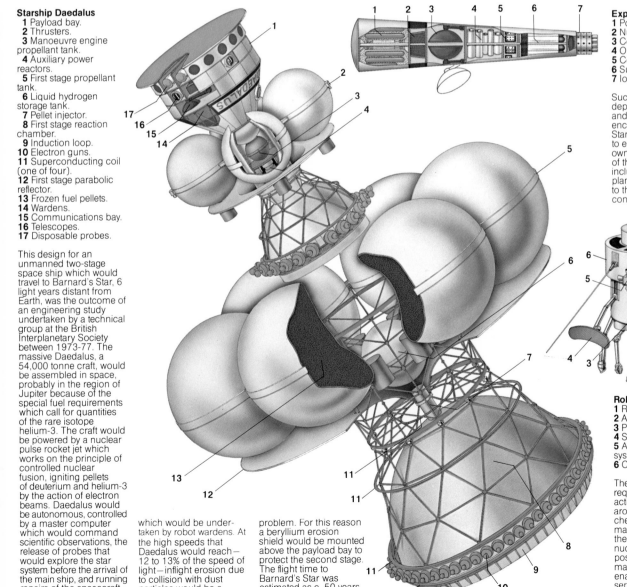

Starship Daedalus
1 Payload bay.
2 Thrusters.
3 Manoeuvre engine propellant tank.
4 Auxiliary power reactors.
5 First stage propellant tank.
6 Liquid hydrogen storage tank.
7 Pellet injector.
8 First stage reaction chamber.
9 Induction loop.
10 Electron guns.
11 Superconducting coil (one of four).
12 First stage parabolic reflector.
13 Frozen fuel pellets.
14 Wardens.
15 Communications bay.
16 Telescopes.
17 Disposable probes.

This design for an unmanned two-stage space ship which would travel to Barnard's Star, 6 light years distant from Earth, was the outcome of an engineering study undertaken by a technical group at the British Interplanetary Society between 1973-77. The massive Daedalus, a 54,000 tonne craft, would be assembled in space, probably in the region of Jupiter because of the special fuel requirements which call for quantities of the rare isotope helium-3. The craft would be powered by a nuclear pulse rocket jet which works on the principle of controlled nuclear fusion, igniting pellets of deuterium and helium-3 by the action of electron beams. Daedalus would be autonomous, controlled by a master computer which would command scientific observations, the release of probes that would explore the star system before the arrival of the main ship, and running repairs of the spacecraft

which would be undertaken by robot wardens. At the high speeds that Daedalus would reach—12 to 13% of the speed of light—inflight erosion due to collision with dust particles would be a

problem. For this reason a beryllium erosion shield would be mounted above the payload bay to protect the second stage. The flight time to Barnard's Star was estimated as c. 50 years.

Exploratory Probes
1 Power supply.
2 Nuclear shield.
3 Communications bay.
4 Optics bay.
5 Computers.
6 Sub-probes bay.
7 Ion engines.

Such probes as this deploy from Daedalus 7·2 and 1·2 years before encounter with Barnard's Star. They are intended to explore under their own propulsion wide areas of the star system, including any possible planets, and report back to the master computer controlling the mission.

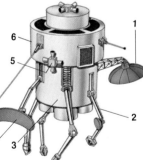

Robot Wardens
1 Radar antenna.
2 Automatic manipulators.
3 Propulsion system.
4 Steady arm.
5 Attitude control system.
6 Computer bay.

The two wardens would be required to check out and activate probes, travel around the parent craft, check for leaks and other malfunctions, and rectify them. They also would be nuclear powered, and possess a high level of machine intelligence to enable them to operate semi-autonomously.

ARTIFICIAL INTELLIGENCE

To most people, the notion of an "intelligent machine" is both fascinating and frightening. Fascinating, because the construction of such a thing seems to pose some ultimate challenge to our own ingenuity. Frightening, because if it was shown that machines could be intelligent, would it not suggest that human intelligence itself is a "mechanical" process and not, as we like to believe, a product of our individuality and free will? It is, moreover, easy to see that the next step after a machine that matched our own intelligence would be one that surpassed it, a super-intelligent machine. If we devised a machine which had more of that quality, intelligence, which makes us superior to other animals, then it would seem to follow that we would be obliged, or perhaps even forced, to yield our position as the dominant species on Earth.

Science fiction has of course been exploring the possibilities of such scenarios for a century or more. But, until about 1950, novelists and scriptwriters were forced to be extremely vague about how or why their robots had become intelligent. There were plenty of machines around that were bigger or stronger than people or, like aircraft or telephones, capable of doing things which people could not do; but there were no machines at all with even a germ of intelligence—indeed the idea that "mechanical" things and "intelligent" things are at opposite ends of the spectrum is entrenched in the language.

All that changed with the arrival of the first computers. Since about 1950 virtually every fictional robot has had a "computer brain." But the computer did more than simplify the life of SF writers and Hollywood special effects departments. It also made the quest for artificial intelligence (usually abbreviated to AI) into a serious scientific endeavour which, some thirty-five years later, has become well established and is beginning to contribute to the design of real-life robots.

It is important to realize that, so far, AI has been little concerned with hardware, the invention of new or better kinds of machinery; virtually all research in the field has concentrated on producing software, novel kinds of program for one sort of existing machine—the digital computer. The reason for this is easy to understand: the digital computer is in principal a universal machine, that is to say, a machine which can do anything for which a clear set of instructions, a pro-

gram, can be provided. This is of course why the same home computer can be used for a whole variety of purposes, from doing the household budget to playing video games. The range of tasks a computer can tackle is limited only by the ingenuity of programmers; just as one can play any kind of music one likes on a piano, so one can run any sort of program one pleases on a computer. Indeed, it could be said that a computer is not, by itself, a machine at all. It is a piece of hardware that is transformed into a machine when a program is loaded into it; at that point it becomes a particular sort of machine, the one required to run that program.

What Is Intelligence?

The challenge facing those involved in AI is to find what sort of programs are required in order for a computer to become an intelligent machine. The first, most obvious, question is: "What do we mean by the word intelligent?" The answer usually provided, that intelligence is what people display when they behave intelligently, merely dodges the question. For the issue is complicated by the fact that we are often extremely vague about what intelligence is. Some would still argue, for example, that it is a single "thing" which different people have in different degrees as a result of inheritance, and which can be measured by IQ tests. Others would disagree, and suggest that intelligence develops or is learned as a result of experience, or that the word describes a whole range of qualities and abilities that may have little to do with one another.

Intelligence indisputably involves thinking, but some kinds of thinking seem more intelligent than others. If, for instance, we believed that the ability to store large amounts of information or to perform long and complex calculations was the crux of intelligence then we would have to acknowledge that long ago computers became more intelligent than we are, for they are undoubtedly superior at such tasks and can be programmed to carry them out without any of the techniques devised in AI laboratories. It is, indeed, this kind of unintelligent "thinking" which

Right: An integrated circuit and a human nerve cell, both enormously magnified. Can two elements seemingly so dissimilar share the secret of intelligence?

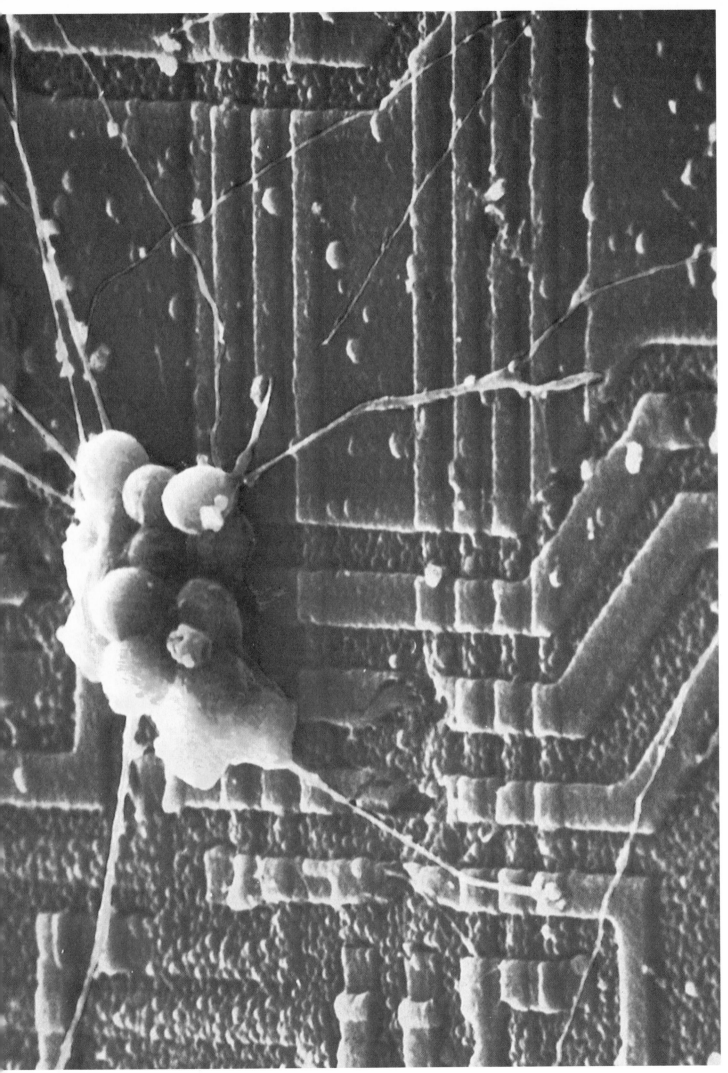

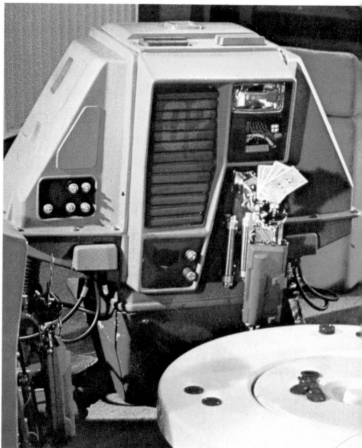

Above: A game-playing robot of a deadly kind: Yul Brynner, the android gunslinger, bares his circuitry in the fantasy film "Westworld".

characterizes the present generation of industrial robots. They can "remember" long sequences of movements, and perform the computations necessary to check they they are being repeated accurately, but they are quite incapable of reacting to unforeseen circumstances or of making decisions, even trivial ones, about how best to achieve an objective. In order to behave intelligently they would seem to need two things—the ability to perceive and understand their surroundings and some sort of skill, perhaps no more than what we call common sense, which would enable them to react to events and make decisions.

The provision of artificial senses, especially vision, a subject discussed in Chapter 3, is indeed one of the main themes of AI research. In this chapter we shall concentrate on developments which aim at giving robots the common sense, or even more elaborate kinds of intelligence, which they will need if they are to make good use of their senses. These developments centre upon three traditional areas of AI research: game-playing, problem-solving, and the use of natural (that is, everyday) language—and upon one comparative newcomer, the specialized types of computer programs that have become known as expert systems.

Problem-solving programs and the game-playing ones to which they are closely related will, it is hoped, allow robots to work out for themselves how to tackle tasks that are described in general

terms rather than, as at present, having to be led through a job step-by-step. The ability to understand and communicate in natural language will be essential if robots are to make use of a sense of hearing (and perhaps of the power of speech) in order to collaborate with human workers who are not versed in computer languages. Finally, expert systems are beginning to show how computers may be able to master the specialized kind of intelligence used by human experts—the sort of combination of knowledge and reasoning based on experience which allows a doctor to diagnose a disease or an engineer to see how to tackle a design problem.

Game-playing

Game-playing had begun to attract the attention of computer programmers even before the term artificial intelligence was coined by John McCarthy of Stanford University in the mid-1950s. Indeed several of the early computer pioneers suggested that when their machines reached the point at which they could play a decent game of chess, sceptics would find it difficult to deny that they were intelligent, and the achievement of an effective chess-playing program became a popular goal. Mechanical chess-playing is, indeed, an idea that predates computers by well over a century. In the early nineteenth century great excitement was aroused by the chess automaton invented by a certain Johann Nepomuk Maelzel (the machine's intelligence, alas, turned out to be entirely "natural"; it was provided by a man concealed within it). Later on, in 1894, one of the first pieces of

robot fiction, a story called "Moxon's Master" by Ambrose Bierce, described a chess automaton which was such a bad loser that, when its inventor threatened it with checkmate, it murdered him.

The attractions of game-playing, and chess-playing in particular, as a field for AI work are clear to see. Most would agree that a high degree of intelligence is required; a chess grandmaster is almost an embodiment of intelligence to most of us. But the world in which the intelligence has to be applied is a constricted and well-defined one. It is not too difficult to see ways in which the state of the game (the position of the pieces at any particular juncture) can be encoded in a form a computer can cope with. The rules are clear. No element of luck or bluff is involved; in theory at least, the question of which move is best can be settled by pure logic. The computer can, therefore, easily understand all it needs to know about the present position or state and it can, by applying a few formal rules, work out all the states that can legally follow from that state. All it needs is an algorithm.

"Algorithm" is a word much used in computer jargon. It means no more than a definite or clear method of working or thinking. We all, for example, learn the algorithms for adding, subtracting, dividing and multiplying numbers when we are first taught simple arithmetic. In terms of cookery, one could think of the list of ingredients that appears at the top of a recipe in a cookbook as the data, and the list of instructions which follows as the algorithm for transforming those ingredients into a particular dish. In AI, as in all other branches of computer programming, an algorithm is a basic requirement.

Above: Alone in his spaceship, an astronaut of the future relies upon his game-playing robot for company: a still from the film "Silent Running".

The programmer must see the way of tackling the problem before he can formalize it as a program. In the case of chess, or other similar game such as draughts or checkers, the basic algorithm is what is called a decision tree.

The key to success is clearly the ability to look ahead to calculate the consequences of a move at the present stage of the game for future play. The winning player will be the one who can carry furthest lines of reasoning that go along the lines of " . . . if I do A then he can do B, C or D; if he does B, I can do E, F, or G; but if he does C, I will have to do H, I or J . . . etc." Such reasoning processes originate with the present state of the game, which can be represented diagrammatically as a

"node", a dot with lines radiating from it to further nodes, each of which represents the state that would result if one particular move was made. Each of these nodes will then have further radiating lines, leading to nodes which represent states that would occur if the opposing player makes a particular answering move.

In theory, such a tree could be constructed reaching out from the opening position before the game has begun to a node which represented a state of the game in which one or other of the players had won. In practice, this is quite beyond the capacity of the largest computer anyone could ever envisage. In even a simple game like noughts and crosses, in which only nine levels separate the starting state and the point at which all nine squares contain a nought or a cross, a decision tree will have sprouted at least 60,000 twigs, or nodes. Within a comparatively few moves the decision tree for a chess game will have spread to totally unmanageable proportions. This is, of course, simply another way of expressing the comparatively well-known fact that the number of board positions or states which can occur in chess is to all intents and purposes infinitely large. It follows, therefore, that until the final stages of the endgame are reached, a chess-playing program cannot look forward to the point at which it actually achieves victory or checkmate. The decision tree algorithm is not, in itself, sufficient.

What is required is some means either of limiting the range of possibilities that are explored, or searched, or some system for allotting values to the states that can be foreseen, the nodes at the extremities of the decision tree. Chess-playing programs make use of combinations of both these expedients. They normally construct decision trees that explore only a limited area of the board, the strategic centre perhaps, or areas which contain key pieces and only move on to look at other areas if the initial search produces no promising move. If a potentially good move is found, then a deeper search may be mounted to explore the possibilities in that area alone to greater depth. If a search of a particular area of the board quickly reveals that all possible moves lead to disaster, then that search may quickly be cut short in favour of examination of other areas.

But, even if such methods are used to limit and prune the decision trees, some scoring system is still required in order that the machine may be able to evaluate the states at the extremities of the tree and decide which are "bad" and which are "good". In other words, it must have some rules of thumb which it can apply when it has searched as far ahead as it can—rules which say, in effect, "this is, from your point of view, a good state for the game to arrive at" or " if the game gets to this state your future looks bleak".

Rules of this kind, which are employed in all branches of AI, are called heuristics, and they are, of course, very similar indeed to the sort of hunches, tactical or strategic instincts, or intuitions based on experience which are used by human players. The question is, how does one equip a machine with them? Some of the more basic and straightforward ones can naturally be provided ready made; but a program relying solely on such prepackaged judgements will never play a game of great subtlety and it will take very little time for an experienced human opponent to see through its reasoning.

The most interesting aspect of game-playing programs is the methods used to allow a machine to refine and revise its heuristics, or even invent completely new ones for itself. One of the first researchers to investigate this possibility was the American, A.L. Samuel, who designed a checkers-playing program in the late 1950s. Although the far greater complexity of chess means that it is impossible to apply Samuel's methods to that game in their entirety, most of today's chess-playing programs have been developed using similar principles.

The essential point is that the program must be given experience. It starts out with a basic set of given heuristics and then plays a series of games against human opponents (interestingly, machines cannot learn by playing against one another, for they will both be applying the same set of heuristics and their games will follow predetermined courses). If the machine loses, then it will backtrack and identify those states which, though it scored them highly on the basis of its existing heuristics, turned out to be bad states in the light of experience. If it wins from what it conceived to be a low scoring state, then it will revise its rules in

A Decision Tree
This diagram represents the sort of decision tree that might be constructed by a noughts-and-crosses playing computer program. At the top is a single "node" representing the starting state of the game—that is, a blank grid consisting of nine squares. The machine can make any one of three possible opening moves. (Because the spaces available on the grid are symmetrical in the early stages of the game, many of the possible moves are equivalent to one another; the blue symbols adopted in this diagram are used to denote these duplicate moves.) Starting from one of the three nodes at level

2 which illustrate possible opening plays, the opposing player can bring about one of the twelve possible states shown at level 3. At this point the tree spreads too widely to be displayed in its entirety, and at level 4 we show only eleven of the sixty or so possible states which the machine may be able to bring about with its second move. It is worth noting that a complete decision tree for a very elementary game like noughts and crosses will, by the time it reaches the final, ninth, level, have sprouted more than 60,000 branches, each representing one possible state of the game.

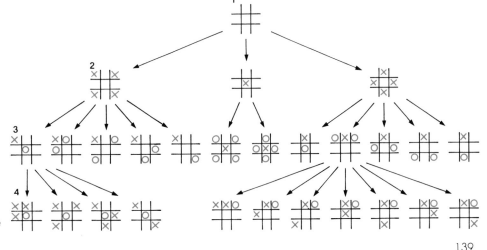

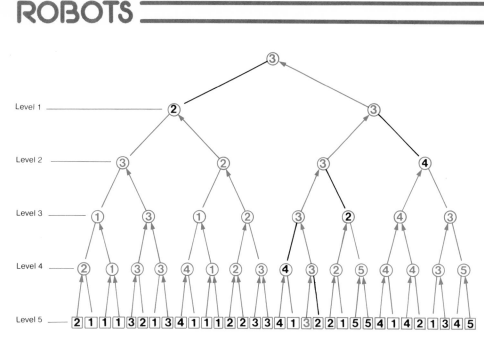

Level 1
Level 2
Level 3
Level 4
Level 5

Mini-maxing
This basic algorithm depends on the idea that the machine will always try to *maximize* its own score when it makes a move, whereas its opponent will always try to *minimize* the machine's scoring possibilities on

his turn. To decide which of the two possible moves open to it is better, the machine looks ahead as far as it can—in this simplified example, level 5. It allots a score to each of the row of nodes there which are grouped in pairs, each pair

emanating from a node on level 4. Assuming it will make the best move, the machine backs up (ie. traces back) the *higher* of each pair of scores to level 4. It then backs up the *lower* score of each pair there to level 3, in effect, acting on the

premise that its opponent will always try to minimize its scoring potential. The red line, along which the best score the machine can hope to achieve has been backed up, follows this zig-zag, mini-max process up the tree.

can now be bought off the shelf is some measure of how far this branch of AI has developed. There are signs, however, that the kind of intelligence used by chess-playing computers on the one hand, and by human chess masters on the other, are very different. Indeed, if one listens to some of the recordings of grand masters talking through their past games, explaining why they made this choice rather than that, or how they planned their strategy, one cannot help feeling that the sort of thinking they employ is altogether subtler, more instinctive or intuitive and less strictly logical than that which can be instilled in a machine. The differences between what can be achieved by the still mysterious process of human reasoning, and those which can be mastered by machine, become even more obvious when we turn to our second area of AI, problem-solving.

the other direction. Over a period of time, the machine's heuristics will be developed to the point at which, perhaps, they could be said to be a product more of its experience than of the basic ones it started with. This does not, of course, mean that every chess-playing computer has to undergo such a laborious training process, for once the program has been brought up to the required standard it can be duplicated as required.

An even earlier development than the learning methods devised by Samuel was the basic technique used in searching a decision tree. This algorithm, known as mini-maxing, is the invention of Claude Shannon, one of the founding fathers of computer science. As a moment's thought will reveal, it is quite fruitless for the machine simply to scan the "bottom line" of its decision tree, the scored nodes which represent all the possible states of the game it can foresee, and try to follow the sequence of moves which leads to the highest score. For this is to assume that its opponent will be accommodating enough, when it is his turn to move, to make the move most advantageous to the machine. A more prudent assumption would be that an opposing player will always select, out of the available moves, the one which is least advantageous to the machine. It is on this principle that mini-maxing operates.

The system works like this. Starting from level one, the single node representing the present state of the game when it is the machine's turn to move, the decision tree is constructed to whatever depth is provided for; this will always be to a level where it is again the machine's move—i.e., level 3, level 5, level 7, etc. (When a machine can be set to play at different levels of skill, then setting it to a more advanced level leads it to construct decision trees that look ahead by a

further two or four or six levels). Using its heuristics, the machine then scores the nodes at the final level only, ignoring intervening nodes whether they represent its own moves or its opponent's.

The machine must then search the scores at this final level to discover which of the nodes represents the best state it can achieve assuming that its opponent will try to frustrate it at every opportunity. As can be seen from the diagram, the scores will be grouped in sets, with each set of nodes representing the possible states resulting from one of the opponent's moves at the previous level. From each group, the machine chooses the highest, the max, score on the assumption that it will make the best move. It then "backs up" this score to the node on the level above; from the new smaller selection of scores, the program selects the worst, or min, score, assuming its opponent will do his best to minimize its score. The process is continued until one final score is backed up to level one; the line along which this last score has been backed up then represents the machine's best move. Backing up on the mini-max system is a time-consuming operation, even for a computer, for if conducted in this fashion it involves the machine in searching every limb of its decision tree. Various expedients have, therefore, been developed to try and cut short the searching process. Perhaps the best known of these is alpha-betaing. Although the mathematics are a little complicated, the idea is relatively simple. If, in the course of backing up one branch of its decision tree, the machine finds that the maxes or mins on any level are less advantageous than those it has already discovered at the same level on other branches, then the search on that limb is abandoned.

The fact that a machine capable of playing chess at tournament standard

Problem-solving

Problems, as every human problem solver knows, come in all shapes and sizes. There are the formal problems of the crossword puzzle or brain-teaser kind; there are the practical problems involved in making things work; the organizational problems of getting people to work together; the human problems of living with each other. Clearly, most of these problems are, as yet, far beyond the scope of AI. The sort of problems AI is concerned with tend to be, in human terms, so elementary as scarcely to merit the description. Yet the fact that they have often proved deeply intractable and resistant to the programming methods available to AI suggests that we, as human beings, must devote a good deal of intelligence to solving them, even if we are unaware of doing so.

One possible approach to problem-solving is the decision tree method used in game-playing. Starting from the existing state of the problem, the machine can use a decision tree to examine all the next states which can be arrived at by taking a single step, then all the states that can follow, if a further step is added to each of the possible first steps, and so on. Again, the difficulty is that even in the case of quite simple problems, the possibilities quickly grow to unmanageable proportions. Moreover, as any human problem solver would see, the machine becomes involved in exploring courses of action which are in common sense terms ridiculous—they bring the problem no nearer to a solution.

One response to this is to attempt to break a problem up into sub-problems, each of which will, when solved, bring the overall solution one step nearer. The basic principle can be illustrated by taking the analogy of map reading. If a human traveller wishes to plan the best route from, say, Paris to Copenhagen, he will not explore on the map every road leading out of Paris to find the one that eventually leads to Copenhagen. Rather, looking at the map as a whole, he will see that if he goes to Brussels, and then to the Hague and then to Hamburg he will be

Left: A typical commercially available chess-playing machine, the Fidelity Electronics "Chess Challenger". Its "intelligence" does not seem to parallel that of a human chess master.

Left: A typical commercially available chess-playing machine, the Fidelity Electronics "Chess Challenger". Its "intelligence" does not seem to parallel that of a human chess master.

logical, step-by-step fashion. One moment, the problem looks impossible, the next we are exclaiming "Aha" because the right answer has lit up in our minds as if in response to some switch being turned on in the unconscious. When compared with the flash of inspiration or insight which leads human beings to the solution of so many problems, the methods employed by AI still seem painstakingly primitive. The fact that they work at all as a practical tool is largely due to the enormous speed, compared with that of the brain, at which computers can operate. But the fact that a computer can solve a simple problem in real time by carrying out tens of thousands of logical processes per second does not mean that it is solving it in the same way as a human being who may arrive at a solution without consciously applying any formal logic to the matter at all.

Using Natural Language

As anyone who has ever tried their hand at computer programming will have realized, the high-level programming languages in which most communication between computers and people is conducted are "languages" by courtesy only. In truth the "words" that make up a language such as BASIC, COBOL or PASCAL are more like the labels on a set of push buttons than the words we use in

moving towards his destination in a reasonably direct fashion making use of the best available roads. He can then look more closely in order to find the best route from Paris to Brussels, the best route from Brussels to the Hague, etc.

Another method takes advantage of the fact that, unlike chess problems, many practical problems of the kind that robots might have to tackle have a clearly defined finishing state as well as a starting state. It is, for example, impossible to define checkmate in terms of the states of a chess game in which it may occur; but it is quite feasible to say that a robot task will be complete when the pile of bricks, say, now stacked in this order have been restacked in that order, or when the robot has moved from point A to point Z via points C, B and Y. It is, therefore, possible to construct a second decision tree, reaching backwards from the target state; when one of the nodes on this tree links up with one of the nodes on the forward-looking tree the solution will have been found.

One of the best-known programs employing this process, known as means-ends analysis, was STRIPS which, in the early 1960s, guided a robot called SHAKEY around a maze at Stanford University (see also page 71). STRIPS was a direct descendant of one of the first problem-solving programs, the General Problem Solver, or GPS, developed by Alan Newell, J.C. Shaw and the Nobel Prize-winning economist, Herbert Simon. The GPS, which was itself a development of the very first problem-solver, a program called Logic Theorist, first explored the process of breaking a problem down into sub-problems and measuring the extent to which a solution of each sub-problem brought nearer a complete solution.

Although these methods have achieved some success, there are numerous kinds

of problems, many of them quite trivial in human terms, for which they are unsuitable. One of the more striking features of human problem-solving is the importance of what might be called the "Aha factor". When we see the answer to a problem—a cryptic crossword clue, perhaps, or the problem of fitting two fiddly components together correctly—we are not aware of having worked towards the solution in a

Means-End Analysis
This diagram shows a typical "robot task" problem: how to convert the upper stack into the lower stack, lifting one block at a time and using the fewest possible moves. The upper decision tree looks forward over the first four moves which can lead to seven possible states (note that the lefthand side of the tree represents a repetitive cycle of moves leading nowhere). Taken to a solution, this tree would become very large and include many sequences of moves that are obviously futile. The process of constructing and searching trees can be cut short in cases like this where there is only one possible "solved state" by constructing a second, backward-looking tree starting from the solution. The lower diagram illustrates such a tree carried back five levels. It can be seen that the states on the rightmost branches of forward- and backward-looking trees are the same, indicating that they can be joined up. The problem will be solved if the machine makes the following moves: 1. Pick up red. 2. Put red on table. 3. Pick up blue. 4. Put blue on table. 5. Pick up black. 6. Put black on blue. 7. Pick up red. 8. Put red on black.

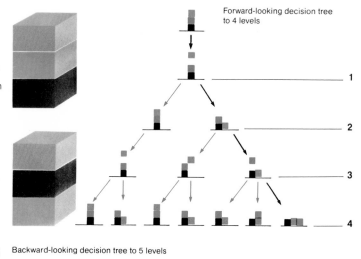

Forward-looking decision tree to 4 levels

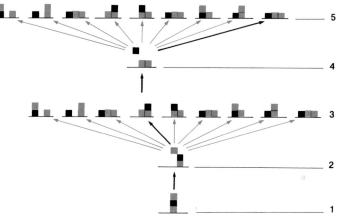

Backward-looking decision tree to 5 levels

everyday speech. That is to say, it is convenient for the user that the instruction "GOTO" should be intelligible to an English speaker, just as it is useful for the switch which turns on a car's windscreen wipers to be labelled "wipers". But in the computer's own terms, the word "GOTO" is not part of a language, it is simply a logical instruction which it can transform into its native machine code of 1s and 0s and act upon. It is behaving more like a dog which sits when told to sit, even though it has no understanding of what sitting means, than like a person who can understand statements such as "I was sitting down when the phone rang" or "I think I shall sit over here".

Natural language is a far more complicated affair. It was extremely fortunate for AI researchers that, just as their minds began to turn towards the difficulties it presented, our understanding was transformed by the work of the American philosopher Noam Chomsky. One of the basic puzzles that confronts anyone who aspires to teach a computer a natural language is how we ourselves achieve our mastery of language. Why is it, for example, that a child with a vocabulary of, say, one hundred words learns (apparently effortlessly) to combine them only in ways which are legitimate—that is, to form only grammatical sentences. There is almost an infinite number of ways in which the words can be combined; and although most of these will be nonsensical, the child can have heard other people use only a small fraction of the legitimate combinations. How then does he or she know how to construct a new legitimate combination while avoiding all the illegitimate ones?

Although traditional grammars attempted to define the legitimate structures of various languages, they did so in a way which looked more like a description of what happened than an explanation of why it happened. Certainly, it would be difficult to convert the rules of French grammar, as set out in a school textbook, into a program that would enable a computer to understand or communicate in French. Essentially, the schoolchild is able to learn French grammar because he or she understands English grammar, and they understand English grammar because they have already learnt to speak English.

Chomsky revolutionized the study of linguistics by arguing that traditional grammars dealt only with what he called the "surface structures" of languages. Beneath the separate sets of surface structures, one for each language, there lay, he suggested, a "deep structure" shared by all languages. From the point of view of AI, the important feature of Chomsky's work was that he described a set of logical rules, "production rules", which he believes are innate to the human brain. These production rules are, in his view, what allows us to "transform" and "generate" sentences that have meaning and are grammatically legitimate.

For example, we can rearrange the words used to ask the question, "was Cinderella at the ball when the clock

struck midnight?'; in order to form the statements "Cinderella was at the ball when the clock struck midnight" or "The clock struck midnight when Cinderella was at the ball." But we cannot transform the question into the statement, "The ball struck midnight when Cinderella was at the clock". The last sentence is illegitimate, not merely because it is nonsensical, but because the way in which the relationships between the elements of the original question have been transformed violates grammatical rules. "Cinderella", who was linked to "the ball" by "at" has now been arbitrarily linked, by the same preposition, to "the clock," and the "midnight" which was linked to "the clock" by the verb "struck" has now been illegitimately linked to "the ball".

Because Chomsky showed how sentences could be broken down into logical building blocks, which could then be manipulated and transformed, independently of the meaning of the words involved, and used to generate new sentences, he made it possible to design

Above: Complex elements like this Inmos transputer (essentially a complete computer, including processor and memory, on a single chip) will make possible a new generation of intelligent machines.

language-using programs which operated at the level of deep structure. At the present stage of research, for example, a typical program might start by being given a simple short story. It parses the sentences as they are fed to it in order to check that they are grammatical, that is, that it can accept them as legitimate components of a grammatical structure and allocate each item of vocabulary to a grammatical category. When the story is complete the computer has, so to speak, decomposed it into a set of logical elements with which it can then manipulate according to the rules of its transformational grammar.

However, although such programs have achieved considerable sophistication when dealing with problems of syntax or

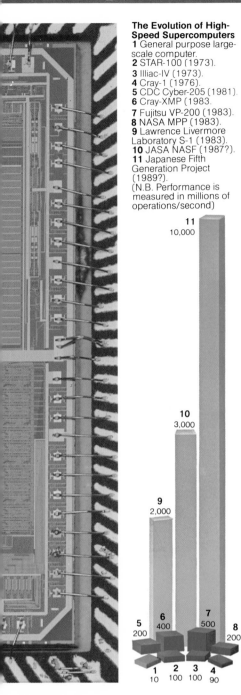

The Evolution of High-Speed Supercomputers
1 General purpose large-scale computer.
2 STAR-100 (1973).
3 Illiac-IV (1973).
4 Cray-1 (1976).
5 CDC Cyber-205 (1981).
6 Cray-XMP (1983.
7 Fujitsu VP-200 (1983).
8 NASA MPP (1983).
9 Lawrence Livermore Laboratory S-1 (1983).
10 JASA NASF (1987?).
11 Japanese Fifth Generation Project (1989?).
(N.B. Performance is measured in millions of operations/second)

11 10,000

10 3,000

9 2,000

6 400 **7** 500

5 200 **8** 200

1 10 **2** 100 **3** 100 **4** 90

grammar, they have revealed that an even more fundamental problem remains unsolved. The point is this: although at one level, that dealt with by Chomsky's grammar, language use can be thought of as a matter of manipulating abstract symbols (something the computer is extremely adept at), at another level, that of human communication, language is a matter of semantics; words have meaning to people because they are about or related to reality. Consider, for instance, the problems that are going to arise if a program which has been provided with the story of Cinderella, and can cope with the elements involved in the sentence "Cinderella was at the ball when the clock struck midnight", is then required to cope with a story about baseball which includes the sentence "The player struck the ball hard".

The most immediately obvious difficulty is that the words "ball" and "struck" are now being used in quite different senses. But the program has further problems. It might well, for example, note that both

midnight and balls were things that, in terms of the logical relationships between the elements in the two stories, could be struck. It would find it perfectly legitimate, therefore, to generate sentences such as "The player struck midnight hard" or "The clock struck the ball Cinderella was at".

One solution to this kind of problem was suggested by the American researchers, Roger Schank and R.P. Abelson. Such confusion would be avoided, they argued, if programs were provided with "scripts" each appropriate to a particular situation. Thus, if a program was able to determine, when asked "what was struck?", whether the question arose in the context of its "Cinderella script" rather than its "baseball script" the danger of a nonsensical reply would be averted. Schank and Abelson indeed argue that such script-using mechanisms are employed by human beings.

It is, however, difficult to avoid the conclusion that script-using, and other ingenious ways of coping with ambiguity, are little more than stop-gap expedients for getting round a very fundamental problem. How can a computer ever "know what it is talking about" in the same sense as a human being does? How, to come back to our example, can one explain to a computer that the ball baseball players strike is a hard spherical object (which will invoke defining the words "hard", "spherical" and even "object") while the ball Cinderella went to was a party at which people danced to music (definitions required for "party", "people", "dancing" and "music")?

Robots may provide one way of getting round these problems. For robots might begin, in some primitive fashion, to experience reality in the same way as people — once they have senses they will be able to see and feel things and to learn the words which describe what they see or feel. They may, ultimately, build up a picture of the world and the ability to talk about it in ways which make sense.

One of the most interesting language-using programs yet devised made a start in exploring this sort of possibility, and got round the snags which are inherent in it, in a particularly ingenious way. SHRDLU, as the program was called, was then the brainchild of Terry Winograd, then a graduate student at the Massachusetts Institute of Technology. The "world" SHRDLU dealt with consisted of a small number of primitive blocks, (cubes, pyramids and boxes) and a robot arm which could be used to move the blocks about. The point of the exercise was to teach SHRDLU the language it needed to cope with this "block world". But the real ingenuity lay in the fact that the "world" itself existed only as a set of programs inside the computer. In other words, right from the start SHRDLU "knew" all there was to know about the world about which it was going to talk. Ultimately, the program became capable of conducting quite sophisticated dialogues about the block world and its own manipulations of it. What has yet to be established, however, is whether such techniques can be extended to cope with the real world, full of

manifold unpredictabilities and the subtle language which human beings use to discuss it. When robotics is in a position to start to tackle that issue, which will in turn depend crucially upon the development of advanced sensory equipment, it may also be able to answer an even deeper question. Is Chomsky right in thinking that the ability to cope with the deep structure of language is an inborn human skill? Or are those who disagree with him right in arguing that language-use is a skill which is learned in infancy? The implications of this controversy are of great importance both to psychology and robotics. If people do not learn language-use from scratch, then the skill with which robots use language will be limited unless and until we fully understand the "language-using program" built into our own brains. But if it proved possible for a robot to learn a language, even up to a fairly elementary level, without the benefit of such a program then one of psychology's central puzzles would have been resolved.

Combinatorial Explosion

The difficulties that arise when AI attempts to transfer the methods it uses to cope with constricted, artificial block worlds or chessboard worlds to the real world, or even some small part of it, have been summed up in a single phrase, the combinatorial explosion. It is not merely that the real world contains many more elements than, say, a set of chessmen, or that our everyday vocabulary is far larger than the limited vocabulary of a script-using program; the real problem arises because the factors that define those elements, or that govern our use of words, can combine in an infinite variety of different ways.

The number of states that can occur on a chessboard may be infinite, but the rules that govern the movements of the pieces are simple and well-defined. But

Below: A scene of SHRDLU's block world. The objects, and the arm which moved them, existed only inside the computer, along with the language-using program which learnt to talk about the tiny world.

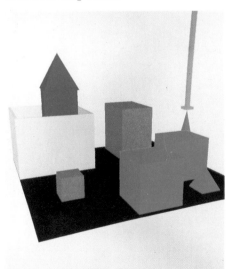

take the same set of chessmen and toss them higgledy-piggledy into a box. Again, the number of ways in which they may arrange themselves is infinite, but this time there are no clear rules. A robot which is instructed to pick out, say, the black pawns, cannot be provided with an algorithm that defines the legitimate positions a black pawn may be in, or which describes which piece to pick up first in order to avoid disturbing the pile.

Similar problems arise with language. To come back to our Cinderella script for a moment, it is quite reasonable to assume that, in retelling the story of Cinderella, a human narrator might say "The prince was immediately struck by Cinderella's beauty", or "Cinderella looked very striking in her magic ball gown", or even "The ugly sister struck a threatening pose". Immediately, the program requires additional definitions of the verb "to strike" that allow it to understand these additional meanings in the Cinderella context. But, to a human being, the choice of the word struck or striking is not accidental—the narrator will have chosen to describe the Prince as struck rather than impressed by Cinderella's beauty precisely because it conveys

Right and below: Set out on the board, the chessmen move according to rules which a program can represent, and apply its intelligence to. But piled higgledy-piggledy in a box, they reflect the infinite untidy variety of the real world, which is as yet too complex for a machine to cope with.

the sense that he was affected instantly, as if he had been physically struck. The word is in fact being used in a sense that is analogous to its use in the baseball script. To separate the two meanings by putting them in different scripts, rather than helping the computer to understand the word, in fact prevents it from doing so. But how, unless the computer is to be part of a robot which experiences baseballs being struck, clocks striking midnight, heroines looking striking, sisters striking poses, etc, will it ever understand the combination

of rules and subtle shades of meanings which govern our own use of the verb?

The interesting point about the combinatorial explosion is that it seems to limit the potential of AI not in areas like chess-playing, which are normally thought to require high intelligence, but in spheres that in our own terms scarcely demand intelligence at all. Perhaps the central problem is that we ourselves have no clear idea of why we are not bewildered and befuddled by the combinatorial explosion when we sort out a pile of

chessmen, listen to a story on the radio or perform a hundred other everyday tasks. One thing does seem to be clear; we do not employ the sort of formal algorithms which AI has tried to make use of. It may be, therefore, that robots will not be capable of matching our skills unless some new approach is developed.

Expert Systems

It is perhaps partly because of the problems posed by the combinatorial explosion that energy and effort has increasingly been concentrated over the past ten years or so on a branch of AI known as expert systems.

We may not understand the sort of rules and algorithms we use to cope with the trivial problems of everyday life, but there are many areas of human knowledge where information and experience have been carefully organized and codified into systematic, regular, algorithmic structures. When a person has acquired a thorough understanding of the structure of knowledge in a particular field, he qualifies as an expert in that field. Expert systems are computer programs which incorporate, and provide access to, bodies of human expertise in, for example, medicine, physics, chemistry, law, geology, etc. Their novelty, and the reason for the excitement which currently surrounds the whole subject, lies in the fact that they attempt not merely to store the knowledge employed by a human expert, but also to reproduce the structure of that knowledge, the processes of reasoning, judgement

Below: Using a graphics tablet to describe a molecular structure, Philip Cook consults a program called LHASA which embodies a range of expertise about chemical processes. Expert systems like this make knowledge widely and easily available.

and even intuition which an expert employs when he brings his knowledge to bear on a particular problem. Using an expert system is thus more like actually consulting a real expert than simply looking up the relevant facts in a database. The program will not only provide an opinion, it will also explain how and why it has come to that opinion (backtracking through its reasoning processes and listing the rules it has made use of), it will ask questions in order to confirm or reject a diagnosis, it may even be able to quantify its opinion, stating for example by what percentage this answer is more likely to be correct than that one.

The actual workings of expert systems are complex, so much so that a whole new discipline, knowledge engineering, is coming into being in order to cope with the task of reformulating human expertise into a shape in which it can be incorporated into programs. The crucial point is that an expert does not follow simple rules of the "If A then B" kind. His judgements are arrived at by weighing up a whole range of factors each of which may have a varying significance according to the circumstances, and many of these factors can only be evaluated in the light of experience. An expert's thinking is much more likely to go along the lines of "If A then B is more likely than C, but checking D and E will settle the issue one way or the other."

Two points are perhaps more fundamental than any others in the construction of expert systems. First, the information provided by the human experts, the material that makes up the program's knowledge base, must be provided in a form which allows statements to be related to each other in terms of the implications which each holds for the other. Technically, such relationships can be formulated in a logical system known as predicate calculus; basically this is simply the system

of Classical logic which deals with the conclusions that can be drawn from two or more statements involving common factors, a familiar example is the schoolroom classic: All Greeks are men. Socrates is a Greek. Therefore Socrates is a man. A new computer language, PROLOG, invented by researchers at the University of Marseilles, allows all information to be communicated to a machine in a form which translates directly into predicate calculus and is already doing much to aid the development of new expert systems.

The second important feature of expert systems is that, unlike most computer programs, the knowledge base, the part of the program which contains data, is separate from the part which controls the manipulation of that data. This latter bit of the program, the knowledge interpreter as it is called, is in turn sub-divided into an inference machine which directs the step-by-step tactics involved in solving a problem, and a control section which oversees the strategy.

The considerable success that expert systems have already achieved, and the even greater potential that they seem to offer in fields like medicine, where knowledge and experience is already accumulating at a rate which far exceeds the capacity of individual human experts to absorb and make use of it, is largely responsible for the resurgence of interest in AI over the past few years. It is not, however, clear that the techniques involved in expert systems have very much to offer to robotics. Much of the progress that has been made with expert systems is due to the fact that they deal with information that has already been organized into formal, abstract systems, and can therefore be handled by programmes which have no knowledge or experience of the "real world" factors on which the abstract structure of expertise was originally based.

Robots, on the other hand, being machines whose whole raison d'être is to understand and act upon the real world, are unlikely to be able to make use of formalized systems of expertise until they have achieved a much fuller understanding of the nuts and bolts of reality. To take a simple example, it would be eminently practicable to build an expert system which could analyse the causes that lead to car breakdowns; given the basic data, and a human assistant to apply tests and report results, such a program would be able to track down, say, the problem which is preventing a car starting on cold winter mornings. But this computerized expertise is going to be of very little help to a robot motor mechanic unless we have first equipped it with the visual and manipulative skills needed to dismantle a carburettor or unscrew a spark plug.

There seems little point in building robots which are mechanical equivalents of that classic figure of fun, the impractical academic, the expert who knows all there is to know about the theory of electromagnetism but is quite incapable of changing a light bulb.

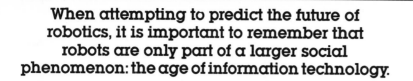

THE FUTURE

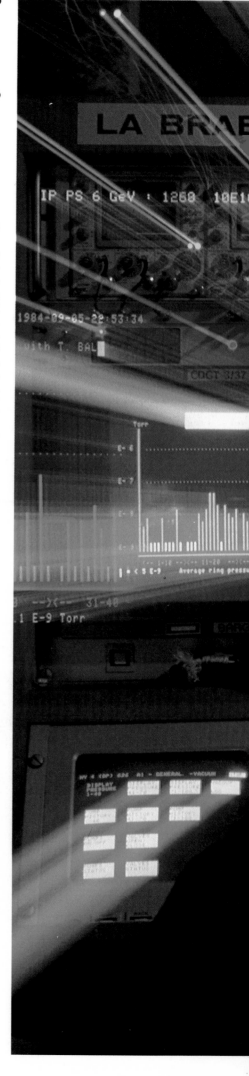

So far, this book has concentrated on describing what robots are, what they can do and how robotics technology is likely to evolve during the next 15 to 20 years. It is important to emphasise that the dramatic advances in robotic technology that have taken place in recent years are linked with similar advances in microelectronics and telecommunications; robots are only one feature of a vast array of computer-controlled devices which have their roots in developments in what is now called information technology.

When we speak of information technology we are referring to technologies relevant to human communication processes and to the handling of the information conveyed in these processes. In the broadest sense of the term, information simply relates to any and all facts that are communicated, learned or stored. Information science is now understood to mean the science by which computers process and store information; information technology is concerned with how computer-based information is stored, processed and transmitted—be it by telephone lines, cable, satellite, teletext or other means.

A key characteristic of modern information technology is that the fusion of information processing (represented by the role of computer technology) and communication (increasingly dominated by telecommunications) has brought about a revolutionary change in the quality of information flow. This means that more communicable information is available than ever before, and it can be processed much more efficiently and flexibly; it can also be transmitted and acted upon more rapidly. It is thus a "heartland technology" which can potentially be applied to every sector and industry.

While the advent of the new "information age" will undoubtedly bring enormous potential opportunities for raising the quality of life, there are real dangers that social inequalities could be extended. The opportunities which open up as a result of the linkage between telecommunications and computers will depend a great deal on who has access to the wide range of databanks which will be created, and how these databanks and their associated monitoring systems are applied to the workplace, and how accessible they are to society generally.

If past experience is anything to go by, the benefits arising from new technological developments will tend to favour those who are at the forefront in the investment and application of scientific and technological innovation. Internationally, countries in the Third World will be at a severe disadvantage compared with their counterparts in Western Europe, the United States and Japan. Projects concerned with social need will take second place to military developments; the most educationally advantaged will benefit more than the least educated; the research efforts of large corporations will receive more government support than that of Universities; and those with the greater resources will derive more from the technology than those who are economically weaker. If this scenario is played out, there is a danger that skill differences will be widened, and the less privileged will be further disadvantaged compared with their richer contemporaries. Moreover, access to the new facilities will inevitably depend as much on education and skills as the ability to pay for the new services.

The Unmanned Factory?

The idea of a completely automated factory as the culmination of technical ingenuity has fascinated engineers and social visionaries (albeit for very different reasons) for a considerable period of time. One of the most famous automated factories is the Yamazaki machine tool plant in Japan; the factory consists of 18 flexible machining centres which can perform a wide range of metal-shaping/cutting operations, plus a variety of other automatic machines. The transfer of work from machine to machine is automatically regulated by computer. The entire operation of the factory, including accounts, the preparation of financial statements, and production control, is performed automatically. The factory reception area contains a flashing number board which gives the latest production total: it changes every 45 minutes, the average time it takes to complete a Mazak machine tool. The factory has three shifts—the first shift

Right: The glamour of the age of information technology is beguiling, but is there a danger that its evolution will only serve further to exacerbate social inequalities?

employs seven people, the second five, and the night shift runs without anybody being present.

However, the notion of a completely automated unmanned factory is seriously misleading; such factories will still need people, but not many. There will still be a need for unskilled labour—at least in the short term—to load and unload parts and to clean and clear the equipment. There will also be some semi-skilled tasks of changing tools where automatic changing is too difficult. Factories in the future will also require three levels of highly trained engineers: planners at the overall programme level, computer operators at the computer production level and technicians at the workshop level.

Moreover, the impact of flexible manufacturing systems (FMS) will not be felt overnight. There are still only around 100 FMS systems in the world and these plants are by no means completely "flexible". They can turn out a variety of products by re-programming the computer, but only within the same family of items. There is a vast difference between a highly automated plant staffed by a group of monitors and machine-minders and a factory with no-one on the shop floor. Perhaps the reality in the foreseeable future will lie somewhere in between these two extremes, although the impact on work and employment will be immense. Most importantly, the labour content of the production process will be drastically reduced.

It is important to recognize that robots only form part of an overall system; they operate in interface with other machines, which themselves are linked into the information flow that directs the technology.

A great deal of interest and concern has centred on the job displacement effects following the introduction of robots into manufacturing. Perhaps the most

dire prediction was published in the US News and World Report in September 1982. This study, which was carried out by Carnegie-Mellon University predicted that: ". . by the year 2000, robots will supplant 3 million factory workers and by 2025, could be handling virtually all manufacturing chores."

A number of sectoral studies have also been carried out in Europe on the employment impact of robots which are also pessimistic, albeit in varying degrees. During the preparation of the Eighth French Plan (1981-1985), it was estimated that the introduction of robots would lead to a loss of about 30,000 jobs, which was not even 1 per cent of the French labour force in 1980. Forecasts in the Federal Republic of Germany are more sombre. Assuming that the utilization of robots will increase from a mere 2 per cent in 1980 to 60 per cent in 1990, the result would be 200,000 lost industrial jobs—about 6 per cent of industrial employment. The trouble with these sectoral studies, of course, is the fact that they are restricted to a particular sector, and they therefore do not take into account the employment effects in other parts of the economy, which are not necessarily negative.

What will jobs be like in the highly robotized plants of the not too distant future? Although it is too early to come to any firm conclusions on the effect of robotic installation on job design and skill levels, the division of labour and the content of jobs will change dramatically as robots become more sophisticated. There will be a greater distance between work stations and less contact between workers. While the conditions of work will probably be safer with the worker more separated from the work process, higher production rates may reintroduce some hazards in the high-speed plant where a

small failure in the system may compound to frightening proportions in a matter of seconds.

It is also likely that workers will have a responsibility for a larger span of the production equipment because there will be greater system integration and fewer workers manning the production equipment. Many workers will merely carry out a monitoring role—patrolling and inspecting a system when all appears to be functioning properly. However, he or she will be expected to react sharply to an incipient crisis and take corrective action when anything goes wrong. This may involve knowledge and competence of a depth essential to handle a highly-integrated system of machines. Thus more jobs will be integrated, and old boundaries between tasks will be wiped out as jobs are combined and enlarged. There is also the possibility that, as robots become more and more sophisticated and complex, many workers will find their jobs less demanding and devoid of interest or satisfaction.

Social contact between workers will also be severely reduced, because there will be a greater physical distance between work stations. The highly robotized plants of tomorrow will no longer be dependent upon the establishment of work-teams with a strong sense of cohesiveness, and isolation from other workers will be a common feature in such plants.

Advanced robotized plants are also likely to demand different kinds of supervisory skills. The traditional human relations skills of the supervisor will become less and less important as a premium is placed on technical competence. There will be fewer levels of supervision and fewer workers. The need to ensure the maximum utilization of costly equipment and the imperative of

The Displaced Workforce

In a much quoted survey which was carried out by researchers from the University of Michigan and the Society of Manufacturing Engineers, it was predicted that by the 1990s the major centres of production in the USA would run on a 32-hour week (or four eight-hour days). Changes in the nature, duration and allocation of work would be negotiated with the workforce in the following stages:

1. From 1980 a new hierarchy of skills, ever more centred on the creation, realization and maintenance of automated equipment, would come into being.

2. By 1985 20 per cent of the workers currently employed in assembly would be replaced by automated systems.

3. By 1988 20 per cent of industrial jobs would be redesigned and 15 per cent of assembly systems automated.

4. By 1988 50 per cent of the labour force employed in assembling would have been replaced.

The process was due to accelerate after that. According to a study presented by the Stanford Research Institute to the United Auto Workers (UAW) in March 1979, 80 per cent of manual work would be automated by the year 2000 which, at present working hours, would amount to the elimination of 20 million jobs from the present total of 25 million.

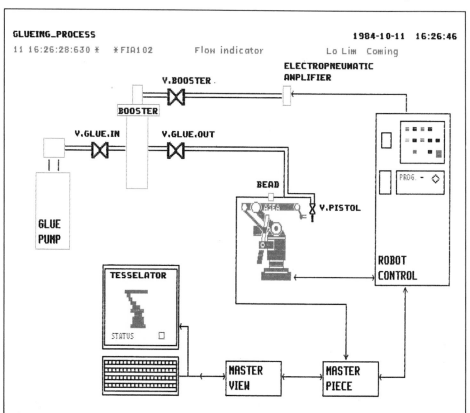

avoiding shut-downs will lead to much closer supervision. Production schedules are also likely to be much more demanding. Supervisors will also find that as their traditional human relations skills are not so important, they will become increasingly dependent on the skills and knowledge of individual workers.

Just as the design and structure of jobs in highly robotized plants will change radically, so too will career patterns, channels of promotion and job security. There will be fewer workers, fewer job classifications, fewer levels of supervision and increasingly complex technical work environments. Many workers will find that the promotional ladders that they planned to climb will be shortened or shattered.

What levels of pay can these workers in advanced robotic plants expect to receive? According to M.S. Katzman (Human resources implications of robots in the United States, "Work and People", Vol. 9, No. 1, 1983): "Work in the highly robotized plants will be generally rewarded with higher pay. While there will be little up-grading of jobs in the new plants, workers will be paid a little more per hour than in less automated plants. With self-regulating mechanisms controlling robots and built-in rates of production, there will be little the worker can do to augment quantity or quality of a product. This will mean that individual or small incentive systems will no longer be useful."

Below: As plants become more automated, more and more human workers will have jobs monitoring rather than manning production equipment. One example of a highly integrated process control and monitoring system is the ASEA Master, and these are "hard" copies of typical displays that are produced by its Tesselator VDUs.

Despite the attention that robots receive from the media, it is important to re-iterate that robots are only one component of a whole series of technological devices which are based on new technology. The impact that they will have on the future of work cannot be considered in isolation from economic changes that are linked with technological innovation.

The long term tendency in all industrial societies—a trend which accelerated during the post-war period—has been for the majority of the working population to be employed in the tertiary sector of the economy, chiefly at the expense of manufacturing and agriculture (see table right). The service sector has constituted the majority of the employed population in Britain since the 1960s and in the United States well before that date. This exodus from industry accelerated in the early 1980s, and is mainly affecting the heavy and material processing or manufacturing industries. This suggests that the advanced industrialized countries are gradually moving towards a kind of "de-materialized" production system where "light" products and processes will be the foundation of their economies for some time to come.

Future Work Patterns?

We can expect a very different form of work organization from the kind we have known in the past. If the present trends are significant, we are likely to see:
1. A situation where full employment cannot be guaranteed, and where fewer and fewer people are involved in paid full-time employment.
2. A manufacturing sector that is smaller in terms of people employed but operating at considerably higher levels of productivity than at present, and more

Changing Work Patterns

	Year	Agriculture	Industry	Services	Women
AUSTRALIA	64	10.3	39.9	49.8	N/A
	73	7.4	35.5	57.1	33.6
	81	6.5	30.6	62.8	36.3
AUSTRIA	60	24.6	40.3	35.1	N/A
	73	16.2	40.6	43.2	38.4
	81	10.3	40.1	50.0	38.2
BELGIUM	60	8.7	46.8	44.6	30.7
	73	3.8	41.5	54.7	34.0
	80	3.0	34.8	62.3	35.9
CANADA	60	13.3	33.2	53.5	26.8
	73	6.5	30.6	62.8	35.2
	81	5.5	28.3	66.2	39.7
DENMARK	60	18.2	36.9	44.8	31.8
	73	9.5	33.8	56.7	41.1
	79	8.3	30.0	61.7	43.6
FINLAND	60	36.4	31.9	31.7	44.8
	73	17.1	35.7	47.1	46.1
	81	11.1	34.8	54.1	47.6
FRANCE	60	22.4	37.8	39.8	35.2[a]
	73	11.4	39.7	48.9	36.0
	81	8.6	35.2	56.2	38.0[b]
GERMANY (Fed. Rep. of)	60	14.0	48.8	37.3	37.8
	73	7.5	47.5	45.0	37.2
	81	5.9	44.1	49.9	38.7
GREECE	61	53.8[c]	18.5	27.7	32.3
	71	38.9	26.3	34.8	27.5
	79	30.8	30.0	39.2	29.7
IRELAND	60	37.3	23.7	39.0	26.6[d]
	73	24.8	30.9	44.2	26.6[e]
	80	19.2	32.4	48.4	28.5
ITALY	60	32.8	36.9	30.2	30.1
	73	18.3	39.2	42.5	28.7
	81	13.4	37.5	49.2	32.3
JAPAN	60	30.2	28.5	41.3	40.7
	73	13.4	37.2	49.3	38.5
	81	10.0	35.3	54.7	38.7
NETHERLANDS[f]	60	11.5	40.4	48.2	N/A
	73	6.8	36.2	57.0	N/A
	80	6.0	31.9	62.1	N/A
NORWAY	60	21.6	35.6	42.9	29.0
	73	11.4	33.9	54.7	36.6
	81	8.5	29.8	61.7	41.4
PORTUGAL	64	42.8	29.5	27.7	18.7
	74	34.8	34.5	30.7	40.0
	80	28.5	36.0	35.5	38.8
SPAIN	60	42.3	32.0	25.7	N/A
	73	24.3	36.7	39.0	28.0
	81	18.2	35.2	46.6	28.6
SWEDEN	62	13.1	42.0	45.0	36.1
	73	7.1	36.8	56.0	40.8
	81	5.6	31.3	63.1	45.9
SWITZERLAND	60	13.2	48.4	38.4	N/A
	73	7.7	44.1	48.1	34.0
	81	7.0	39.3	53.6	35.2
TURKEY	60	81.1	8.6	10.2	45.2
	73	64.5	15.1	20.4	N/A
	80	60.4	16.3	23.3	N/A
UK	60	4.1	48.8	47.0	34.4
	73	2.9	42.6	54.5	37.6
	81	2.8	36.3	60.9	40.3
USA	60	8.3	33.6	58.1	33.3
	73	4.2	33.2	62.6	38.5
	81	3.5	30.1	66.4	42.8
OECD	60	21.7	35.3	43.0	34.3
	73	12.1	36.4	51.5	36.2
	81	10.0[g]	33.7[g]	56.3[g]	38.6[g]

a: 1968. b: 1980. c: 1964. d: 1961. e: 1971. f: In work-years. g: Estimated. This table of the structure of civilian employment throughout the member nations of the Organization for Economic Co-operation and Development (OECD) 1960-1981 is based on International Labour Office definitions and is reproduced from "World Labour Report 1", © 1984, International Labour Organization, Geneva.

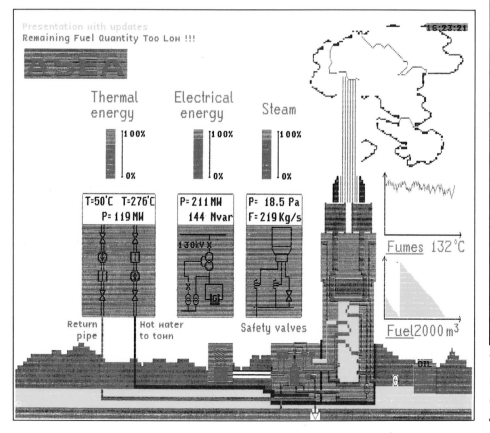

Presentation with updates
Remaining Fuel Quantity Too Low !!!

ASEA   16:23:21

Thermal energy   Electrical energy   Steam

100%   100%   100%

0%   0%   0%

T=50°C T=276°C   P=211 MW   P= 18,5 Pa
P=119 MW   144 Mvar   F=219 Kg/s

130kV

Return pipe   Hot water to town   Safety valves

Fumes 132°C

Fuel 2000 m³

reliance on shift-work and sub-contracting.

3. A demand for more highly technically qualified people to service the growing "telematics" sector as well as more specialists and professionals, but fewer and fewer less qualified workers.

4. Shorter working lives, increasing flexibility in work tasks, more part-time and home-working, short-term contracts based on fees rather than guaranteed life-time employment, and more self-employment.

5. Work organizations in the future will be much smaller both in physical terms and also in the number of people they employ.

6. The boundaries between leisure and work will become increasingly blurred and much more importance will be placed on the "informal" economy of the home and the community.

7. There will be an increased demand for education at all levels.

8. A smaller earning population and a larger dependent population.

9. Fewer manual jobs and a much smaller (and weakened) trade union movement.

10. More "self-servicing" in the home and the community.

11. New forms of social organization and government to complement the changes in the organization of work.

Unemployment Threat

Concern about unemployment being induced by automation stretches back over a long period. Long before the microprocessor had been invented in the early 1960s a debate was already in progress about the effects of computers on employment levels. Then, as now, there was a great deal of disagreement among the experts, ranging from the optimists to the pessimists. Many experts still assume that even though jobs will be increasingly lost in manufacturing and other traditional industries, the expansion of the service sector would easily maintain employment levels. Many still believe that the current levels of unemployment are just temporary products of the worldwide recession. The coming of the "post-industrial society" is seen as providing new forms of job creation.

However, there is no guarantee that a smooth transition will take place; employment has already begun to decrease in some traditional branches of services as well as final marketed services. The continued expansion of the public sector and government employment is at best uncertain and the new information tech-

nology will displace jobs in the service sector as well as in traditional industries, if only because the tertiary and secondary sectors are both automating at the same time. Despite the growth in the service sector of the economy coupled with the increase in clerical and office employment in the 1950s-1970s, a large number of occupations in these areas are ripe for automation. Nor is there much support for the view that the new "information sector" will be a growth employment area. There may well be a growth of jobs in the so-called "personal services" sector, such as providing people with food, drink, holidays, leisure, sport, heat, light, transport, cleaning, maintenance etc., but here too there is scope for a considerable degree of automation, and there are limits to demand for such services. Of course, an accurate forecast of the likely growth/decline of different occupations in different sectors is notoriously difficult to predict, but the prospects for a return to full employment are bleak.

Moreover, there is a strong possibility that we will see an increasing tendency for labour segmentation to emerge, where an increasing number of jobs become less secure, more flexible and increasingly isolated from the external labour market and the wider trade union movement. Most of the new jobs that are created will come from information services and particularly from personal services; such jobs will be few and far between and will be

Above and right: The old and the new—in the 1920s Cadbury employed women to pack their confectionery; nowadays (right) this task is performed by dedicated "pick-and-place" robot hands. As can be seen, the human involvement has been minimized.

Kondratiev's Economic Cycles

N. Kondratiev was a Russian economist who in 1926 pointed out that economic activity moved in "long waves" of fifty or so years in duration. The first long wave was from 1789 to 1849 (going up until 1814 then down); the second from 1849 to 1896 (up until 1873) and the third from 1896 to 1945 (although Kondratiev only identified the upswing until 1920 and did not venture to predict the future). Carrying on his time sequence produces a fourth wave from 1945 to 1995 (probably exacerbated or accelerated by the jump in energy prices in the 1970s); 1970-95 are the years of decline leading into the beginning of a fifth wave at the end of the century.

Kondratiev did not think that the waves were accidental. "Important discoveries and inventions" were made during the downswings and then applied to the upswings. What Kondratiev did not comment on, but which is of perhaps the greatest social importance, is the fact that the principal focus of industrial activity tended to change with each successive wave. What is the relevance of Kondratiev's work? New products and new technologies are crucial, but where is the evidence that they will produce more rather than fewer jobs than the businesses they replace? Kondratiev was talking about *output*, not *jobs*. As long as manufacturing was labour-intensive the two were the same. Now they are not. The new businesses think in terms of hundreds of people, not thousands, even when they have big new plants.

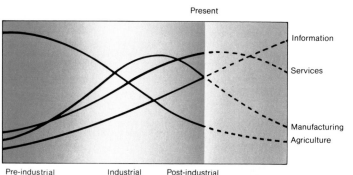

The Waves of Work
The graph illustrates the proportion of the labour force that has been employed in four different types of work during the 19th and 20th Centuries. The present decline in agriculture and manufacturing industry is mirrored by a rise in the service and IT sectors. Projections of future trends reveal the gap between the rising and falling curves widening for some time yet, until services peak, and begin to decline.

Present

Information

Services

Manufacturing

Agriculture

Pre-industrial   Industrial   Post-industrial

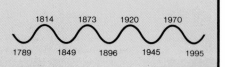

Although we are still in the embryonic phase of the so-called information revolution, current technological developments point to a number of challenges:

1. Technological innovation is proceeding so rapidly that the life-cycle of products is becoming much shorter than previously. This means that a premium is placed on flexibility in production and marketing planning.

2. The need to locate industrial sites according to the most favourable labour and product market criteria will become less and less important as time goes on. Proximity to component supply centres and technological know-how will be more important.

3. There is likely to be a diversification of business organization towards complementary mechanical and electronic activities in order to absorb overmanning and improve profitability, by creating a network of small enterprises which are highly specialized in specific fields.

4. There is likely to be less emphasis on production itself with a greater commitment to pre-production (Research and Development), and post-production areas of the business—such as marketing, technical assistance and applicative software. All this will have profound implications for management structure and functional responsibility in enterprises.

5. We can expect to see a continuous appraisal of "make or buy" decisions in enterprises because enterprise management will be aware of the risk of finding that component parts are unavailable—thus jeopardizing the success of an entire range of its products.

6. The increasing importance of information in management decision-making is an inevitable consequence of advances in technological development. This will be true in the cases of incorporating microelectronics in products, the provision of services and in product manufacture.

The prolific growth in paper-work which has been a feature of the growth in office and administrative functions during the twentieth century could eventually slow down significantly as it is gradually replaced by electronic data storage, processing and transmission. The "paperless" office is by no means an unlikely possibility. Enterprises will need to be able to take advantage of the availability of very cheap microelectronic data technology by integrating the vast increase in information available into the planning, decision-making and control functions. In manpower terms, it is worth remembering that the capital investment per employee in office jobs is much lower than for factory workers. Thus the office and administrative sector is ripe for automation, and we can expect substantial job losses to occur, especially in routine office activities where many women are presently employed.

nowhere near sufficient to return us to anything resembling the full employment that we experienced during the 1950s and 1960s. Finally, most of the new jobs (with the exception of those requiring very high technical skills) are likely to be inferior in job content and in terms of working conditions.

Weakened Trade Unions

The trade unions have had limited success in their policy of seeking to influence the direction of the new technology by bringing it within the ambit of collective bargaining through new technology agreements. They rightly emphasise that certain groups of workers were particularly vulnerable to changes stemming from the new technology, particularly women (who work in large numbers in the office sector), the unskilled, older workers and young people seeking to enter the labour market for the first time. They have been severely hampered by the fact the microelectronics has emerged during a period of recession, and their bargaining power has consequently been reduced. Most technical change is taking place without any kind of agreement, and where trade unions have succeeded in securing new technology agreements, such agreements have fallen far short of their model aspirations. In any case, trade unionists find themselves facing an insoluble dilemma on jobs. If the new technology is introduced then jobs will disappear, but if new forms of automation are ignored then jobs will be eliminated as the market position of the firms that employ them is eroded by more innovative competitors.

Changes in the use of work time are already taking place throughout Western industrialized societies. While full-time paid work is still the predominant form of work, part-time and temporary work has expanded considerably since the 1950s as a result of women's entry to the labour market (on average, more than 60 per cent of employed women are working part-time). In addition, of those workers who are in full-time employment, an increasing number are occupied in shift-work. There has also been a shortening of the length of the working day, a growth in annual holidays, and a decrease in the number of years spent in the labour force.

We can expect to see a continuation of the trend towards a gradual reduction in the average length of people's working lives, largely because of more flexible and more "portable" pension schemes; the years from 16 to 19 being increasingly seen as a period of education, training and work experience; more older workers being able to work on a part-time basis without loss of pension rights; and the likelihood that more and more people will be able to take periods off work for raising children, undergoing retraining or attending educational classes without the loss of pension rights.

Likely Effects

Nearly every enterprise will be affected in one way or another by the new technology, regardless of its activities. The impact of the new technology will spread across the entire structure of an enterprise from manufacturing to administration, and from planning to marketing.

Small is Beautiful

The realization of the "small is beautiful" notion is linked with the implementation of computer automated manufacturing. It is likely that plants, possibly even large

situated under one roof, co-ordinated by a vertically integrated management hierarchy is no longer a necessity once the new technology is fully implemented. Enterprises could be widely dispersed without any consequent loss in managerial co-ordination and control as a result of new technology. When information technology is combined with computer-aided design and computer-aided manufacturing (CAD/CAM), whole segments of the production process could be spatially and organizationally separated. Once computers begin to specify the requirements for parts fabrication in a standardized language and once the automated facilities exist to turn these specifications into a part, the need to have all the stages of engineering within the same location, or even in the same enterprise, diminishes. Thus the problems of managing large production units would thereby be avoided. It is likely that CAE will enable vertically-integrated operations to uncouple their production processes— leading to the emergence of many small single-product or single-function companies. A logical extension of this is one where workers, either employees or freelance, can operate their word processors, CAD systems etc from home.

Much speculation has taken place about the potential that information technology offers for the development of homeworking or some form of self-employment. The main attraction of homeworking for employers is financial: there is no need to provide factory or office facilities. In most cases lower wages or salaries can be paid because of the reduced ability of homeworkers to take collective action through trade unions. In any case, it is much easier to lay

corporations, will shrink in terms of numbers employed quite substantially. Moreover, the availability of relatively cheap forms of automation by reprogrammable computer-aided engineering (CAE) devices will enable enterprises to batch-produce items that were previously produced with "hard-wired" automation and to reduce the size of economic

batches. Thus, in the not too distant future, smaller firms may be able to take on business that was previously carried out only by large companies.

Information technology will enable rapid co-ordination to take place throughout different management functions in the enterprise. Thus the need for the various stages of the production process to be

Right: CAD is very much a technology of the 1980s. Here a designer is using the interactive graphics of Marconi-Quest's Q-Design system to refine the circuit diagram for a PCB.

Below: The ability of CAD to simulate a robot's actions on a CRT allows the designer to debug the program before the machine is required to run it.

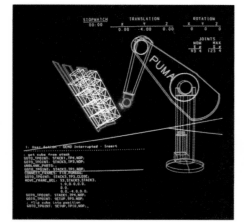

Left: Computers are certainly labour-saving devices, but does their advent herald the rupture of the sense of social community that is one of the attractions of work today?

become more common, as firms refuse to take on the responsibility of employing an expensive specialist for forty years or more; flexible time contracts will be introduced to make part-time work more feasible when an organization does not need the full-time services of certain specialists, many of whom will be pleased to be employed for part of their time; and education and training will become an ever increasing priority in organizations, partly because training will be a way of harmonizing the interests of the individual being trained with the interests of the organization.

The scenario which has been outlined above may be an attractive one for senior management insofar as it enables managerial overheads to be drastically reduced. It may also be attractive for those relatively few key staff who will retain prospects of full-time employment and for those who are willing to accept the risks of working independently on short-term contracts. But what about everybody else?

The Work Ethic

Perhaps one of the biggest problems facing society in adapting to the changes that are on the horizon is the central importance that paid work has occupied in Western societies for the last 150 years or so. The status and identity of individuals in the wider society have been largely influenced by their occupation. Indeed, the terms work, occupation and employment are frequently used inter-changeably in everyday speech. It is difficult to conceive of a future where "work" in the traditional sense of the word becomes less and less important both for the individual and society as a whole. Our self-esteem and the opinion that others hold of us is measured almost entirely by what we do rather than what we are. Thus an employed person of sixty perceives himself (and is perceived by others) as being of much greater worth than he will be as an unemployed person of sixty-five, five years hence. People who have to retire early for medical reasons or who opt to take early retirement as part of a redundancy scheme are immediately seen as having lower status and value in the eyes of others.

Similarly, unemployment and leisure are seen as opposite sides of the same coin but psychologically their impact is totally different: one is feared and the other is eagerly sought. Unemployment has disastrous personal implications for the individual, and is identified with rejection, uselessness, dependence on others, laziness and social isolation. Leisure is sought and enjoyed and is equated with self-sufficiency and the ability to make choices. The work ethic defines work as making leisure meaningful and conversely, leisure is seen as

workers off when they are not based on the employer's premises. Information technology considerably expands the number of occupations that can be suitable candidates for homeworking.

In the manufacturing area, a major constraint which has prevented factory workers from carrying out their work at home until now has been the need to operate large and/or complex machinery which needs factory backup facilities or the availability of rapid access to information. Computer-integrated manufacturing (CIM) removes many of these impediments.

Similarly, a large amount of office work can easily be carried out at home by means of computer terminals which are linked to a central computer via the telecommunications system. Work can therefore be carried out at home and be monitored and controlled in a central office. This obviates the necessity for exercising managerial control, which has always provided a major constraint for the expansion of homeworking. Many areas of female clerical work lend themselves readily to homeworking, and the consequent dangers of social isolation for women within the home are obvious.

Higher levels of management are also likely to be affected by the trend towards homeworking. The future development of information systems should eventually permit communication of a high quality over distances. "Teleconferencing", which substitutes for the need to bring staff

physically together for management meetings by providing video linkages, is still very costly and rather inconvenient.

However, according to a survey of 255 among the largest 1,000 UK companies, almost two-thirds believe that by 1988 they will be employing executives working from home.

New technology is spawning novel ways of dealing with the problems of managerial complexity. There is a general expectation that it will permit the contraction of management hierarchies and a radical simplification of management structures. The new technology will enable managerial overheads to be significantly reduced and we can expect management hierarchies to shrink as large organizations sub-contract many of their activities to other smaller organizations. This is partly connected with new technology but it is also a reflection of a change in managerial philosophy generally.

Ultimately the adoption of new technology will facilitate the emergence of what can be called the "professional" organization. The repetitive bits of work will be progressively automated. The accessory bits to the core of the organization's work will be gradually contracted out. What will be left? The specialists, the experts and the co-ordinators with a few helpers and dial watchers. More and more the organizations of industry and business will come to resemble organizations of professionals. Fixed-term contracts will

making work meaningful. The exaggeratedly absolute position asserts that work, however debased, is always good, while non-work, however welcome, is almost always bad, a form of incapacity and humiliation. It is as if work were seen as a raft in a shark-infested sea: being on the raft means safety and security, being in the sea means disaster; the idea of moving on and off the raft voluntarily has no appeal. There are winners and losers: no intermediate position is possible.

The changes which will come about as a result of the introduction of information technology will provide a major challenge to the work ethic. Jobs will become increasingly difficult to find: an increasing number of economists are claiming that full employment will never return to Western societies. The International Labour Organization (International Labour Office) estimates that 1,000 million new jobs would have to be created between now and the year 2000 to achieve full employment worldwide.

Somehow or other we will have to find alternative solutions to cope with the radical changes that are on the horizon. There has been no shortage of suggestions, ranging from increased government expenditure, reducing the length of the working week, job sharing, early retirement, workers co-operatives, reducing the proportion of time that people spend as part of the labour force during their lifetime etc. Some of these options have already been adopted to a small degree over the last decade; but these have usually been seen as ad hoc "temporary" responses to rising levels of unemployment rather than as serious long term measures to adjust society to a prospect of continuing job losses. Few experts believe that any of these suggestions would bring us back to full employment.

Above: A multi-weld station going full blast on the Austin Rover Metro line, Longbridge. Such automation is more and more in evidence in industry today.

What is "Taylorism"?

"Taylorism" refers to the ideas of F. W. Taylor, an American management consultant, who advanced a number of principles about job design which are sometimes known as "Scientific Management". He attempted to transform the administration of the workplace so as to increase management control according to three principles:

1. Greater division of labour: production processes were to be analysed systematically and broken down into their component parts, so that each worker's job was simplified and preferably reduced to a single, simple task. Greater specialization would lead to greater efficiency, while the de-skilling that followed simplification of tasks would also allow cheaper, unskilled labour to be hired. Greater division of labour would in turn remove the planning, organizing and hiring functions from the shop floor.

2. Full managerial control of the workplace was to be established for the first time, and managers were to be responsible for the co-ordination of the production process that greater division of labour had fragmented.

3. Cost accounting based on systematic time-and-motion study was to be introduced to provide managers with the information they needed in their new roles as the controllers of the workplace.

Scientific Management, or Taylorism, proposed two major transformations of industry simultaneously: the removal of manual skills and organizational autonomy from the work of lower-level employees; and the establishment of managing as a role distinct from ownership, with a set of technical functions to do with organization.

New Designs for Jobs

Not only do we need to have a vision of how society can adjust to all the changes stemming from information technology and how work can be re-defined and redistributed, but we also need to consider ways of redesigning jobs to make work itself more intrinsically satisfying and using the new technology in such a way so that it matches human ability and fosters skill, rather than seeking to eliminate it. There has been a long tradition of "Taylorism" in manufacturing industry whereby jobs were progressively fragmented and operator skills were reduced wherever possible.

Robots are now being introduced to carry out functions such as paint-spraying, repetitive spot-welding etc—all of them tasks which are generally considered to be dirty, dehumanizing, dangerous and repetitive. But why were these jobs which were formerly done by human operators so designed in the first place? It was precisely because they were the result of a long process of fragmentation and simplification to fit in with the imperatives of Taylorism. It is ironic that the early applications of robotics in many cases allow us to automate such tasks out of existence. While most of us would applaud the fact that robots are now taking over such demeaning tasks, it does not alter the fact that technology is still seen by many managers, designers and engineers as a means of making human beings subservient to the dictats of the machine—with the intention of eliminating human judgement and discretion wherever possible. There is no reason why engineers and managers should continue to follow this path of subordinating work to the machine, fragmenting work into rigid components which result in tedious and

Above: Might this be an image of the workplace of the future? This computer network controls a power station on the Isle of Grain in Kent.

Below: This is the NC lathe developed by Howard Rosenbrock and his team at UMIST as part of a flexible system designed to integrate the craftsman with computer-controlled tools.

demeaning tasks for millions of working people until the best thing that can be done with the jobs that remain is to automate them out of existence! A path can be followed through which human skill can be preserved, not necessarily by becoming fossilized in old patterns, but by evolving into new skills in relation to new machines and systems. This can only be done, however, at the beginning of the process of technological application. It is at that time when choices can be made. If new technology takes the alternative path of being used to draw upon and foster human skills instead of seeking to

eliminate them by a gradual process of simplification and fragmentation, then there might not be such a need to consult social scientists about suggestions for some form of job redesign which might alleviate the monotony or the pressure inherent in so many jobs!

The design of the technology can either limit the organization of work around it or it can be used to provide alternatives for management in the way in which it is used. For example, a research team at the University of Manchester Institute of Science and Technology under the direction of Professor H. Rosenbrock, is currently working on the development of a flexible manufacturing system with the intention of creating a system which allows for a "computer-aided" craftsperson who would be responsible for the whole job of making a part, once it had been designed. He or she would make the first part in a batch using the numerically-controlled machine tools and interacting with them through computer interfaces. His or her operations would be recorded and repeated automatically to make the remaining parts of the batch. The robot, too, would be programmed by the operator.

The system is reported as having the technical advantages of easier programming of the robot because the full three-dimensional situation is evident to the operators, and also rendering separate verification of programs unnecessary because making the first component automatically verifies the program which results. The system is more flexible because the operator skill is available to deal with the multitude of difficulties and special situations which arise. Such flexibility is of positive economic benefit in allowing a greater deal of product variety (eg tailored specifically to the require-

ments of different markets) and quicker production changes (compared with conventional mass markets).

The above example provides evidence that it is possible—providing that the appropriate objectives are set and appropriate choices made by management, systems designers and trade unions/employees—to incorporate skilled work and facilitate decision-making on the shop-floor in concert with the introduction of new technology. There is no inherent reason why designers of new technology systems should produce machinery and computer systems which deskill and trivialize the tasks of those that work with them. In all probability, many engineers and designers are usually unaware that social choices have already been made in the design process itself, largely because it is often carried out in isolation from the particular point of application, without reference to payment systems, skill hierarchies, established working practices and the politics of the work-place.

Finally . . .

We are still in the early stages of the information technology revolution. Despite the rapid pace of development there is still time to make choices which will ultimately determine the kind of society that our children and grandchildren will live in and the kind of work they do. Technology can be used to promote greater economic equity, more freedom of choice, and a quality of life which far exceeds anything we can possibly envisage. Conversely, it can be used to intensify the worst aspects of a competitive society, to widen the gaps between rich and poor, and be used by a small powerful elite to exercise control in an Orwellian fashion over the rest of the population.

We are on the threshold of a technological revolution which is more far-reaching and is developing more rapidly than any previous technological change in history. It is much easier to allow technological innovation to take its own course, than it is to understand or deal with its social consequences. The pervasiveness of this technology, together with the rapid pace of its introduction, highlights the importance of finding ways to deal with its possible consequences for the future of work. So far, few nations—with the notable exception of the Scandinavian countries—have taken positive steps to ensure that technology is used to the benefit of society as a whole, instead of being limited only by the laws of the "free market" and thereby benefitting only the most powerful groups in society. The control and application of new technology is a political issue, and the threats and the opportunities it offers, not only in terms of its implications for the future of work, but also for the future of society itself, are too important to be left to market forces alone. There is an urgent need to find a solution to the problems posed by the new technology—before society is torn apart in a bitter struggle between those who have jobs, and those who have not.

GLOSSARY

A

ACOMS Automated component optical measurement system.

Actuator Device which translates energy into motion and which is responsible for a specific action in an automation system, eg a servo motor.

AGV Automated guided vehicle.

AI Artificial intelligence: discipline in which scientists are attempting to give computers reasoning power approaching that of people.

Algorithm Procedure used in computing to solve a mathematically-expressed problem in a set number of steps.

Analogue Representation of information by a value that changes continuously with time (see also digital).

Android Robot similar in appearance to a human.

APOMS Automated propeller optical measurement system.

ARCS Autonomous remote-controlled submersible.

ARS Autonomous robot submersible.

ASV Adaptive suspension vehicle: unmanned transport mechanism under development for US Department of Defense.

Automaton Device that carries out a number of set routines under automatic control.

B

BASIC Popular computer language used, for example, by hobbyists on home computers.

Batch manufacture Production process in which items are made in small runs of a few hundred components at a time. Applies to the majority of manufactured items.

Binary Representation of information by code which uses a combination of two numbers—0 and 1. Virtually all modern computers process information using the binary code.

Bit Abbreviation of binary digit, either a 0 or a 1.

Bugs Errors in software.

C

CAD Computer-aided design.

CAM Computer-aided manufacture.

Cartesian coordinates System of values that defines the position of an object in space according to the distance from the convergence of a set of mutually perpendicular axes. Three values (x, y and z) are needed to define position in three dimensions.

Cartesian coordinate robot A robot arm that can move along the three basic translational axes, ie up and down, from side to side, and in and out.

Chip Small sliver of semiconductor material turned by a variety of chemical and physical processes into integrated circuits.

CIAM Computerized, integrated and automated manufacturing system.

CIM Computer-integrated manufacture.

CLIP Cellular Logic Image Processor: very fast computer for processing images.

CMU Carnegie-Mellon University.

CNC Computer-numerically controlled (applied to manufacturing device such as machine tool or robot).

Continuous path control Technique to control movement of robot arm by specifying position of arm in every point in space between its beginning and end positions.

CRT Cathode ray tube which is required for most computer displays.

CURV Cable-controlled underwater recovery vehicle.

Cybernetics Theory of communications and control with special emphasis on feedback (see feedback).

Cylindrical coordinate robot Robot whose arm operates in the three Cartesian axes (x, y and z), but with the added ability of swivelling around its base so it can handle jobs within a cylindrical work envelope.

D

DARPA Defense Advanced Research Projects Agency, a division of US Department of Defense.

Debugging Technique to rid computer programs of bugs.

Deburring Operation to remove unwanted segments of metal from cast or machined object.

Degrees of freedom Number of axes about which device such as a robot arm can move.

Digital Representation of information by code based on series of numbers.

Disk Storage medium for computers, based on altering magnetic properties of a material to code information in a series of binary digits.

Domino effect Jargon term for the way introduction of robots into manufacturing affects other areas of production.

E

End effectors (also **end of arm tooling**) Tools such as drills, cutting edges or screwdrivers attached to the end of a robot arm to do specific jobs.

EOD Explosive ordnance disposal.

EVA Extra-vehicular activity: used in space flight when an astronaut ventures outside space craft.

F

Feedback Technique whereby a device alters its activity according to information that it receives about external circumstances.

Feedforward Transfer of information to alert computer or other device about coming events.

First-generation robot Robot without sensory ability, sometimes called "blind, deaf, dumb" machines.

Fixed stop robot Unsophisticated form of robot in which the extent of the motion of the arm is defined by mechanical stops. The arm can only stop at these pre-defined limits.

FMS Flexible manufacturing system, an advanced automation system used in batch manufacture.

FORTH Sophisticated computer language in which many of the terms are similar to English phrases.

G

GPS General problem solver; an advanced computer program devised in the USA in 1960.

Gripper End tool of robot used for handling jobs.

H

Hard automation Relatively unsophisticated form of automation in which the function of machines can be changed only by altering mechanical components, not by programming.

Hardware Mechanical parts of computer or automation system (see also software).

Heuristics Set of rules for problem-solving employed in many branches of AI.

Hexadecimal keypad Keyboard with 16 keys, including 0 to 9 and A to F to represent 10-15.

I

Integrated circuit Set of electronic functions built into a small segment of semiconductor.

Interface Mechanical connection between two machines, eg machine tool and supervisory computer.

IOSS Integrated orbiting servicing system, an automated system designed for remote, unmanned repair of spacecraft.

J

JAMSTEC Japan Marine Science and Technology Centre.

Joystick control Control of the movement of a robot or other actuator by manipulation of a small stick, similar to that used by pilots to control the position of an aircraft.

JPL Jet Propulsion Laboratory: NASA base in California operated by California Institute of Technology.

L

LCD Liquid-crystal display.

LED Light-emitting diode.

LMF Lunar manufacturing facility.

LOGO Simple computer language, widely used in schools to control the movements of a mobile robot, or "turtle".

M

Manipulator The arm of an industrial-type robot.

Manufacturing cell Array of computerized and interconnected production hardware used to turn out specific families of products.

MBB Messerschmitt-Bölkow-Blohm, a German aerospace manufacturing concern.

Menu List of options, eg for different movement of robot arm, often displayed on a CRT, from which users of computers or automated systems can select their choice.

Microprocessors Integrated circuits with processing capabilities, ie which can operate as the central-processing units of computers.

MUC Mobile universal constructor: part of a proposed automated lunar manufacturing facility.

156

N

NC Numerical control, eg of machine tools.

Noise Electrical interference in the form of stray signals.

O

Off-line programming Provision of software commands to devices such as computerized machine tools by means other than a direct interaction with the machine. Once defined, the program can be loaded into the robot's controller which will then instruct the manipulator to operate automatically.

OMV Orbital maneuvering vehicle: US transportation tug in space for jobs such as transfer of payloads between low and high orbits.

P

Parallel processing Operation of computer in which the machine digests several streams of instructions simultaneously (see also serial processing).

PCB Printed circuit board: contains integrated circuits and other electronic components and is the basic building block of computers and other electronic mechanisms.

PDRS Payload deployment and retrieval system, comprising the Space Shuttle's Remote Manipulator System, the controlling computer software, and the manipulator positioning and retention mechanisms.

PFMA Protoflight manipulator arm, a 7 degree of freedom manipulator.

Pick-and-place robot Rudimentary form of robot that can be programmed only to transfer objects between two sites with little trajectory control.

Pitch Movement of object such as robot arm up and down in the vertical plane.

Pixel Picture element in a display screen; the more pixels in the display, the better the resolution.

Point-to-point control Technique to program robot arm by defining series of points along the trajectory which the device is required to travel.

Polar coordinate robot A cylindrical coordinate robot with extra sophistication of

Playback robot Robot controlled by programs so that its activities can be varied according to the instructions within the programs.

Program Set of commands written in binary language of 0s and 1s that instruct computerized machines such as robots in specific modes of action.

PROLOG Computer language used in artificial intelligence studies, particularly in relation to expert systems.

Proximity sensor Device that senses position and relative distance of objects, for example by recording changes in electrical properties of a circuit due to a nearby metal component.

PUMA Programmable universal machine for assembly: robot devices sold by Unimation robot company, now owned by Westinghouse.

R

RAM Random-access memory: integrated circuit used as computer storage facility.

Rectangular coordinate robot Same as Cartesian coordinate robot.

Repeatability Measure of accuracy of a robot arm which indicates the precision with which a movement or position can be repeated once registered in the robot's memory.

Resolution The accuracy with which a robot can place its end effector within a known minimum distance from a desired position.

RMS Remote manipulator system, the teleoperated arm used aboard NASA Space Shuttles.

Revolute coordinate robot A robot of the jointed arm type, which is articulated at shoulder, elbow and wrist.

Robot (general) A machine that in appearance or behaviour imitates either a person or a specific action of a person, such as limb movement.

Robot (industrial) A programmable, computer-controlled mechanical arm capable of a range of handling tasks, such as lifting, deploying tools etc.

Roll Movement of device such as robot arm about its longitudinal axis.

RRV Robotic research vehicle (now cancelled, but previously under development at Jet Propulsion Laboratory for Mars exploration).

RUM Remote underwater manipulator.

S

SCARA Selective compliance assembly robot arm.

Second-generation robot Robot with feedback as a result of being equipped with sensory perception.

Self replication Postulated ability of a device such as a robot to fashion an identical device from a supply of raw parts.

Sensor Device such as TV camera, touch pad, or thermometer that obtains information and feeds it to the control system.

Serial processing Operation of computer in which machine performs mathematical steps one instruction at a time.

Servo control Mechanism for converting a small mechanical force to a larger force for control purposes.

Servo manipulator Manipulator that can be controlled very accurately by servo mechanisms.

Shaft encoder A device that enables a robot's controlling computer to obtain information about the position of the robot's various components.

Soft automation System of factory equipment that can be programmed to do different jobs.

Software Instructions in binary code that inform a computerized machine of required modes of action (see also hardware).

Spherical coordinate robot Same as polar coordinate robot.

Spotty automation Automation process that leaves many low-skilled jobs (eg cleaning) to be done by people.

SRS Self replicating system.

Stepper motor Electric motor controlled by electronic mechanism to change torque in series of clearly defined stages.

Strain gauge Device to measure force—used in sensors in feedback systems.

STRIPS Stanford Research Institute Problem Solver; a

SUC Stationary universal constructor: part of a proposed lunar manufacturing facility.

Syntaxeur Machine which enables operator to teach robot a set of actions by leading a control device through the same actions.

T

Teach pendant Keypad by which a robot is guided through a specific sequence of movements which can then be stored in the computer memory.

Telechiric device Mechanical arm that is "driven" through a sequence of movements controlled by a remote human operator.

Teleoperator As telechiric device.

Telepresence Act of operating remotely a telechiric device, with the operator obtaining information about the device's surroundings through TV cameras and other sensors.

Terraforming Act of changing climate of other planets to make them like the Earth, and so capable of habitation by humans.

Third-generation robot Robot that can make decisions, using principles of artificial intelligence.

Transputer Novel type of microprocessor devised by Inmos Ltd.

Turtle Small mobile robot used in teaching, and programmed by languages such as LOGO.

U

UC Universal constructor: part of a proposed lunar manufacturing facility.

V

VDU Visual display unit.

Vision Act of seeing, as in robots endowed with "sight" due to TV cameras.

VTOL Vertical take-off and landing (aircraft, RPVs etc).

W

WAC Water, air and current system (associated with robot welders).

Work envelope Area of reach of a robot arm, in which it can perform tasks.

Wrist articulation Ability of robot hand to move about "wrist" joint.

INDEX

Page references set in **bold** type refer to subjects that are mentioned in picture captions.

INDEX

PICTURE CREDITS

24